# Barth

## BLOOMSBURY GUIDES FOR THE PERPLEXED

Bloomsbury's *Guides for the Perplexed* are clear, concise and accessible introductions to thinkers, writers and subjects that students and readers can find especially challenging. Concentrating specifically on what it is that makes the subject difficult to grasp, these books explain and explore key themes and ideas, guiding the reader towards a thorough understanding of demanding material.

**Guides for the Perplexed available from Bloomsbury include:**

A GUIDE FOR THE PERPLEXED

# Barth

## PAUL T. NIMMO

Bloomsbury T&T Clark
An imprint of Bloomsbury Publishing Plc

B L O O M S B U R Y
LONDON · OXFORD · NEW YORK · NEW DELHI · SYDNEY

**Bloomsbury T&T Clark**

An imprint of Bloomsbury Publishing Plc

Imprint previously known as T&T Clark

50 Bedford Square
London
WC1B 3DP
UK

1385 Broadway
New York
NY 10018
USA

**www.bloomsbury.com**

**BLOOMSBURY, T&T CLARK and the Diana logo are trademarks
of Bloomsbury Publishing Plc**

First published 2017

© Paul T. Nimmo, 2017

**British Library Cataloguing-in-Publication Data**
A catalogue record for this book is available from the British Library.

ISBN: HB: 978-0-5670-3263-8
PB: 978-0-5670-3264-5
ePDF: 978-0-5673-0736-1
ePub: 978-0-5672-1369-3

**Library of Congress Cataloging-in-Publication Data**
A catalog record for this book is available from the Library of Congress

Cover image © Siede Preis/Getty Images

Typeset by Deanta Global Publishing Services, Chennai, India
Printed and bound in India

*To Jill*
*with love*

# CONTENTS

# ACKNOWLEDGEMENTS

To write an introduction to Karl Barth is to engage an extraordinary theologian and an extraordinary task, but also to be the bearer of an extraordinary privilege.

I am thus very grateful to the publisher of this book, Bloomsbury/ T&T Clark, for inviting me to undertake this work in the first place, and for tolerating with great patience the many delays arising en route to publication. I would like to express my warm thanks to Tom Kraft, who originally commissioned the book, and to Grishma Fredric and Beth Williams, for all their work in bringing the manuscript to production. In particular, I would like above all to thank Anna Turton, for being the most professional and most supportive editor a writer could want.

This book is a revised and expanded version of material on Karl Barth which was originally delivered in the Kerr Lectures at the University of Glasgow in 2008. I would like to record my profound gratitude to George Newlands, who invited me to give the lectures, as well as to his colleagues at that time – Julie Clague, Ian Hazlett and Werner Jeanrond – for hospitality and conversation in the course of my visits to Glasgow. I am also indebted to the many students who attended the series of lectures, and who provided challenging and insightful questions.

The material in this book has greatly benefitted from its reception and critique by a series of students at all levels who have participated in courses on the theology of Karl Barth that I have taught in Göttingen, in Edinburgh and in Aberdeen. It has also improved immeasurably as a result of direct comment from profoundly gracious colleagues on various drafts, above all from Tyler Frick, Declan Kelly, Daniel McDowell, Mike Rea and Simeon Zahl. I am deeply grateful for all these conversations; the remaining errors and infelicities in the text are entirely my own.

In the course of the many years during which this book has slowly taken shape, I have known to value the support and kindness of many colleagues both near and far. This is an appropriate place, therefore, to express my appreciation of and respect for David Fergusson, David Ford, Paul Foster, Jason Fout, Tom Greggs, Paul Dafydd Jones, Robert McKay, Bruce McCormack, Suzanne McDonald, George Newlands, Ryan Reeves, Iain Torrance, Don Wood, Simeon Zahl and Phil Ziegler, as well as my lasting indebtedness to the late and greatly missed John Webster.

I have been supported over the same period by the companionship, patience and humour of many friends – in particular Derek Browning, Keith Graham, Anette Hagan, Nikki Macdonald, Colin Macpherson, Stephen Manders, the late Ernest Marvin, Joshua Mikelson, David Plews, Carsten Schleisiek and Nicola Whyte, and the original Cambridge 1405. Above all I would like to thank Mark and Jenny Russell and their family for the hospitality and sanctuary they continue to offer me, and Tom Greggs, for warm collegiality, wise counsel and cherished friendship.

My family has – now as always – provided the rock on which I stand, and I would like to express once again my love and gratitude to my parents Robert and Hilary Nimmo, and to my siblings Robin, Stephen and Elise and their families. My own family is the greatest of blessings, bringing joy and wonder in abundance to every day of my life, particularly in the adventure, discovery and laughter of my beloved children – Samuel, Daniel and Rebekah; but this book is dedicated to my wife, Jill, with love and admiration, and with prayerful thanks for all that she is to me.

And finally, may this flawed work in some small measure serve the greater glory of God, the Father of lights, with whom there is no change or shadow of turning.

Paul T. Nimmo
King's College, Aberdeen
June 2016

# FOREWORD

This guide aims to introduce readers to the theology of Karl Barth, perhaps the most significant theologian of the twentieth century. It seeks to achieve this goal by means of careful attention to the structure and content of *Church Dogmatics*, the work which Barth himself considered to represent the most detailed and comprehensive account of his thought. In tracing a path through the many volumes of this landmark text, this guide seeks faithfully to represent the key contours of Barth's theology, highlighting those features which are particularly decisive or distinctive, and articulating the relationships which exist between the different doctrines explored. In this way, it is hoped that the theological instincts and dogmatic concerns which lie at the heart of the work of Barth will be rendered clear, even to the student approaching his writings for the first time.

The first chapter provides a concise biography of Barth, noting the key events in his professional and personal life and the major events in world history which formed the backdrop to his theology, and offers counsel on how to approach *Church Dogmatics*. There follow a series of chapters exploring the different sections of *Church Dogmatics*, starting from the doctrine of the Word of God, moving through the doctrines of God, of creation and of reconciliation, and ending with the sections on theological ethics that are integral to the dogmatic enterprise of Barth. The final chapter concludes with a brief reflection upon the enduring impact and contemporary interpretation of the theology of Barth. At the close of the book, there appears a concise list of suggestions for further reading for those who wish to continue exploring the theology of Barth.

Given that the primary focus of this guide is to present the ideas of Barth, little space beyond the first chapter is devoted to detailed exposition of his historical context: to relate his context to his work beyond superficially correlating the two is a detailed task beyond the scope of an introduction. Similarly little room beyond the first chapter is given to tracing the diachronic development of the theology of Barth: though an important area of research, there is insufficient space in an introductory work for any extensive engagement with the attendant material and issues. And finally, similarly little attention is given to the vast array of available secondary literature: to do even modest justice to the reams of such material is again beyond the scope of an introduction, though significant trajectories of response to the work of Barth are indicated and considered at certain points.

In the quest to understand the theology of Barth, there is – of course – no substitute for engaging with his work in *Church Dogmatics* and beyond at first hand. And there is no way in which an introductory guide can hope to be remotely comprehensive; every reader of Barth will, in any event, develop their own, particular interpretation of his work. Nevertheless, if this modest work offers a way for newcomers to Barth to gain a holistic sense of his theological legacy, and encourages and fortifies them to open the pages of *Church Dogmatics* for themselves, it will more than have achieved its purpose. And if it leads any reader further, to turn from *Church Dogmatics* to the text of Scripture through which Barth encountered the Word of God and with which *Church Dogmatics* wrestles over its many pages, it will have achieved something for which it can only hope.

# ABBREVIATIONS

Texts from *Church Dogmatics* are referenced inline, by volume, then part-volume, then page number. The following edition of the text has been used:

Barth, Karl. *Church Dogmatics*. Edited by G. W. Bromiley and T. F. Torrance. Translated by G. W. Bromiley and others. 4 volumes in 13 parts. Edinburgh: T&T Clark, 1956–75.

Texts from *The Christian Life* are also referenced inline, by the annotation TCL and then the page number. The following edition of the text has been used:

Barth, Karl. *The Christian Life: Church Dogmatics Volume IV, Part 4, Lecture Fragments*. Translated by Geoffrey W. Bromiley. Edinburgh: T&T Clark, 1981.

In citations of these translations of the work of Barth, the original capitalization and the exclusive use of masculine pronouns has generally been preserved, however infelicitous they may be. In the remaining text, efforts have been made to avoid gender-exclusive language in respect of God or human beings – efforts which may have given rise to stylistic infelicities of their own. Given the limitations of the English language, one can only do the best one can and hope that others will be able to do better.

# CHAPTER ONE

# The life and work of Karl Barth

This chapter provides a concise outline of the life and work of Karl Barth, moving from his early years in Switzerland as a student and as a pastor through his time working as an academic in inter-war Germany to his return to Switzerland in later years to university teaching. The chapter concludes with some introductory suggestions for approaching and reading *Church Dogmatics*.

## I  A life in outline

### *The early years of Karl Barth in Switzerland*

Karl Barth was born on 10 May, 1886 in Basel, Switzerland. He was the eldest of five children born to Johann Friedrich ('Fritz') and Katharina (Sartorius) Barth. Katharina Barth belonged to a notable family of Basel theologians, while Fritz Barth was a Reformed minister who taught at the College of Preachers in the city. When Karl was still an infant, the family left Basel and moved to Bern, when Fritz Barth was called to a position in the University of Bern in 1889. They enjoyed a comfortable life in the new city, and the family home was a busy place of books, music and guests. The family remained in Bern throughout Karl's childhood, and his father enjoyed a distinguished career there until his premature death in 1912. While a teenager, in 1901–2, Karl went to confirmation classes under the charismatic minister Robert Aeschbacher, and it was during this time that he decided to study theology.

In the autumn of 1904, Barth enrolled as a student of theology at the University of Bern, and rapidly proved himself to be both industrious and gifted. After two years of introductory work in Bern, he moved to Germany for advanced studies in theology. This sojourn was interrupted by a semester back in Bern in 1907, as the president of the local branch of the Zofingia student society of which he was a member, and by successive summer vacations back in Switzerland undertaking placements in parish ministry. While in Germany, Barth spent a semester in Berlin under Adolf von Harnack and Julius Kaftan, a semester in Tübingen under Adolf Schlatter and Theodor Haering, and finally a semester in Marburg under Wilhelm Herrmann. Barth's education thus involved some of the major figures in the theological world of the late nineteenth and early twentieth centuries, figures often described as being 'liberal Protestants'. Many years later, Barth suggested that that their work was over-rationalist, making too many concessions to modern culture and modern science, and making the human being to be the measure of all things. The result, for Barth, was a theology which focused on the human experience of God rather than with God's address to humanity, and which bypassed the real questions of faith.

Though his studies were completed in 1908, Barth remained in Marburg for a further year, working as assistant to Martin Rade and as editorial assistant to Rade's influential theological journal *Die Christliche Welt* (*The Christian World*). At this time, a strong friendship developed between Barth and his compatriot Eduard Thurneysen, and Barth also began a lifelong relationship with Rudolf Bultmann. In September 1909, having been ordained in Bern (by his father) the previous year, Barth became the assistant pastor of the German-speaking Reformed congregation in Geneva, working with Adolf Keller, later a renowned ecumenist. At this point in time, Barth had apparently discounted the possibility of an academic career, though he continued to give academic papers, publish scholarly articles and undertake theological reading.

Barth remained almost two years in Geneva before moving in 1911 to become a pastor in the industrial village of Safenwil in the Aargau region. Of significance to the early period of Barth's ministry in the village was his support for the local workers' movement and his wider interest in religious socialism. It is no surprise, then, that he was nicknamed 'The Red Pastor', and he accepted invitations to address workers' meetings around the country. However, he always advocated reform and co-operation in place of rebellion and antagonism, and never became a thorough-going socialist. His interest in social democracy was far more practically oriented than theoretically grounded, and the kingdom of God always posed a limit to the power and validity of human political orders. By the time of a lecture in Tambach in 1919, he had become rather critical of the religious socialist movement which he had once admired.

In 1913, after a two-year engagement, Barth married Nelly Hoffmann, an aspirant violinist and a member of his first-year confirmation class in Geneva. Over the ensuing decade or so, the couple had five children – a daughter, Franziska, and four sons, Markus, Christoph, Matthias and Hans Jakob. Even amidst growing family commitments, Nelly Barth was an active supporter of her husband's work in the early phase of his career. Some years later, in 1924, Barth came to know Charlotte von Kirschbaum, a Red Cross nurse with an interest in theology, and in 1929, she moved in with the Barth family. She took on the role of secretary and assistant to Barth, significantly enhancing both the extensity and the intensity of his endeavours. In 1933, Barth and von Kirschbaum desired to marry; however, his wife would not consent to a divorce, and instead their uneasy co-existence in the same house continued.

The outbreak of the First World War in 1914, and the unquestioned support for the German war effort both from his previous teachers of theology and from the social democratic politicians in Germany, caused Barth to question seriously the theological inheritance that had been bequeathed to him. He considered the war unjust, unnecessary and sinful, and criticized the churches for their acquiescence in the war and inattentiveness to the Gospel. The theology of the day, meanwhile, had proven itself unfit for service in face of the evils of this war. In the course of the following seasons, therefore, and in conversation with his neighbouring pastor and close friend Thurneysen, Barth discovered a new starting point for the enterprise of theology. Departing from any easy identification of God with individual nations, cultural movements, moral practices, human achievements or Christian religiosity, Barth sought to begin again with the true and living Word of God that was corrupted by such idols. And central to this quest was the recognition that Scripture spoke primarily of God and God's relation with humanity, and not of humanity and its relation to God.

In this way, Barth distanced himself from the Protestant theology of the late nineteenth century, drawing particular encouragement from his conversations with the Pietist pastor Christoph Blumhardt. A year after the end of the First World War, in 1919, Barth published a commentary on Paul's Epistle to the Romans that he had written between 1916 and 1918. The work represented a radical departure from the then-prevalent mode of scriptural exegesis: instead of trying to think *about* Paul, it sought to think *with* Paul, recognizing that the message of the apostle was not simply for his own time, and that the prevailing historical-critical method for the interpretation of Scripture had its limits. Paul presented a dramatic picture of the inbreaking of the work of God from above, a process of transformation of the old world into the new going far beyond merely changing individual behaviour patterns or sociopolitical arrangements. Although the volume was rather critically received, it was nonetheless widely noticed, and raised awareness of Barth's name both in Switzerland and in Germany. And some readers, including the Swiss theologian Emil Brunner, were delighted with the radicality of the text and its fresh starting point with God.

Soon thereafter, however, Barth became unsatisfied with his first venture at a commentary on Romans and worked between 1920 and 1921 on a second, radically revised edition, published early in 1922. This willingness to be critical of his own writings and to begin again from the beginning in his theological work is characteristic of Barth's approach as a whole. In the new edition of the commentary, he sought to offer an even more thoroughgoing account of the radicality of the inbreaking of the kingdom of God, not only of its interrogation and destruction of any human effort at righteousness, but also of the impossibility and paradoxicality of the divine grace meeting humanity from above. God is to be recognized and acknowledged *as God*, and only God can and does make Godself known to human beings in history. In the preface to the new edition, Barth acknowledged both the assistance of Thurneysen and the influence of figures as diverse as Franz Overbeck, Plato, Immanuel Kant, Søren Kierkegaard and Fyodor Dostoevsky, but above all he emphasized his attending once again to the words of the Apostle Paul. By the time of the appearance of this second edition, however, Barth was no longer in Safenwil.

## *Karl Barth as academic in Germany*

In 1921, with the success of the first edition of the commentary on Romans fresh in the air, Barth was called to the newly created position of Honorary Professor in Reformed Theology at the University of Göttingen in Germany, a country in the midst of deepening economic catastrophe and significant cultural upheaval. He did not have an easy entry into academic life. He was the only Reformed theologian in a largely Lutheran faculty, which made for difficult collegial relations that were further strained by political differences. And he was also rather underprepared for the task of teaching, such that much of his time was spent producing material for new courses under great pressure. During his four years in Göttingen, Barth offered lecture courses on a series of texts and figures in Reformed theology – the Heidelberg Catechism, John Calvin, Huldrych Zwingli, Friedrich Schleiermacher and the Reformed confessions – and three sequential lecture courses on dogmatics, his first constructive dogmatic venture, later published as the *Göttingen Dogmatics*. He also offered a series of further courses on exegesis, covering the texts of Ephesians, James, 1 Corinthians 15, 1 John, Philippians and Colossians, as well as the Sermon on the Mount. This combination of theological and biblical offerings became a feature of Barth's teaching and writing from this early point onwards, but it also served to effect a rapid extending of the scope of Barth's knowledge of theology and a profound deepening of the intensity of Barth's theological reflections.

Around this time there arose a group of theologians who shared certain theological instincts with Barth – the so-called 'dialectical theologians'. A new journal, co-founded by Barth, Thurneysen and Friedrich Gogarten, edited by Georg Merz, and entitled *Zwischen den Zeiten* (*Between the Times*), offered a forum for like-minded theologians to publish their work, and members of the wider circle of its supporters included Bultmann and Brunner. Yet despite some similarities in approach and view, there were differences between the editors from the start, and Barth became increasingly disaffected with the directions which Gogarten and Bultmann were pursuing in their work. Against a backdrop of growing theological and political differences, together with attendant interpersonal issues, the journal ceased publishing in 1933, though in reality the movement had effectively split around three years earlier.

Central to Barth's theological thinking at this time were a continuing insistence on the inability of human beings, in and of their own power, to speak of God, and a continuing confidence that the event of revelation in which God speaks of Godself is the only possible foundation for Christian preaching and Christian theology. Against the backdrop of this dynamic understanding of revelation, Barth sought to recover the importance of the Scripture principle in and for constructive theology. But he also came to an understanding of the inbreaking of the kingdom of God that was increasingly tethered to the incarnate Jesus Christ, rendering his theology more thoroughly Christocentric.

In 1925, Barth accepted a call to become a Regular Professor of Dogmatics and New Testament Exegesis at the University of Münster, leaving behind his previous status as an honorary professor. Amidst a period of relative social and economic stability in Germany, his teaching duties continued unabated. In the following five years he gave lectures on eschatology, the history of Protestant theology, ethics (over two semesters) and dogmatics (over three semesters). This second venture in dogmatics is commonly known as the 'Münster Dogmatics', though only one volume of material was published, as the first part of a proposed multi-volume *Christian Dogmatics in Outline*. Barth also delivered exegetical lectures on John, Philippians, Colossians and James, and offered seminars on a series of significant texts – Calvin's *Institutes*, Anselm's *Cur Deus homo?*, Schleiermacher's *Christian Faith* and Thomas Aquinas' *Summa Theologiae* part I – and on the work of Albrecht Ritschl, the readings of Galatians of Martin Luther and Calvin, and the Reformation doctrine of justification.

During this period, there took place an expansion in Barth's circle of conversation. In Münster, he was surrounded by Roman Catholic scholars. And he increasingly found that while liberal Protestant interpreters of his work were engaging his theology with the tools of psychology, sociology and philosophy of religion, which Barth considered irrelevant, a more critical yet more theological reception of his work was emerging among Roman Catholic scholars. Especially important among the latter was Erich Przywara, who instilled in Barth a desire to consider the question of the relationship between nature and grace with particular vigour, and – finally – to deny Przywara's view of analogy.

For Barth, it was crucial to understand divine revelation as an utterly transcendent act that is beyond all human grasp and power, in order to recognize its utterly gracious nature: there was no way from creaturely being to knowing God, and no analogy of being (*analogia entis*) between God and humanity. In truth, this was the same broad concern which distanced Barth from the other dialectical theologians: the denial of the idea that faith was a human possibility. In the course of the subsequent and lifelong conversation with Roman Catholic theology which he pursued, Barth was no stranger to using robust and polemic language. At the same time, however, the intensity and depth of his interaction with Roman Catholic theology is indicative of the compelling significance and great appreciation which he accorded it.

In late 1929, amidst increasingly volatile political and social circumstances in Germany, Barth was called to the University of Bonn, where he began teaching in the spring of 1930. As his reputation grew, so too did the size of his student audiences. Over the following years, he delivered lectures on ethics (again over two semesters) and sermon preparation, as well as exegetical lectures on the Sermon on the Mount, John, James and Philippians. His seminars attended to various significant texts – Anselm's *Cur Deus Homo?*, Luther's *Large Catechism*, the Lutheran *Formula of Concord*, Schleiermacher's *Christian Faith* and Ritschl's *Institutes of the Christian Religion* – as well as to the doctrine of justification, the Protestant doctrine of sanctification, the problem of natural theology and the theology of the nineteenth century (two semesters). Most significantly, he gave five semesters of lectures on 'Prolegomena to Dogmatics', as part of a new dogmatics venture distinct from the Münster Dogmatics; this material would later be revised and form much of the first volume of *Church Dogmatics*.

This period also saw the break-up of the movement of dialectical theologians, with Barth and Brunner particularly crossing theological swords. Against Brunner's claim that all human beings were in some way seeking God, Barth contended that human striving had lost all meaning. Therefore the church – and theology – could only ever begin from the Word of God, not from the human situation. There is no 'point of contact' between God and humanity that exists as a human capacity or potency, and thus no human possibility of knowledge of God; instead, Christian faith is a divine possibility, arising in an encounter with divine revelation, and theology exists only as human reflection upon that divine revelation. The rejection of natural theology which this position entails famously led to Barth's 1934 treatise against the work of Brunner, written against the backdrop of the rise of National Socialism in Germany, and entitled simply *No!*

Barth drew explicit encouragement at this point from Anselm, whose work – in Barth's view – confirmed the theological agenda which Barth had pursued for some years. For Barth, the so-called 'proof' of God's existence that Anselm provides in *Proslogion* is no such thing: the work is rather the investigation and explication of what must be said about God given the faith of the church. Yet here Barth reasserts his view that the faith of the church, while relatively true, is nevertheless constantly questioned by the ever-new revelation of God as to whether it corresponds to the truth of God that is revealed. Theology is thus never an activity that finds completion or resolution. And it is correspondingly with this core insight that Barth begins the work of *Church Dogmatics* – that Jesus Christ is the source and the criterion of all theological knowledge, as the One in whom God is both revealed and reconciled to humanity.

In 1933, amidst growing economic and political chaos, the National Socialist party came to power in Germany, led by Adolf Hitler. Using violence where necessary, the new regime sought to extend its powers over all areas of human society, including religion. Consequently, the Protestant churches in Germany – a separate concordat was concluded in 1933 between the National Socialist government and the Roman Catholic Church – were quickly brought under the control of the regime, supported by a popular movement which sought to combine National Socialism and Christianity, the *Deutsche Christen* ('German Christians').

Barth recognized from the outset that Hitler's party threatened genuine Christian belief and its expression, and thus decried the teaching of the 'German Christians' as heresy. He encouraged the theological resistance to the ideology of the regime, supporting first the Pastors' Emergency League and then the Confessing Church, but challenged the latter for being too narrowly focused on the church, and for failing to recognize the exercise of the sovereignty of God over every sphere of human existence. In 1933, Barth started a new theological journal entitled *Theologische Existenz Heute* (*Theological Existence Today*), to which he was the primary contributor. The forum allowed him to record publicly his theological response to the events taking place around him.

Most famously, in May 1934, Barth drafted the Theological Declaration of Barmen for the Confessing Church. This document confessed the position of the true church of Jesus Christ as being one of obedience to the one Word of God in Jesus Christ and, as a corollary, one of opposition to false doctrine from other sources of 'revelation'. The Word of God alone binds Christians, and does so in every sphere of life. Particularly prominent in the text was a thinly veiled rejection of the corrupt and heretical 'German Christian' understanding of the church and the state and how they inter-related. Sadly lacking in the text, however, in Barth's retrospective view, was any direct thematization of the plight of the Jewish people, who were already experiencing state discrimination.

In November 1934, Barth was suspended from his teaching duties for refusing to take the required oath of loyalty to Adolf Hitler. In March 1935, he was banned from speaking in public, and a formal dismissal from his position followed in June. Almost immediately, Barth was offered a chair in systematic theology at the University of Basel, and the family returned to the city at the beginning of July, where Barth would live for the rest of his life. Three years later, in 1938, the writings of Barth were banned in Germany.

## The later years of Karl Barth in Switzerland

Once back in Basel in 1935, Barth adopted a pattern of university work which would broadly accompany him until his official retirement in 1962. Work on *Church Dogmatics* continued to be the central focus of his endeavours as a theologian, and he devoted significant energies to writing material for the class lectures that would later, in revised form, become the further volumes of the series. In preparing the necessary reams of scriptural, historical and theological material, Barth was deeply indebted to von Kirschbaum, whose labours and insights contributed greatly to the work. New volumes were published regularly over the ensuing years, though never quite as regularly as Barth would ideally have liked.

Beyond lecturing towards *Church Dogmatics* in particular, Barth continued with a demanding general schedule of teaching in the university, from undergraduate lecturing through seminar offerings and discussion groups to research supervision. During these years, he reprised many of the courses that he had taught during his time in Germany, revising and correcting the material as he went. And he also took up for instruction and edification a wide variety of new theological topics (such as the church, baptism, the Lord's Supper and natural theology) and a broad array of new texts (such as *On True and False Religion* by Zwingli, the *Compendium of Theology* of Johannes Wollebius, the *Spiritual Exercises* of Ignatius of Loyola and *Verbum Dei* from the Second Vatican Council). As his reputation grew, so too did the number of students wishing to work with him, and following the end of the Second World War, an increasing number of international students arrived in Basel.

In the course of his latter years, Barth continued theological conversations with many of his former dialogue partners, such as Brunner, Bultmann, Thurneysen, Willem Visser 't Hooft, Martin Niemöller and Josef Hromádka. But he also joined in the conversations developing among a new and younger generation of theologians. In this connection, he engaged with the work of a whole host of renowned international scholars such as Hans Küng, Hans Urs von Balthasar, Jürgen Moltmann, Eberhard Jüngel, Thomas F. Torrance, Helmut Gollwitzer, Hans-Joachim Iwand and Keiji Ogawa.

Family life carried on throughout this time in Basel. In 1936, Barth became a grandfather for the first, though far from the last, time. In 1941, his brother Peter died suddenly, and in the same year, his son Matthias died from a climbing accident; Karl Barth preached on the occasion of both funerals. For all the complexities of his domestic situation, Barth always took both a great pride and a great interest in the lives of his children and, in due time, grandchildren.

And beyond the work of the university and the busyness of the family, Barth was prominently active in a diverse number of arenas, with a vigorous array of public lectures, church commitments, political activities, media engagements and wider events requiring of his time and energy in demanding fashion.

From his new home in Switzerland, Barth continued his active opposition to the National Socialist regime in Germany. Even before the outbreak of the war, Barth was an advocate of armed resistance to Hitler, in contrast to the official neutrality of the Swiss government. In 1938, he founded an organization which sought to help the Confessing Church in Germany, and he worked with others to offer assistance to and raise finance for Jewish refugees who managed to escape from Germany. That same year, he began a new journal entitled *Theologische Studien* (*Theological Studies*), which contained theological material opposing National Socialism and led to suspicion at home in neutral Switzerland.

One year following the outbreak of war in 1939, Barth volunteered for armed military service in defence of Switzerland's borders, though in the event the country was never attacked. And he continued throughout the war both to encourage Allied military action against Germany and to pose critical challenges to the position of the Swiss government and to the attitude of the Swiss people. The government subsequently restricted his public activities, banning him from speaking in public on political issues from 1941. Following the war, Barth was a strong advocate of reconciliation in Europe, and he returned to Germany to teach two semesters amidst the ruins of post-war Bonn in 1945–6, and to give lectures throughout the country, much of which had been devastated.

Rather different in tone was Barth's response after the Second World War to the developing Cold War between capitalist west and communist east. To the frustration of many in the west, Barth refused to offer outright condemnation of communism: he appreciated its clear recognition of the importance of social issues, though he acknowledged explicitly that the communist regime in the Soviet Union was despotic and ruthless. At the same time, he refused to offer unhesitating endorsement of capitalism, being strongly aware from his time in Safenwil of the human cost of that alternative economic system, and being strongly resistant to any identification of political system with Christian truth. In the highly charged political environment of the post-war era, the resultant stance – broadly neutral and seeking a third way between opposed ideological views – was deeply controversial on both sides of the emerging Iron Curtain.

During these later decades in Basel, Barth also continued to pursue his interest in and engagement with the growing ecumenical movement, while at the same time believing that church unity was too important to leave in the hands of any mere movement. In 1937, he prepared a lecture for the Edinburgh Faith and Order Conference on 'The Church and the Churches', in which he observed that the unity of the church consists in the common task of proclamation to which all churches and Christians are called. Such events helped lead to the formation of the World Council of Churches (WCC) in 1948. Barth delivered the opening address at the First WCC Assembly in Amsterdam in that year, and played a significant role in preparing materials for the Second WCC Assembly at Evanston in the United States in 1954.

A few years later, Barth was invited to be a guest observer at the third session of the Second Vatican Council. The Council took place between 1962 and 1965, and was called with the intention of addressing the relationship between the Roman Catholic Church and the modern world. Barth was one of a select group of non-Roman Catholics to be invited, but was unable to attend owing to his diminishing health and energies. Nevertheless, Barth followed the Council's developments with interest, and even visited Rome in 1966 for a personal audience with Pope Paul VI and conversations with Roman Catholic scholars. He was very pleased by, though not uncritical of, the progress made by the Council.

From his base in Basel, Barth regularly travelled throughout Switzerland to deliver lectures and conduct conversations. In addition, with the exception of the years 1939–45, he travelled extensively around Europe, visiting friends, and attending and addressing academic conferences, ministers' gatherings, church groups and secular organizations. From his base in Basel, he also regularly contributed to academic journals, church periodicals and secular publications, and gave a number of radio and television interviews. He was a regular, if not frequent, preacher, and delivered a large number of sermons in the State Prison of Basel between 1954 and 1964. Finally, he continued to communicate with a range of correspondents around Europe and beyond, including many former students and colleagues, and received a number of them at his home in Basel. His willingness and his ability to commit on so many fronts diminished over time, both as his desire to focus on *Church Dogmatics* increased, and as the inevitable limitations of health and age told.

In 1962, Barth officially retired from the University of Basel, although work on new material for *Church Dogmatics* had in truth ceased a couple of years beforehand. One of his first acts after retirement was to visit the United States for the first time: there he lectured at diverse seminaries, met Martin Luther King, and appeared on the front cover of *Time* magazine. Once home, he continued to fulfil other commitments and engagements as health allowed, even continuing to lead a small number of seminars over ensuing years. His constitution was weakened by a series of health setbacks between 1964 and 1966, though he recovered somewhat thereafter, resuming some of his theological activities, overseeing the publication of one further fragment of *Church Dogmatics* (IV/4), and making his trip to Rome. In the night of 9–10 December 1968, however, Barth died peacefully at home in his sleep.

## II On reading *Church Dogmatics*

*Church Dogmatics* is the work with reference to which Barth asked his theology to be understood and judged. Yet for a number of reasons, it is not an easy text to approach for the first time, and can prove quite daunting.

One of the possible reasons for this difficulty is that wherever you begin reading in *Church Dogmatics*, it can feel as if you have jumped in at the deep end. From the first page of the first volume, the work sits deep within the world of Christian belief and practice: there is no gentle introduction and no apologetic preamble. Instead, Barth always and immediately takes his orientation from the reality that God is known in the church and the world because of God's Self-revelation in Jesus Christ. This orientation has two direct and notable consequences for how Barth proceeds. First, it means that the doctrinal content of every theological topic is derived from this basic reality. There is no primary recourse to general observation, natural theology, human experience or secular philosophy. And second, it means that the movement of thought in every theological topic is always from this reality to its possibility – precisely the opposite movement from that which you might intuitively expect.

A further possible reason for this difficulty is that the tone which Barth employs in his writing can seem robust and assertive, even polemical at points. There is no doubt that Barth was a vigorous writer, who cared passionately about his theme and was determined to oppose that with which he disagreed. Yet for all the unyielding quality of his style, Barth himself was well aware of the *provisional* nature of all theology as a human undertaking. Indeed, for Barth, it could not be otherwise, given that theology can only ever move from and return to the Self-revelation of God in Jesus Christ, which is never under human control or command. For this reason, Barth considered that a true mark of progress in theology was that it always begin again at the beginning, such that it could and should never hope to arrive in any final sense at a completed system of doctrine. Theology remains a pilgrim discipline, for Barth, reflecting the pilgrim existence of the church as a people on the path of discipleship.

This notion of beginning again at the beginning goes part-way to explaining the physical bulk of *Church Dogmatics* – both as a whole and in each volume – that can render it rather daunting from the outset. One of the typical ways in which Barth writes is to consider a particular matter from one angle, and then to reconsider it from a further angle or even angles – sometimes with the aim of gradually expanding the argument with new material and other times with the aim of successively focusing the argument to pinpoint clarity. Either way, the procedure might be compared to a long mountain walk where a hiker traverses a long ridge encircling one central mountain, pausing to consider the changing view at regular intervals. Such an analogy perhaps captures something of the joy *and* the ardour of the procedure. And beyond this, there is the carefully systematic nature of Barth's writing, by virtue of which an exposition of one theological topic necessarily incurs mention or discussion of other topics.

At the same time, *Church Dogmatics* is carefully structured at every level, and for all the theological development in Barth's thinking over the years which the volumes attest, is written with a remarkable degree of internal consistency. The overall work is divided into five volumes, though the fourth volume was incomplete and the fifth volume was unstarted when Barth died. The following chart shows the overall structure of *Church Dogmatics*:

Structure of *Church Dogmatics*

| Volume I | The Doctrine of the Word of God | |
|---|---|---|
| *volume I/1* | | |
| Introduction | §1 | The Task of Dogmatics |
| | §2 | The Task of Prolegomena to Dogmatics |
| Chapter I: | §§3–7 | The Word as the Criterion of Dogmatics |
| Chapter II: | §§8–18 | The Revelation of God |
| | §§8–12 | The Triune God |
| *volume I/2* | | |
| | §§13–15 | The Incarnation of the Word |
| | §§16–18 | The Outpouring of the Holy Spirit |
| Chapter III: | §§19–21 | Holy Scripture |
| Chapter IV: | §§22–24 | The Proclamation of the Church |

As this chart shows, each volume of *Church Dogmatics* treats primarily of one doctrine, and each is divided physically into two or more part-volumes. Each volume is also divided first into chapters and then into sections (called paragraphs, though they can be many pages long, and are indicated with a '§' mark).

Each individual paragraph begins with a thesis statement in bold that is then expounded over the subsequent pages. This thesis statement is crucial: it serves as an orientation to both the content and the structure of the argument that follows, and in it no word is wasted. They thus reward careful attention. In the material which follows the thesis statement, Barth's own constructive position is exposited in the main text in regular font; the small-print sections which interrupt this main text at frequent intervals introduce a variety of further material, most often a selection or combination of biblical exegesis, historical theology and critical comment. A clear sense of Barth's constructive position can generally be derived from the main text alone. Yet the small-print sections should not be disregarded: they are instructive not only in explaining the constructive position in greater detail, but also in indicating its exegetical and doctrinal background and in explaining the rejection of alternatives.

As he works through the different paragraphs, Barth sometimes indicates the steps in his argument by way of numbered sections or additional breaks. Yet even where no explicit signs appear, Barth tends to offer an indication of some sort at those moments when the argument is transitioning from one point to another. It is helpful to look out for these moments, for those turns of phrase or interjections, for they allow the reader to gain a sharper awareness of the overall movement of the argument and the details of its trajectory. It is also helpful to look out for the regular points at which Barth explores the theological implications of the same phrase or clause time after time, but highlighting a different word on each occasion. And finally, it is important to look out for those places where Barth indicates that he is exploring *false* routes forward – sometimes over several pages – before setting out the *right* path to take, and to avoid an incorrect reading by missing such rhetorical devices.

Though *Church Dogmatics* is most often encountered in academic settings, it should always be remembered that the primary audience of the underlying material in its original setting was the *church* – or, more precisely, those students first in Bonn and then in Basel who were training to be pastors and teachers in the church. For Barth, therefore, theology is not primarily a discipline in the academy, but a discipline of the church. Certainly, Barth self-consciously located himself and his work within a particular church tradition – Protestant and Reformed. However, the substance of his work not only draws on but also speaks to the church universal. *Church Dogmatics*, then, is not a theology for one individual church or confessional group; it has instead implications for all traditions. In this sense it might be described as an *ecumenical* theology, thinking from, with and for the church as a whole.

Theology undertaken correctly, for Barth, has implications for what the church thinks and believes; and more than this, it has implications for what the church confesses and does, and for how individual Christians live and work and witness in the world. It is no wonder, then, that *Church Dogmatics* includes as an integral part of its text a series of major sections on ethics. Far from being confined to some ivory tower, theology is a deeply *practical* undertaking which at times can be radical and even dangerous. And precisely as a practical discipline of the church, Barth stated, theology can only be undertaken within the context of prayer. In its seeking after and reliance upon the truth of the revealed Word of God, theology can only ever be an exercise in petition, in humility and in need. And as a response to the good news of Jesus Christ, theology can only ever be an exercise of praise, of joy and of exaltation.

In what follows, successive chapters work sequentially through the different volumes of *Church Dogmatics*, expositing and explaining the key contours of Barth's theological position and indicating the relationships between the different doctrines explored. For ease of use, they contain no footnotes that might encumber the text; instead, all references for quotations from *Church Dogmatics* are given inline. In addition, lengthy quotations are avoided, in order to encourage readers to venture to open the original volumes for themselves. At the end of this book, a short list of suggestions for further reading in the primary and secondary literature is given.

# CHAPTER TWO

# The doctrine of the Word of God

The first volume of *Church Dogmatics* is based on lectures in Christian dogmatics that Barth delivered in Bonn and in Basel in the 1930s. The material was thus composed at a time of political and economic turmoil in Germany, including the end of the Weimar Republic and the emergence and election of the National Socialist party. The first part-volume appeared in 1932, while the second part-volume followed in 1938. The overarching theme of this volume – after two brief sections of Introduction – is the doctrine of the Word of God. The first section addresses the Word of God as the criterion of dogmatics, while the remaining sections attend sequentially three different aspects of the revelation of God: the divine revelation itself, including material on the triune God, the incarnation of the Word, and the outpouring of the Spirit; Scripture; and church proclamation. Each of these will be considered below in turn, and it will be seen that Barth's systematic approach results in all manner of Christian doctrines already being broached and explored within this first volume.

## I Introduction

At the outset of *Church Dogmatics*, Barth considers both the task of dogmatics and the task of prolegomena (introductory material) to dogmatics.

Barth begins by observing that dogmatics is a theological discipline, and that theology is a function of the church. Theology basically means to speak of God, and speaking about God takes place, by the grace of God, in the church – in the words and actions both of individuals and of the community. That there exists such talk of God in the church in the first place is simply assumed by Barth.

Barth observes that in all human talk of God, there exists both a vulnerability (to temptation) and a responsibility (before God). In view of this predicament, the church must be able to criticize and correct its speech about God. This task falls to theology in the strictest sense of the word, which means, to dogmatics. Barth thus offers this initial definition: 'Dogmatics is the self-examination of the Christian Church in respect of the content of its distinctive talk about God' (I/1, 11).

The criterion for all the church's talk about God – including dogmatics – is 'the being of the Church, Jesus Christ' – in other words, 'God in His gracious revealing and reconciling address to humanity' (I/1, 4). In seeking to ensure that the church's talk about God conforms with Jesus Christ as its basis, goal and content, dogmatics has the character of a science. Yet it is a 'science' which does not have its subject matter – Jesus Christ – at its disposal: instead, for Barth, dogmatics must ever and again *receive* Jesus Christ, as God *addresses* humanity in a new event of revelation. Indeed, dogmatics is only possible on the basis of faith that God can and will do this, in accordance with the promise God has given to the church. For this reason, every statement in dogmatics is a statement of faith; yet in view of its subject matter, dogmatics must venture to speak with the assurance of communicating not just human truth but also divine truth.

At the same time, for Barth, the human activity of dogmatics in which this revelation of Jesus Christ is appropriated and expressed is fallible. And so Barth posits that dogmatics itself must be open to critique and correction, and that it must be ventured in humility and obedience. It cannot begin with a set of fixed ideas – not even church confessions or biblical texts – that it can simply presuppose, assemble and rehearse. Instead, it must always begin again at the beginning, absolutely dependent upon the ever-new address of God and upon the faith and obedience which this event brings. It is therefore always a divine matter whether our hearing and obedience are real and thus whether our dogmatic work is sanctified. In view of this genuine difficulty, Barth writes of prayer as 'the attitude without which there can be no dogmatic work' (I/1, 23).

Given this concept of dogmatics, it is no surprise that Barth does not affirm that there can be any prolegomena to dogmatics, that is, any discussion of the path of knowledge to be followed in dogmatics, that are not part of dogmatics itself. For Barth, there is no route from knowledge in other disciplines to dogmatic knowledge, and no 'point of contact' for knowledge of God in human beings that can serve as a starting point for dogmatics – at least not outwith the event of revelation and faith. From the start, then, Barth opposes the possibility of a programme of apologetics which proceeds as if such a point did exist.

Barth recognizes here that there are other ways of pursuing dogmatic enquiry – ways formally the same in respect of their desire to refer to Jesus Christ and the church, but materially different in terms of their way of understanding the same themes. These ways he describes as 'heresy'. Particularly in view for Barth here are the theologies of Roman Catholicism and liberal Protestantism – two forms of Christianity which will be dialogue partners throughout this volume of *Church Dogmatics*, but whose presence as Barth's principal antagonists fades somewhat in later volumes. Barth considers the former to conceive dogmatic knowledge as an innate possibility of humanity, and the latter to conceive dogmatic knowledge as an existing reality in the church. In both cases, then, it seems to Barth that the truth of dogmatics is already at our disposal. By contrast, Barth contends once more that the true starting point for dogmatic knowledge can only ever be 'the present moment of the speaking and hearing of Jesus Christ Himself' (I/1, 41).

## Comment

In this opening section, Barth begins in the middle of things. He simply assumes that there *is* in actuality talk about God in the church, and presents his vision of dogmatics as a human activity which serves to critique and correct that discourse. Dogmatics is an activity that is both grounded in and judged by the Word of God revealed to humanity in Jesus Christ. And it is dependent on the event of revelation in which this Word is received ever anew, and upon the faith and obedience which is gifted by God in the same event. For these reasons, there can be no prolegomena to dogmatics that are not already part of dogmatics: no recourse to general anthropology, as Barth sees in liberal Protestantism, or to church dogma, as Barth sees in Roman Catholicism. Instead, any initial discussion in the prolegomena of the way of knowledge to be followed can only have recourse, prayerfully yet expectantly, to the Word of God. This construal of dogmatics is certainly contentious, particularly in view of its emphatically Christocentric way of proceeding, but Barth follows it in practice – the rest of the first volume of *Church Dogmatics* is an exposition of the doctrine of the Word of God. The result is that much of the volume is given to issues in theological epistemology, as Barth clarifies and defends his position.

# II The Word of God as the criterion of dogmatics

In the first chapter proper of *Church Dogmatics*, Barth takes a closer look at the Word of God and the way it serves as the criterion of dogmatics. In successive sections, he explores the task of proclamation, and then in turn the three forms, the nature, and the knowability of the Word of God, before turning to the relationship between the Word of God, dogma and dogmatics.

## *Church proclamation as the material of dogmatics*

That there is human speech about God in the church is a matter, as indicated above, of the grace of God. And though there are various types of human speech about God in the church, it is in proclamation – in preaching and sacrament – that the church is *specifically* commissioned to declare the Word of God. Of itself, Barth notes, human speech lacks any innate capacity to declare the Word of God, and can only seek to serve the Word of God. In the event of divine revelation, however, the proclamation of the church can actually *become* and be this divine Word, as God reveals Godself through human words, working in and through them to announce the promise of God.

Barth acknowledges that God can also reveal Godself outside the church: God can speak through any medium to reveal Godself. However, the church has for Barth a divine *commission* to proclaim God by way of preaching and sacrament. To consider preaching as self-exposition, as Barth sees in liberal Protestantism, or as optional extra, as Barth sees in Roman Catholicism, will not suffice. At issue in church proclamation is instead the repetition of the divine promise of the future revelation, reconciliation and vocation of God, and the fulfilment of this promise in the event of the new coming of the Word of God.

By the grace of God, then, the human word of proclamation that seeks to serve the Word of God can become and be the Word of God; yet in all this, it remains a deeply human word, and thus both vulnerable to temptation and responsible to God. The dogmatic task of criticism and correction finds its central locus here, as the church questions whether its proclamation in preaching and sacrament conformed to its divine commission yesterday and whether it will conform to its divine commission tomorrow. In its service of proclamation, dogmatics thus seeks to offer to the church 'guidelines, directions, insights, principles, and limits' (I/1, 86).

## The Word of God in its threefold form

One of Barth's central insights in his prolegomena is that the Word of God has three forms – as proclaimed (by the church), as written (in Scripture) and as revealed (in Jesus Christ). This is not a new insight, but it is an insight which Barth conceives in a new way.

As noted above, the proclaimed words of the church can *become* the proclaimed Word of God in the event of revelation: hence Barth writes that 'Proclamation must ever and again become proclamation' (I/1, 88). If this is to take place, then it is necessary that the church's proclamation is commissioned by the Word of God, that its theme of discourse is the Word of God and that its criterion of judgement is the Word of God. But over and above all this, for proclamation to reveal the Word of God then an *event* of the Word of God is necessary. In this event, without the human words of proclamation losing their freedom or integrity, they become words in and through which God speaks.

In proclamation, the church must recall the revelation of God that has taken place in the past, and in particular the witness to past revelation that confronts the church in the text of Scripture. Just as in the case of proclamation, the human words of Scripture can *become* words in and through which God speaks, in an event of divine revelation. Yet there is a significant difference, for the words of Scripture are absolutely determinative of and foundational for all subsequent proclamation: 'The prophetic and apostolic word [is] the necessary rule of every word that is valid in the Church' (I/1, 104). There is no church writing or tradition outwith the canon of Scripture that has the same authoritative status. Instead, the canon of Scripture alone imposes itself upon the church by virtue of its content – 'the word, witness, proclamation and preaching of Jesus Christ' (I/1, 107).

Scripture attests past revelation, and proclamation promises future revelation, and in the event of divine action, both can become the Word of God. Yet neither is *of itself* directly identical with revelation: both can only point towards revelation, for in revelation, Barth writes, our concern is with 'God's own Word spoken by God Himself' – with Jesus Christ (I/1, 113). It is this revelation which has given rise to Scripture and which calls forth proclamation: revelation is originally and directly what Scripture and proclamation are derivatively and indirectly. Revelation is the divine event of the Word of God being spoken in time – the making present of the person of Jesus Christ and his reconciliation.

For all their distinction, there are not then three different words of God, but one Word of God in three forms. Scripture and proclamation are God's Word as they become so in revelation; Jesus Christ simply is God's eternal Word.

## *The nature of the Word of God*

God and the Word of God are never given to us in the same way as other things around us. Rather, for Barth, 'God's Word means that God speaks' (I/1, 132). For all the natural means in and through which this Word *speaks* to us, addressing us from beyond our own possibilities as the Word to us of the Lord who is our Creator, Reconciler and Redeemer, Barth is emphatic that it is truly *God* who acts to address us here and now in a specific and concrete way.

The Word of God addresses us with sovereign power, rendering us – and indeed the church and the world – hearers of this Word, claiming our very being, and deciding upon and asking after our obedience or disobedience in response.

The characterization of the nature of the Word of God which Barth deploys here is *mystery*, as he writes that 'Our concept of God and His Word can only be an indication of the limits of our conceiving' (I/1, 164). The Word of God is never at our disposal as an object in the world. Even as it is spoken to us, it always comes to us as veiled, not just in a creaturely form but in a creaturely form that is fallen. Hence in revelation, there is both an unveiling of God in this veiling and a veiling of God in this unveiling – in both cases, it is only in faith that we hear the full and true Word of God. There is here a rejection of both a naïve realism which considers the Word of God materially graspable and a base idealism which considers the materiality of revelation dispensable – such crudely realistic or idealistic theologies are unacceptable to Barth.

This dialectic of veiling and unveiling in the revelation of the Word of God is one of a number of dialectics – patterns of thought in which contrasting ideas must be held in tension but in which, often, a definite order is to be recognized – that Barth mentions here. He also alludes to Law and Gospel, demand and promise, letter and spirit. In each case, Barth suggests, we think or experience only one member of the pair at a time, but we must simultaneously hear the other member in faith. This hearing, like faith in general, is not within our own innate possibilities, but is rather the work of the Spirit, 'the Lord by whose act the openness and readiness of man for the Word are true and actual' (I/1, 182).

## *The knowability of the Word of God*

Barth starts out from the assumption that it is possible for us to hear and speak and know the Word of God. But the particular knowledge of the Word of God is not bare factual knowledge; rather it is knowledge that claims us and determines us, and calls us to be responsible witnesses to its content. And this knowledge of the Word of God is not possible, for Barth, on the basis of any human predisposition to or innate capacity for the Word. Instead, it is and becomes possible for human beings only 'when the ability is given to them by the Word itself' (I/1, 196). This takes place in the event of divine revelation.

In revelation, we *experience* God's Word, as it comes to us and determines our being in a primary and unique way completely different to our own acts of self-determination. This divine determination certainly affects our intellect, but it also affects our feeling and our will. Yet in this experience of determination we are not simply receptive or passive, for it is precisely our *active* self-determination that is now determined by God's Word. The result, for Barth, is that our self-determination has its meaning, basis, seriousness, content, truth and reality, not in ourselves, but rather *outside ourselves*, in Jesus Christ. It is ultimately this real *experience* of being addressed by God's Word that decides and proves that the possibility of this address lies not within ourselves but in the divine grace.

The possibility of knowledge of God can therefore only be known and affirmed in *faith*, as our self-determination is actually determined by God. True faith arises when the Word of God is given to us 'as the object of acknowledgment, and therefore as the basis of real faith' (I/1, 230). Thus though there is genuine human action and experience at stake in speaking of true faith, it is action and experience that is utterly determined by its Object, by Jesus Christ.

In the event of faith, and only there, and not on the grounds of any human capacity, there arises a *conformity* of the human person to God. This adapting of our person to and by the Word of God is not a question of an *analogia entis* (analogy of being) between God and humanity that can be surveyed and perceived – this Barth considered to be the deeply problematic Roman Catholic position. Instead, the conformity for Barth takes place – in faith – between the address of divine grace in revelation and the corresponding human act of hearing and confessing. This *analogia fidei* (analogy of faith) takes place as an *event* in which, in faith and confession, 'the Word of God becomes a human thought and a human word, certainly in infinite dissimilarity and inadequacy, ... but a true copy for all its human and sinful perversion' (I/1, 241). This is, again, not a human possibility, but a divine possibility, and takes place as an 'opening up from above that takes place in the event of real faith' (I/1, 243). Even and precisely here, then, in the genuine and free human action of faith, the creature is enclosed and determined by the gracious action of God.

## *The Word of God, dogma and dogmatics*

At this point, Barth returns to the task of dogmatics – the criticism and correction of the proclamation of the church in light of the Word of God. Barth considers that in modern Protestantism, criteria from other disciplines have regularly been used alongside the Word of God in the dogmatic task, while in Roman Catholicism, the external criterion of the Word of God has been conflated with the internal tradition and teaching of the church. By contrast, writes Barth, 'seeing we face the task of dogmatics, we decide … to accept the Bible as the absolute authority set up over against Church proclamation' (I/1, 265). It is, after all, Scripture which attests the revelation of the Word of God, and which speaks to us as the Word of God in the event of revelation.

## *Comment*

In this chapter of *Church Dogmatics* on the Word of God as criterion of dogmatics, Barth covers much ground, offering an expansive account of the way of knowing to be followed in his work. It begins by listening for and attending to the revelation of the Word of God that is attested in Scripture. It is only in the present event of revelation that the creature by grace has the possibility of hearing and knowing this Word, and of acknowledging it in faith. Dogmatics, and the church, must therefore always begin by hearing this Word, for it is the Word of the Lord of all humanity, and is thus a Word radically different from any word which the creature can say to itself.

A number of features of this presentation are worthy of further reflection.

The first is the sheer radicality of Barth's position in its context. The rejection of liberal Protestant and Roman Catholic ideas, which appears as a regular refrain throughout this section, indicates that Barth is consciously setting forth an alternative understanding of the criterion and task of dogmatics. There are two points in particular which have proven controverted in this connection.

On the one hand, Barth insists that the sole criterion of dogmatics is the revealed Word of God, as attested in Scripture. The exclusive focus on Jesus Christ which this entails renders any programme of theological apologetics redundant, and rules out any way of natural theology – of seeking knowledge of God by other means. Barth recognizes explicitly that the validity of his path cannot be empirically proven. Instead, Barth posits, it can only prove itself to be correct in the event of faith, in which the revelation of God actually occurs.

On the other hand, Barth also insists that the sole criterion of dogmatics is not given to it as possession, but can only be received by it in the divine act of revelation. We can only have knowledge of God by way of recollection of past revelation and in expectation of future revelation: it is never something given to us over which we can dispose. Though our human words can conform to the Word of God in an event of grace and revelation, this is not an event within our power and control but only a promise which we can strive to claim.

The result of this position is that dogmatics emerges as a deeply necessary yet rather humble discipline, the task of which 'cannot be to tear down the barriers of faith that are set for the Church' (I/1, 249). Not only for its basis and its criterion, but also for its success, it is deeply dependent on the Word of God revealed in Jesus Christ and attested in Scripture and proclaimed in the church.

The second is the way in which much of this material is rather *formal* in exposition – there is little material *content* in respect of the issues considered. Hence Barth recognizes the need for more explicit accounts of the Word of God, of Scripture and of proclamation as part of an analysis of 'the concrete concept of revelation which the Bible attests to have taken place and proclamation promises will come' (I/1, 290). It is to this task that Barth turns next.

# III  The revelation of God

In this extensive chapter, Barth exposits the concept of divine revelation. This leads him to consider the doctrine of the Trinity, and thence to explore first the incarnation of the Word, and then the outpouring of the Spirit. The doctrines of Word and Spirit are central to the exposition of Barth's doctrine of reconciliation, which is discussed in Chapters 5 and 6; here, however, the focus is on these doctrines in their relation to the knowledge of God in revelation.

# *The triune God*

To understand the doctrine of revelation correctly means to start with the doctrine of the Trinity. The reason, for Barth, is that it is only 'by observing the unity and the differentiation of God in His biblically attested revelation that we are set before the problem of the doctrine of the Trinity' (I/1, 299). To put this particular doctrine at the *beginning* of dogmatics is for Barth an essential move – for all that it has not been a move regularly made in the history of the tradition – in order to safeguard that the revelation of God which is in view is *Christian* revelation. It is, Barth emphasizes, on the basis of the revelation of God that is attested in Scripture that 'our understanding of revelation, or of the God who reveals Himself, must be the doctrine of the Trinity' (I/1, 312).

The revelation of God has no higher or deeper ground than itself, and its reality and truth is its own. This view, which summarizes Barth's understanding of the scriptural witness on this point, underlies his programmatic statement that 'God reveals Himself as the Lord' (I/1, 306). In the divine freedom in which revelation takes place, the lordship of God is evidenced in three ways. First, in revelation, God reveals Godself as God the Son in an event of Self-*unveiling*, making God present and known in creation by means of a form that is not God. Second, God is by nature *veiled* to humanity, different to and hidden from the world, such that even in the event of revelation, God the Father remains *veiled* and does not take form. And third, the event of revelation occurs as a concrete historical event in which revelation is *imparted* to a specific creature who, in and of themselves, cannot receive this revelation, but in the power of God the Spirit is empowered to hear, believe and obey. For Barth, the biblical witness to revelation comprises these elements of unveiling, veiling and impartation, and in this way offers both an indication and an outline of the doctrine of the Trinity.

At this point, Barth turns briefly to consider the theological tradition of the *vestigia Trinitatis* ('vestiges of the Trinity') – purported analogies of the Trinity in creation which are distinct from God and from the revelation of God, yet which are said somehow to bear a similarity to the doctrine of the Trinity and are thus considered an image of the triune God. It should come as no surprise that Barth rejects this tradition as it relates to created objects in themselves. Any inherent similarity of such a kind could only be by way of an *analogia entis* – an analogy of being, exactly the mode of analogy that Barth denies. By contrast, the only analogy of the Trinity in creation which Barth endorses is that which occurs in the event of revelation, in which God makes Godself present as Father, Son and Spirit.

From this starting point in the biblical witness to revelation, Barth moves to consider the doctrine of the Trinity in the church. Barth acknowledges that the doctrine of the Trinity itself does not stand in Scripture, but posits that it is a faithful *interpretation* of the biblical texts. His subsequent presentation broadly follows the traditional patterns of orthodox Trinitarian doctrine.

Barth treats first of the unity of God, emphasizing that God is one in essence, and that this oneness is not abrogated by the threeness of the divine 'persons'. In this way, he writes, Christian monotheism simply is Trinitarian: 'God is the one God in threefold repetition' (I/1, 350). Moving to the triunity of God, Barth posits that the oneness of God denotes neither singularity nor isolation, but does include distinction – of Father, Son and Spirit. These distinctions are not a matter of essence or thought or will; instead the distinctions are a matter of distinctive *relations* to one another. In referring to these distinctions, Barth advocates the term 'mode of being' over the usual term 'person': the former has a long theological heritage, and avoids the latter's risk of thinking about the divine 'persons' after the fashion of human persons. Yet Barth also recognizes that human language simply fails here, as 'none of the terms used … can adequately say what we ought to say and are trying to say in using it' (I/1, 367). And more broadly, Barth here recognizes the difficulties that the Christian doctrine of the Trinity will always face in view of the dangers posed by modalism and tritheism.

The fact that God's essence is one, together with the fact that no separation between the modes of being of God follows from their distinct relations to one another, leads Barth to affirm the doctrine of *perichoresis* – 'a complete participation of each mode of being in the other modes of being' (I/1, 370). To this unity corresponds the unity of the work of God, which truly reveals God's essence. God's work, however, takes place in the *freedom* of God and thus a distinction is to be made between the divine essence and the divine work. In revelation, we can only ever grasp the *works* of God; hence we can understand the triunity of the *essence* of God only by grace and within creaturely limits. With this in mind, the doctrine of appropriations follows Scripture in attributing particular *works* of God to particular *persons* of the Trinity, but in truth recognizes explicitly that God always works in all three modes of being.

In three further sections, Barth explores the three modes of being of the triune God: God as Father, God as Son and God as Spirit.

First, on God as Father, Barth observes that in the revelation attested in Scripture, God encounters humanity as its Lord, and the climax of its witness is that Jesus of Nazareth is the Lord. Yet precisely here, Barth writes, 'the lordship of Jesus as the Son of God is obviously only a manifestation, exercise and application of the lordship of God the Father' (I/1, 386). The Father whom Jesus reveals is, for Barth, the Lord of our existence, who not only wills our life but leads it through death to eternal life, and thus God the Creator. That God is our Father *in time* corresponds with God *eternally* being in Godself the Father of the Son, in and as a mode of being of the divine essence.

Second, on God as Son, Barth returns to the theme of Jesus of Nazareth as the Lord. To speak of Jesus as Lord is, for Barth, to indicate the deity of Jesus Christ, for he is the true revelation of God the Father. Yet in the Son we have to do not simply with the divine ruling of our created existence, but with a new miracle in which God turns to and addresses us as not only created but also sinful, in the same movement restoring our relationship with God. In Jesus Christ, then, we have to do with God the Reconciler, and thus 'revelation is itself reconciliation' (I/1, 409). That Jesus Christ can *in time* both reveal to us the Father and reconcile us to the Father rests, for Barth, on Jesus Christ being *eternally* the Son of the Father and thus eternally God. Both true revelation and true reconciliation would be jeopardized, for Barth, if the deity of the Reconciler were to be called into question. Once again, however, Barth recognizes that to confess the deity of the the Son rests on the appropriate interpretation of the biblical witness to revelation.

Finally, on God as Spirit, Barth returns again to the theme of Jesus of Nazareth as the Lord, to enquire as to how we are able to make this confession. In the event of revelation, God is not only present to us externally, from above, but also internally, from below – not only objectively, but also subjectively. God's freedom to be present in this way, and to effect this encounter, is the Spirit of God. The Spirit allows us to believe, know and confess the Word spoken in revelation, gives us instruction and guidance, and empowers our own witness to Jesus Christ. By the work of the Spirit who is also the Lord, we are set free to become children of God: this is the work of God the Redeemer, even as 'we can regard it only as future, ... as the redemption that comes to us from God' (I/1, 463) and have it in the present only in faith. That the Spirit is the communion of God and humanity *in time* rests on the fact that the Spirit is the communion of the Father and of the Son *in eternity*. The work of the Spirit in our redemption thus rests, once again, on the Spirit being itself eternal and divine – another confession which Barth recognizes to be based on the appropriate interpretation of the scriptural witness to revelation.

In the conclusions of the sections on the Son and the Spirit, Barth explores the statements on the Son and the Spirit in the Niceno-Constantinopolitan Creed (325/381). His treatment of both this material and its implications is broadly traditional, at least in a western sense. Yet it is significant that Barth does not accept the Creed on any other basis than that it is a faithful interpretation of Scripture and thus of revelation. And he recognizes that in speaking of the eternal and the incomprehensible, even the Creed can only indicate and not explain or prove the divine mystery.

## *The incarnation of the Word*

Having answered the question of the *Subject* of revelation in the doctrine of the Trinity at the end of the first part-volume of *Church Dogmatics*, Barth turns at the start of the second part-volume to the objective and subjective *fulfilments* of the event of revelation. This leads him, first, to the incarnation of the Word, and second, to the outpouring of the Spirit. For Barth, the central claim of these doctrines is that God 'is free for us and in us' (I/2, 2).

Barth begins with the incarnation of the Word in Jesus Christ, and – in accord with his method – he considers first the *reality* of the incarnation as it is attested in Scripture and only then the *possibility* of the incarnation. Scripture attests that the Word or Son of God becomes human in Jesus of Nazareth. And it is for Barth this *particular* name of Jesus Christ which is central to the New Testament, and not any concept of incarnation in general; thus it is this once-for-all reality which must guide our dogmatic thinking.

It is only on the basis of Jesus Christ that we can infer that God is *free* to be God in and among us in such a way that the Son of God becomes a man. This possibility, Barth writes, 'is eternally grounded within God Himself' (I/2, 34). The divine freedom encompasses God's ability to condescend to us, and to become known by us in the veiling (and unveiling) of the Word of God in human flesh. And this freedom encompasses God's ability to remain God in this event of the Son becoming human, of becoming like us in all respects except sin. In this way, Jesus Christ reveals not only true God, but also true humanity – the latter is the starting point for Barth's theological anthropology, treated in Chapter 4 below.

That God reveals Godself to us in Jesus Christ suggests, for Barth, that God has time for us, which further implies that we should understand what *time* is from this event of revelation. In revelation, Barth writes, God assumes the veil of our old time 'in order to make it – and this is the unveiling – His own time, the new time' (I/2, 56). The event of revelation only ever takes place in history in the form of a miracle. But when it occurs, we are transposed from our fallen time into the time of Jesus Christ, and we become 'contemporary with it, a partner in this time and so a time-partner or contemporary of Jesus Christ, of the prophets and apostles' (I/2, 59). Even though of ourselves we remain thirled to fallen time, we now recognize that this fallen time will not last forever.

Prior to the incarnation, Barth notes, there was a time of *expectation* of revelation, attested in the Old Testament; following the incarnation, there was a time of *recollection* of revelation, attested in the New Testament. Both Testaments witness to the one covenant of grace between God and humanity, to the hiddenness of God in revelation, and to the divine presence coming to humanity. Yet though the times of expectation and recollection relate closely to the fulfilled time of Jesus Christ, they are not identical with it: fulfilled time is a matter of revelation, and revelation always enters our sphere from above.

At this point, Barth enters into matters of Christology, but only in so far as they pertain to revelation; Christology will receive a fuller treatment in the doctrine of reconciliation, treated below in Chapters 5 and 6. The revelation of God in Jesus Christ, Barth writes, is a mystery: 'It can be contemplated, acknowledged, worshipped and confessed as such, but it cannot be solved, or transformed into a non-mystery' (I/2, 124–5). And it is Scripture – in its expectation and recollection – which confronts us with this mystery of the incarnation.

Barth begins by considering each part of the Gospel claim that 'the Word became flesh' (Jn 1.14). First, *the Word* who becomes flesh is the eternal Word, acting in divine sovereignty and divine freedom, and retaining – even as incarnate – this sovereignty and freedom as 'very God'. For this reason, the tradition is right to affirm Mary as 'Mother of God' – though wrong to claim for Mary any more than this. Second, the Word who becomes *flesh* becomes truly human in the sphere of history, and thus God becomes 'the Subject of a real human being and acting' (I/2, 151). In becoming flesh, the Word also becomes liable to the judgement of God upon sinful flesh; yet in this position, the Word made flesh does not sin but is obedient to God. And third, that the Word *becomes* flesh by the miraculous will and work of God suggests both that the Word is to be sought and found only in the flesh assumed *and* that there is to be found in the flesh also the complete transcendence of the Word. These last claims may indeed lie in tension, but Barth indicates that both are necessary.

Barth rounds off this treatment of the incarnation with an affirmation of the church teaching that Jesus is conceived by the Spirit and born of the Virgin Mary. For Barth, this teaching, 'the miracle of Christmas', points to 'the mystery of Christmas' – the true divinity and true humanity of Jesus Christ.

## *The outpouring of the Spirit*

Having explored the *objective* aspect of revelation in the doctrine of the incarnation, Barth turns to contemplate the *subjective* aspect – the *revealedness* – of revelation in the outpouring of the Spirit. This subjective correspondence on the human side to the divine event of revelation is, for Barth, 'just as seriously the content of the biblical witness to revelation' (I/2, 206).

While God is free to reveal Godself to humanity, it is not the case that of itself humanity is free to receive this revelation: for Barth, the witness of Scripture attests that 'man's freedom for God … cannot be explained from man's side' (I/2, 205). Therefore our freedom for God is not a human possibility but a *divine* possibility. And we know of this possibility, Barth continues, only because it is already a *reality*, and – more precisely – a reality in the church. The church is the unique place in history where the revelation of God is received. Both the existence and the unity of the church derive from the Word of God, and for all that the church may be visible in the world, the truth of its existence and unity can only ever be a matter of divine revelation.

God reveals Godself to us by way of signs in creation, taking up creaturely instruments in ever-new ways to reveal Godself afresh in every generation. As we receive these signs as signs of revelation, as we recognize and acknowledge them, so in this event our very existence as children of God is given anew. That this takes place, for Barth, is the mystery that is the work of the Spirit, and the subjective reality of revelation. And as this activity of the Spirit completes the movement of God towards us in Jesus Christ, so we come to know that 'we are in Christ by Christ' and so 'hearers and doers of the Word of God' (I/2, 240).

Again, it is from the reality of God's revelation reaching us in the work of the Spirit that we infer that God is *free* to do this. In the outpouring of the Spirit, the Word comes to our hearing and bestows the freedom necessary for this hearing. And there is no other freedom of humanity for God than this freedom that is created by the Spirit. In this act of God, Barth writes, 'Our existence is confronted by something outside and over against it, by which it is determined, and indeed totally determined' (I/2, 266). Even as this event itself remains a mystery to us, we know ourselves to be set before God with Jesus Christ as our Lord. And the goal of this event is that 'out of man's life there should come a repetition, an analogy, a parallel to [Christ's] own being' (I/2, 277).

As revelation encounters human beings, as a specific determination of their existence, it enters the sphere of *religion*. And so there arises the question of whether revelation should be interpreted by the category of religion, or whether religion should be interpreted by the event of revelation. In contrast with many modern Protestant approaches, but in line with his confession of the unsurpassable character and determining power of revelation, Barth opts for the latter strategy. He thus regards not only non-Christian religions but also – and above all – the Christian religion itself through the lens of revelation.

The result is that Barth characterizes religion as 'the contradiction of revelation, the concentrated expression of human unbelief'

(I/2, 302–3). In religion, instead of listening to revelation, *we* speak; instead of receiving our salvation in revelation, we seek to save ourselves. Throughout this discussion, Barth is relentlessly negative about the possibilities of human religion. Certainly, he acknowledges, religion is capable of self-criticism, which may lead us either to mysticism or to atheism. But only true revelation in Jesus Christ demonstrates the unbelief of all religion, and thereby opposes, contradicts and displaces it.

The Christian religion, like all religions, is in and of itself unbelief; however, by the grace of God, Barth writes, 'the Christian religion is the true religion' (I/2, 326). This is because it is in the church alone that the revelation and grace of God confronts human beings and enables them to live as children of God. Such an affirmation is only valid as a statement of faith, and only possible in the context of the miracle of divine revelation. Moreover, such an affirmation is only valid if the truth of the Christian religion is conceived not as a creaturely possession or disposition but as 'an event in the act of the grace of God in Jesus Christ' (I/2, 344). It is Jesus Christ alone who creates, elects, justifies and sanctifies the Christian religion. Hence the Christian religion should at all times recognize in humility its weakness and its dependence on grace.

Barth concludes this chapter by turning to those who receive the revelation of God – those who have been adopted as children of God and who are now called to conform their lives to the will of God. For Barth, the new freedom of the children of God, their act and work, is 'revealed in the fulfilment of revelation as the outpouring of the Holy Spirit' (I/2, 368). Those whom God has found and freed in revelation cannot exist in faith without both seeking after God and testifying to God. And hence, the Christian life consists of love and praise.

As Barth explores aspects of the basis, context, content and purpose of our love of God, and of our love of neighbour which is praise of God, so he insists that love and praise are genuine creaturely realities, acts of our self-determination which correspond to the grace of God in Jesus Christ. In these events, which occur only by way of the miracle and activity of God, we become what we truly are as those who are loved by God. In this way, Barth writes, 'in our very existence we become a sign and testimony' (I/2, 414). Our corresponding creaturely disposition must thus be one of humility and prayer.

# *Comment*

At the end of this lengthy section of *Church Dogmatics*, it is helpful to review the road travelled. In order to provide a thorough analysis of the biblical concept of revelation, Barth has discoursed upon the doctrine of the Trinity, the doctrine of God, Christology and pneumatology, and has also outlined positions in ecclesiology and ethics and provided a theological analysis of religion. As will be seen again in future chapters, Barth's systematic approach to individual questions inevitably leads him to reflect widely on various matters at every point.

At the same time, given the rubric of revelation under which this chapter is presented, it is noticeable that much of the analysis here is rather *formal* in tone. The overriding focus is on issues of epistemology – of knowledge of God, and on the Trinitarian account of Word and Spirit which enables our present knowledge of God. The foundations that are laid here govern the material in the remaining volumes of *Church Dogmatics*, particularly the Christocentric conception of the Word of God as the absolutely exclusive locus of revelation. Where confessional statements are encountered in this material, they tend to receive simple acceptance rather than real engagement. As *Church Dogmatics* proceeds, this focus will shift somewhat, as more attention is given to the Gospel accounts of the history of Jesus Christ who is truly divine and truly human. This will lead Barth later to engage more extensively with issues in theological ontology and more critically with the substance of existing Christian confessions.

Three features of this treatment of revelation deserve comment at this point.

First, this chapter exemplifies clearly the way in which Barth always begins in dogmatics with the actuality and reality of a given event and only then moves to consider its possibility. This is a reversal of the dominant modern mode of thinking, and may at first seem counter-intuitive. But it reflects the fact that Barth does not start his dogmatics with a blank slate, but from a position within the church and its commitment to the confession of the Christian faith. And it brings with it Barth's ready acknowledgement that the positions that he describes and advocates cannot be proven empirically; rather they are implicates of faith, and dogmatics – correspondingly – is that faith seeking understanding.

Second, Barth recognizes that the traditional beliefs of the church – such as the doctrine of the Trinity and the deity of Jesus Christ – cannot simply be read off the surface of the text of Scripture. However, Barth is not concerned by this, and instead works with a cheerful confidence that these doctrines both represent a faithful exegesis of Scripture and are indicated by the nature of revelation which Scripture attests. The authority of the ancient creeds of the church thus rests on their conformity with Scripture. And Barth recognizes explicitly that – for dogmatics and for Christians – what is at stake in these creeds, as in revelation as a whole, has the character of miracle and mystery.

And third, Barth characterizes revelation in every aspect as a divine possibility, insisting that both the objective aspect *and* the subjective aspect of revelation are the prerogative of God. He thus denies any innate point of contact for human knowledge of God. However, precisely here, Barth indicates a clear space for human agency: the response of faith, love and praise which is evoked in the one to whom revelation comes represents a genuine event of creaturely self-determination, for all that it is circumscribed by the divine determination. For Barth, human freedom and divine freedom are thus not in a competitive relation: what it is to be truly human is to be under the lordship of God.

# IV  Scripture

Having explored at length the event of the revelation of God in the Word of God, Barth now turns once again, and now in more detail, to the second and third forms of the Word of God – Scripture and proclamation. The broad position in respect of each has been advanced already: these forms are the Word of God only as they *become* the Word of God in the context of an event of revelation. Barth turns first to offer greater and deeper elucidation of Scripture.

As Barth has already outlined, Scripture has especial authority in and over the church in general and its proclamation in particular. This is true, for Barth, 'to the extent that it is a witness of divine revelation' (I/2, 457). The authority of Scripture is therefore not a quality of Scripture in itself. Instead, if Scripture acquires in the church the dignity and validity of the Word of God – and does so no less than the revelation that it attests – then this is due to the power of revelation. Scripture is vindicated as an authority for the church in and by what takes place, as 'the witness to divine revelation which we have heard in it ... repeat[s] itself in such a way that it can again be apprehended' (I/2, 458).

It is within the church alone that there arises the consequent *confession* that Scripture is the witness of revelation. Barth writes that 'there is a Word of God for the Church: in that it receives in the Bible the witness of divine revelation' (I/2, 463). Both this reception of the Word of God in Scripture, and the confession of and obedience to Scripture which result are, for Barth, events which take place miraculously, in the power of the free grace of the Spirit of God. That Scripture becomes in and for the church the Word of God is a matter of faith, to be indicated and affirmed, but not able to be proven empirically.

The term 'witness' is thus central to Barth's conception of Scripture. A witness is not *identical* to that to which it witnesses, and, correspondingly, Scripture is not *itself* the revelation of God, but simply human words and human speech. Scripture does not set God's revelation at our disposal in any kind of static revealedness, and its text is thus as open to historical and critical study as any other human text. Moreover, Barth observes, as a human text Scripture also bears a capacity for errors, not only in matters of history or science, but also in matters of religion or theology: all that it says is related to and conditioned by history. The Word of God may be infallible; but the biblical words of human beings are in and of themselves entirely fallible.

However, Barth insists, as a real witness, Scripture nevertheless sets the revelation of God before us, and that infallible revelation is its basis, object and content. Therefore, analysis of a historical or critical nature remains insufficient in so far as it fails to attend to that of which Scripture speaks as a human word. And this subject matter of which Scripture speaks is nothing other than the revelation of God. Hence it is not a question of us grasping the subject matter of the text of Scripture, but of the subject matter of the text – the revelation of God in Word and Spirit – grasping us. In the event of divine revelation, Scripture truly becomes the Word of God and speaks revelation, and that revelation is heard as the real subject matter of the text in all its freedom and authority over us. And so, Barth writes, the church 'lives by the fact that Christ is revealed in the Bible by the work of the Holy Spirit' (I/2, 513).

The relation between Scripture and the Spirit, indicated in the doctrine of inspiration, is thus for Barth always a matter of the free grace of God. The result, Barth notes, is that the church can only pray that, in the power of the Spirit, 'the Bible may be the Word of God here and now' (I/2, 514). Yet the church does not pray this without hope and confidence, and it does not pray this without taking up and reading Scripture for itself. The biblical witnesses have not spoken in vain, and we must dare to attend to what their texts now say to us today, praying that God will once again work in and through them to reveal Godself to us in Word and Spirit. Hence, for Barth, we are summoned to persistence as we wait and knock at the door of Scripture.

The confession that Scripture is the witness of the divine revelation could not, for Barth, adequately be received without listening to the past and present voices of the church. At this point, Barth considers the authority of Scripture *in* the church, and the authority of the church *under* Scripture – what he calls the *objective* side of the church's obedience to the Word of God attested in Scripture. There is, for Barth, no possibility of the church and Scripture having equal authority: the church only exists at all and only has authority at all as it is obedient to the Word of God in Scripture. Barth thus rejects the traditional Roman Catholic position which posits two sources of revelation – Scripture and church tradition. By contrast, for Barth, it is in Scripture alone, for all its 'mediate, relative, and formal quantity', that the church has to do with the Word of God – 'with the self-subsistent and self-maintaining direct and absolute and material authority, with its own existence, nature, and basis' (I/2, 544). Hence the church cannot evade the claim of Scripture on its obedience.

At the same time, Barth recognizes that the tradition of the church is important. As the Word of God speaks through Scripture, it demands to be attested by the church: past voices in the church thus have a particular authority as prior *witnesses* of that same Word, just as the present *witness* of the church has a particular authority in its response to that same Word. However, Barth notes, the authority of the Word of God 'cannot be assimilated by the Church, to reappear as the divine authority of the Church' (I/2, 579). The genuine authority of the church is thus not direct, material and absolute, but is instead indirect, formal and relative. The authority of the church exists only as the church is constituted as the church – in the common hearing and receiving of the Word of God. This event is made concrete in the act of *confession*.

Our present individual acts of confessing the faith can happen only in attending respectfully to the past acts in which the church has confessed its faith. The common confession of the church aims at the common proclamation of the Word of God, and may indeed be human, partial and provisional. Yet as it seeks to ask and answer questions about the hearing and receiving of the Word of God in the church, it must be respected and heeded. In short, for Barth, we can only speak to the church once we have first listened to it.

Barth then proceeds to explore in detail examples of specific historical forms in which the authority of the church encounters the contemporary church. The first is the content of Scripture – the inherited 'canon' of authoritative texts recognized by the church; the second is the work of 'church fathers' – specific teachers whose work is recognized as broadly authoritative; and the third is the confessional statements of the church. In the case of each historical form, the authority of the church is to be carefully heard and seriously respected; yet in each case, 'respect for its authority has necessarily to be conjoined with a basic readiness to envisage a possible alteration' of its claims (I/2, 659). Such changes can only occur in obedience to the Word of God attested in Scripture.

The confession that Scripture is the witness of the divine revelation could not, for Barth, adequately be received without also reading and considering Scripture for ourselves. At this point, Barth considers the freedom of Scripture *in* the church, and the freedom of the church *under* Scripture – what he calls the *subjective* side of the church's obedience to the Word of God attested in Scripture. For Barth, the respective authorities of the Word of God and of the church would be tyrannical, were it not for the fact that the human obedience involved is 'both spontaneous and receptive, … obedience from the heart' (I/2, 661). Here, then, authority and freedom are not mutually exclusive: precisely the one who is *obedient* to the authority of the Word of God is drawn to stand on their own feet and made *free* and *responsible*. Both authority *and* freedom, Barth observes, must be considered predicates of the Word of God.

To recognize the freedom of the Word of God *in* the church itself means for Barth to recognize that 'Scripture itself is a really truly living, acting and speaking subject which only as such can be truly heard and received by the Church and in the Church' (I/2, 672). The freedom of the Word of God is the freedom to establish this church, over against the sinfulness and the diversity of humanity. And it is the freedom to preserve this church, without which preservation the church would dissolve and perish. In response to this freedom, the church must unceasingly submit to the living authority of Scripture.

The activity of exegesis must therefore be an ongoing work in the church, as the church seeks to trace out 'the particular freedom which the Word of God takes today in the course of its government of the Church' (I/2, 695). Barth describes the corresponding willingness to assume responsibility for this task as freedom *under* the Word of God. This freedom to be responsible for the interpretation and application of the Word of God is neither a possession of the church nor a possibility of humanity. It is rather a gift of the freedom of God in the event of the divine governance of the church, a gift of grace for which one can only pray and give thanks. By virtue of this miraculous event, the Word of God that is attested by the apostles and prophets is received and accepted by us, becoming *our* word. Divine freedom thus neither suspends nor destroys human freedom; rather, in the event of revelation, it evokes and even *establishes* our genuine human freedom. This freedom of ours under the Word thus remains – parallel to the authority of the church – indirect, relative and formal.

Responsibility for the interpretation and application of Scripture in the church is a calling for all Christians. In contemplating this task, Barth notes, there must first take place 'the freely performed act of the subordinating all human concepts, ideas and convictions to the witness of revelation supplied to us in Scripture' (I/2, 715). This act of obedience recognizes the superiority of the Word of God which Scripture attests. There then unfold the three aspects of biblical exegesis: the explanation (*explicatio*), which attends to the subject matter of the text; the reflection (*meditatio*), which adopts and adapts our own thoughts to that subject matter; and the application (*applicatio*), which conforms our act of witness and our very existence to that subject matter. Each of these aspects takes place in the true freedom given under the Word of God.

## *Comment*

In this full articulation of his doctrine of Scripture, Barth sets forth an account which is not only powerful and innovative, but also controversial. There are four particular aspects of this doctrine which merit further comment.

First, the doctrine presented here confirms many of the theological impulses evidenced earlier in *Church Dogmatics*. It is thus evident again that Barth conceives God as the living Lord who addresses human beings in the present. And it is also evident again that Barth conceives of both the objective and the subjective dimensions of revelation to be a matter of divine possibility alone, with human authority and human freedom in the church only deriving their actuality and possibility from the gift of grace and from the prior authority and freedom of the Word of God. Central to each stage of this discourse is the motif of witness: Scripture is not identical to the Word of God, but a human witness to it; yet precisely as human witness, God takes up Scripture ever again to address us in and through its human words. As it bears the reality and possibility of true human existence in genuine freedom, the Word of God attested in Scripture is once again both revelation and reconciliation.

Second, the doctrine presented here is distinct from accounts in the classical Protestant tradition in two striking ways. On the one hand, Barth's denial of any givenness to revelation, of any sense in which the Word of God in Scripture stands in the possession or at the disposal of the church, has been rejected by many theologians, particularly those in evangelical traditions. It is charged that this denial underplays the claims of Scripture itself, and erases any sense of a qualitative distinction between Scripture and other texts. In response, one might note Barth insists that Scripture does retain a unique authority, yet that this authority lies not in the hands of the *church* but in the free grace of *God* alone. On the other hand, Barth's acknowledgement of the possibility of error in the human words of Scripture has also been deeply opposed by many Protestants. It is charged that this acknowledgement again underplays the claims of Scripture itself, and renders the text fallible, errant and untrustworthy. In response, one might note that Barth insists that the Word of God which speaks in and through Scripture is utterly infallible and inerrant, and that – though he regularly describes passages of Scripture as being 'remarkable' – he never once points out any actual error in Scripture.

Third, the doctrine presented here is distinct from accounts in the classical Roman Catholic tradition and in modern Protestantism. In respect of the former, Barth affirms the absolute superiority of revelation (and its witness in Scripture) over and against the authority of the church, its dogma and its tradition, in a way resisted by traditional Roman Catholic teaching. In passing, one might note that more recent statements of Roman Catholic teaching – such as from the Second Vatican Council – seem to evidence greater resonances with Barth's doctrine. In respect of the latter, Barth rejects the idea that the text of Scripture must be interpreted in line with the criteria of modern enquiry – the self-consciousness and historical consciousness of modern humanity. Instead, Barth sees the genuine freedom of obedience to the Word of God as in opposition to any modern notions of the absolute freedom of humanity. To suggest otherwise, for Barth, relativizes the particular role of Scripture within the divine economy, disregards the freedom and authority of the Word of God, and misconstrues the nature of true human freedom. In both cases, Barth seeks to preserve the full *authority* of Scripture in its full *freedom*.

Finally, the doctrine presented here betrays a robust confidence in the actuality and possibility of the living God speaking concretely in and through Scripture to the church today. For all that this is a divine possibility for which we can only pray, and for all that our human words remain fallible and faulty in and of themselves, still the Word of God has the authority and freedom to take up the words of Scripture in a fresh event of revelation and to allow us to receive, accept and respond to them in authority and freedom. For this reason, it is the responsibility of all church members to continue to read Scripture prayerfully.

# V  Church proclamation

In turning to the proclamation of the church, Barth arrives at the third form of the Word of God and thus what he calls 'the final and really critical point in the doctrine of the Word of God' (I/2, 743). Here too, we have to do with the one Word of God, Jesus Christ, as the church is commissioned to proclaim the Word of God in the authority and freedom accorded to it by the grace of God. And precisely here the task of dogmatics – to explore the conformity of the proclamation of the church to the Word of God – arises as an issue again.

Barth starts – as should be no surprise by now – from the *actuality* of the identity between the proclamation of the church and the

Word of God. This relationship is a divine actuality, and thus a divine possibility, resting on God's decision to appoint and authorize witnesses in the world to divine revelation. This is not a general truth or an empirical finding. By contrast, where proclamation truly occurs, there takes place a divine event in which God overcomes the attendant human incapacity to speak and to hear the Word of God, as the human words of proclamation are inspired and used by the Spirit. And so, Barth writes, 'both those who speak and those who hear … necessarily rely on the free grace of God and therefore on prayer' (I/2, 755). Yet in light of the reality of this event, the church cannot fall into arrogant complacency; instead, it must devote itself to the task of preaching in humility and in prayer.

The human task of church proclamation thus stands under a necessity and a promise: it is both commanded by God and empowered by God. The aim of the preacher within this situation is, in Barth's words, 'to incite and inspire the hearers to hear for themselves what the Word of God … has to say to them' (I/2, 763). The word of proclamation seeks therefore to be a *transparent* human word – it seeks to point towards and to compel the hearing of the Word of God itself, without distracting from it by idolatry or arrogance. If it succeeds in this, becoming what Barth calls 'pure doctrine', it does so in an event of grace in which God acts by Word and Spirit to fulfil the promise given to the church. But to recognize the miracle of this event is not to absolve the responsibility of the preacher in the work of proclamation: 'pure doctrine' is a *task* that faces us.

The task of dogmatics in particular is to concern itself with the 'purity' of church proclamation. This is the question of whether the different aspects of proclamation 'have or have not the quality of serving the Word of God and becoming transparent for it' (I/2, 777). For Barth, whatever stimulates, sustains and guides the striving of the church for purity of doctrine is good dogmatics.

In the material which here follows, Barth will take up first the formal task and norm of dogmatics and then the material task and method of dogmatics. Ahead of this, he reflects briefly on the relationship between dogmatics and ethics.

The key question Barth treats initially is whether or not there can be a Christian ethics that is independent of dogmatics. To posit that there *can* would be to suggest that the goodness of Christian character can be *directly* perceived, and that such Christian character can be described within a *general* account of human conduct. For

Barth, with his starting point in the revealed Word of God and his dialectical view of revelation as both veiling and unveiling, such a position is untenable, and leads to dogmatics being transformed into and controlled by ethics. By contrast, for Barth, the question of ethical human conduct can only be addressed within the context of the revelation of the God *who is good*. And, conversely, dogmatics loses not only its object but also its meaning if it does not attend to human existence as it is determined by the Word of God. Hence, Barth concludes, 'Dogmatics itself is ethics; and ethics is also dogmatics' (I/2, 793). Barth thus proceeds to include a section on ethics within each volume of *Church Dogmatics*, as will be seen in detail in Chapter 7.

In turning to the formal task and norm of dogmatics, Barth reflects upon the church as the 'hearing church'. The primary function of dogmatics consists, in Barth's words, 'in inviting and guiding the Church … to listen afresh to the Word of God' (I/2, 797). Dogmatics reminds the church in this way that before the church proclaims anything, and before dogmatics itself ventures a word, God spoke – and still speaks – in Jesus Christ and in the witness of Scripture. The church must therefore continually strive to hear the Word of God – the basis and law both of the church itself and of its proclamation. And where there is a danger that the Word of God is being ignored, the task of dogmatics is to warn the church and to call it back to this act of listening. Dogmatics thus reminds the church – critically yet positively – of the essential relation between the human word of proclamation and the Word of God. It does not, however, have the Word of God at its disposal, any more than the church itself does. It is merely a human discipline alongside proclamation, and is thus *itself* subject to the judgement of the Word of God and called to listen for the Word of God.

The norm of dogmatics (just as of proclamation) is thus the revelation of the Word of God attested in Scripture. It is this norm which informs the character of dogmatic work, guiding its critical reception both of the 'church fathers' and confessional statements of the past, and of the proclamation of the church and its changing situation today. In its subjection to the Word of God, Barth sees his dogmatics to be distinctively *Protestant* – rejecting the 'heresies' of modern Protestantism, Roman Catholicism and Eastern Orthodoxy – and, within Protestantism, to be a distinctively *Reformed* rather than Lutheran or Anglican dogmatics.

In turning to the material task and method of dogmatics, Barth reflects upon the church as the 'teaching church'. The task of dogmatics is not only to call the church back to the hearing of the Word of God, but to call the church forward to the proclamation of the Word of God. Barth asserts that the church cannot be silent or inactive in light of the revelation of Jesus Christ: 'By reason of this hearing, the church which hears the Word of God is called to teach' (I/2, 844).

Yet dogmatics at this point not only reminds the church of its duty to proclaim the Word of God; it also has a material significance, in so far as it has a duty to test the proclamation of the Word of God for its purity of doctrine. It can do so only in a limited and provisional way, for ultimately the purity of doctrine, as we saw above, lies only in an event of grace. Nevertheless, by way of its own presenting and unfolding of the Word of God and in obedience to it, dogmatics seeks itself to teach as far as its capacity allows. And consequently, dogmatics seeks, in Barth's words, 'to mark off the boundary between the Church and its doctrine on the one hand and error and falsehood on the other' (I/2, 852). This is the human act of *witness* which the discipline of dogmatics requires.

The decision on which dogmatic method to adopt is, in the sense already noted in this chapter, a decision to be taken both in freedom and obedience before the Word of God. Barth denies here the possibility of any dogmatic 'system', in the sense of a self-contained set of principles and consequences, of the kind seen in some post-Reformation Protestant writers. Rather, while dogmatics has to proceed in an ordered and coherent fashion, it must always remain open to the work and activity of the Word of God which cannot be systematized. For his own part, and having explored various alternative options, Barth outlines his intention to treat in turn in the following volumes of *Church Dogmatics* the doctrines of God, creation, reconciliation and redemption. These, Barth notes, are 'the things which dogmatics has to say about the content of the Word and therefore about the work and activity of God' (I/2, 883).

## *Comment*

In reaching the proclamation of the church, Barth arrives not only at the conclusion of the doctrine of the Word of God, but also at its most critical point. And in so doing, he also reprises afresh the theme of the Introduction to *Church Dogmatics* as whole – the relation of dogmatics and proclamation.

The preaching of the church is, for Barth, a task that is divinely commissioned; and in the event of revelation, it is divinely empowered. That event does not lie within the power or control of the church or the preacher: we can only pray for it humbly and wait for it expectantly. And yet the task of proclamation must be undertaken responsibly, and not complacently. The dynamic relationship between the proclamation of the church and the event of revelation is thus formally parallel to that between the reading of Scripture and the event of revelation.

The material vigilance of the church in respect of proclamation is effected in dogmatics, the second-order reflective task which seeks to critique and correct the first-order proclamation of the church in light of the divine revelation. It seeks as best it can to ensure that talk of God in the church is as pure – in other words, as transparent to the Word of God – as possible. In this venture, dogmatics, like proclamation, begins with the hearing of the Word of God in the church, and must be characterized by unceasing prayerful invocation of the Spirit.

There are two consequences of this view which deserve particular mention at this point. First, this conception of both proclamation and dogmatics is an entirely *dynamic* one. Both ventures are undertakings which are a necessary work of the church in each new day in respect of their differently targeted activities of guiding and correcting. There is, then, no possibility of a timeless dogmatics for Barth, no possibility of a simple slavery to an entrenched past (or to a domineering present); rather, in dogmatic work one must 'continually begin again at the beginning in every point' (I/2, 868). And thus, it is also a *provisional* task, for its results are always open to question and reformulation. Second, this conception of both proclamation and dogmatics is an entirely *ecumenical* one. Barth explicitly posits that 'Where dogmatics exists at all, it exists only with the will to be a Church dogmatics, a dogmatics of the ecumenical Church' (I/2, 823). Thus for all Barth's strong and explicit inclination towards theological positions more consonant with Protestantism, and Reformed Protestantism, in this volume, this is more a matter of empirical characterization than of dogmatic agenda. Barth, after all, considers this work to be part of a *church* dogmatics.

# CHAPTER THREE

# The doctrine of God

When Barth moves from volume I of *Church Dogmatics* to volume II, he leaves behind the prolegomena of dogmatic work and enters immediately into unfolding his understanding of the doctrine of God – not, of course, that the doctrine of God had not been present in a sustained way in the first volume; there, however, it was considered in light of a different set of concerns, and was not the central topic of investigation. The second volume was written in Basel just before and also during the Second World War, a conflict of unprecedented extensity and brutality. It contains some of the most significant material in *Church Dogmatics*, but also gives rise to certain vexed questions of interpretation. Volume II consists of two part-volumes, each of which contains two sections: volume II/1 has 'The Knowledge of God' and 'The Reality of God', while volume II/2 has 'The Election of God' and 'The Command of God'. The first three of these sections will be explored below; the final section – which attends to Christian ethics – will be explored in Chapter 7.

## I  The knowledge of God

In his section on the knowledge of God, Barth sets forth his understanding of theological epistemology – how we come to know God. Barth's view is utterly theocentric, for our knowledge of God depends exclusively on the divine revelation: we know God, because God reveals Godself to us. We do not know God on the basis of our own efforts or practices, and we do not know God on the basis of creation; we know God becomes God comes to us in Jesus Christ by the power of the Spirit. There is therefore no knowledge of God other than that gained when *God reveals God* and we respond in faith. Correspondingly, Barth follows closely in this section the procedure of Anselm – that of faith seeking understanding.

## The fulfilment of the knowledge of God

Barth's starting point in his theological epistemology is quite particular: 'We start out from the fact that through His Word God is actually known and will be known again' (II/1, 4). It is, for Barth, a present reality that people in the church speak about and hear about both God and the grace and command of God. The presupposition of all this discourse being true is the activity of God, for God is objectively and actively present when and where true knowledge of God exists. Without this divine presence, there can be no knowledge of God, for God can only be known through the Word and the Spirit.

Human speech about God is not only established and empowered by God, however; it is also called into question by God. This highlights the issue of the *criteria* of true knowledge of God. Barth is adamant that the only valid criterion for this is the Word of God itself. There is no conceivable *external* criterion for judging whether knowledge of God is genuine or not: this can only be ascertained by reflection on and response to the Word of God itself.

What Barth is doing is to attend first to the actuality of knowledge of God and only then to its possibility. This is the opposite of the way modernity has often proceeded in matters of knowledge, which tends to move from the possibility of knowledge to its actuality. Correspondingly, Barth contends that the first question in theological epistemology is not 'Can we know God?', for God already *is* known. There is therefore no need to proceed hypothetically by way of any abstract reasoning or speculative logic; instead, we can move forward on the existing basis of the concrete knowledge of God in the church. On this basis, the only legitimate questions in this field are 'How is God known?' and 'How is God knowable?', and Barth unfolds answers to each question in turn.

To answer the first question, 'How is God known?', Barth first observes that the original Subject of knowledge of God is Godself:

God knows Godself *immediately* and *eternally*. In this way, God is first and foremost objective to Godself: Barth describes this as God's 'primary objectivity'. When creatures have knowledge of God, we *participate* in this original divine *Self*-knowledge. However, we can only do so *mediately* and *temporally*. We can only know God as Object, and Barth describes this as knowledge of God's 'secondary objectivity'.

What this means is that God is never *directly* revealed to us, but only *indirectly*, through signs and objects other than God. In an act of condescension, God comes to us in lowliness, taking up created realities in an event of revelation to act as vehicles for and witnesses to Godself. In themselves, these created realities had, have and will have no special quality or ability to reveal God. However, God can *use* them in revelation. There is therefore an important *dialectic* in operation here: precisely in the event of revelation, God remains hidden in creaturely media. In other words, in the event of unveiling, God remains veiled; in the clarity of revelation, God remains a mystery to us. There is thus no identification of God with the medium of revelation.

The central locus of the secondary objectivity of God is the human nature of Jesus Christ. This is, for Barth, 'the first sacrament' – 'the foundation of everything that God instituted and used in His revelation as a secondary objectivity both before and after the epiphany of Jesus Christ' (II/1, 54). Jesus Christ is the paradigmatic event of the dialectic of the simultaneity of revelation and hiddenness. The humanity of Jesus Christ is not *in itself* revelation or real knowledge of God, which explains why so many did not recognize him as the Son of God. However, the humanity of Jesus Christ is able to *serve* revelation as God makes Godself known through that veil.

Our guarantee that the knowledge of God gained in revelation is true knowledge is, Barth writes, that there is a perfect *correspondence* between the truth of the secondary objectivity and our knowledge of God on the one hand and the truth of the primary objectivity of God and the triune God's Self-knowledge on the other. Hence, in revelation, God makes Godself known to us as the Lord, while the inner truth of that lordship is that God eternally knows Godself as Father, Son and Spirit. In revelation, then, we genuinely receive a share in the true knowledge of God and confront the fullness of the true being of God. God is distinct from us, but also genuinely relates to us: real knowledge of God as the One who is to be loved and thus feared above all is revealed to us, even as God remains simultaneously hidden.

The corollary of the dialectic of veiling and unveiling is that there are no events or objects at our disposal that reveal God by themselves: neither creation, nor Scripture, nor the church, nor proclamation, nor the sacraments. Divine revelation is a matter of an event of grace, in which God renders Godself as an *Object* of knowledge to us. Even where this happens, God remains the *Subject*: God precedes and our knowledge can only follow. There can be no domestification of the knowledge of God. All that we can do is pray for grace and revelation, confident in the promise that God will not cease to bear witness to Godself in ever-new revelations of God's presence.

For Barth, the human knowledge of God which results from the being and action of God in revelation is a very particular kind of knowledge – the knowledge of faith. Just as God is unique among possible 'objects' of knowledge, so too the knowledge of God that results from revelation is unique: it demands a very particular human response, that of turning to God in faith. This new determination of the individual involves love, trust and obedience. It is this free, obedient human response of faith that *corresponds* to the gracious divine act of revelation. Echoing the language of the Jewish philosopher Martin Buber, Barth posits that God addresses us as a 'thou', allowing us in turn to address God as 'Thou'. Knowledge of God is therefore not a matter of dispassionate intellectualism, but is a life-involving and life-changing event: in face of it, there can be no neutrality. The only alternative to a response of faith and obedience is disobedience, a turning away from God.

## The knowability of God

Having investigated the *actuality* of human knowledge of God, Barth proceeds to explore its *possibility*, thereby addressing his second question: 'How is God knowable?' Barth recognizes that, in one sense, human knowledge of God is as uncertain and provisional as any other type of human knowledge. At the same time, however, knowledge of God is grounded uniquely and entirely in revelation, and thus in a divine possibility and actuality.

As such, there is another sense in which our knowledge of God has no analogy at all.

Consequently, Barth dissents from two alternative views of revelation which in his view tend to undervalue it. First, he opposes the nineteenth-century Protestant tendency to devalue and disregard the *possibility* of revelation, as if, Barth comments, it were *bored* of revelation. Second, he opposes the desire of natural theology to ground a measure of knowledge of God on the basis of creaturely reason acting *independently* of revelation. In opposition to this latter position, Barth is insistent that there is no *analogia entis* (analogy of being) between creation and God on the basis of which knowledge of God is possible. Instead, the only analogy that exists here is one effected in the event of revelation. This analogy is 'to be created by God's grace, the analogy of grace and faith to which we say Yes as to the inaccessible which is made accessible to us in incomprehensible reality' (II/1, 85).

At this point, however, Barth has to reckon both with the vibrant presence of natural theology in the Christian tradition and with texts in Scripture which may be read to support it. Barth begins by highlighting what he considers an internal contradiction that afflicts any Christian natural theology: it aims to be 'Christian', but tries to disguise this by being 'natural'. He further argues that the Scripture verses in question ultimately pertain to nothing other than God's revelation of grace, and thus do not indicate an alternative route to knowledge of God. Finally, he locates the vitality of natural theology in the fact that we are at war with grace and thus wish to be closed to God's revelation. Rather than allowing revelation to pose a question to us, our sinful desire for self-affirmation and self-preservation leads us to domesticate and absorb revelation, treating it as an answer to our questions.

Despite this sinful opposition to the revelation of God, however, Barth maintains that there *is* a true human readiness and openness for the knowledge of God. This is not found in us, but in Jesus Christ, in whom we participate. He has not only assumed our enmity towards God's grace and revelation but he has also obliterated it, and by the work of the Spirit we participate in his person and work through faith in the reconciliation that he has accomplished. Here lies the foundation of Barth's view – which we will see again in his later doctrines – that there is no such thing as an independent human being as such, for 'The truth of his existence is simply this – that Jesus Christ has died and risen again for him' (II/1, 167). From this perspective, Barth concludes, natural theology can only be repudiated and excised.

This rejection of natural theology is probably the most controversial part of this section of Barth's theology. His work has come under sustained criticism from various theological perspectives from those who want to assert that a measure of knowledge of God can be derived from sources of general revelation. It is undoubtedly the case that Barth's way of understanding knowledge of God has significant implications both for the way in which theology engages other disciplines and for the way in which Christians address those who are not Christians. And it is also the case that Barth and his followers have been accused of 'fideism' in this connection: of relying exclusively on revelation and faith to the exclusion of reason.

It is certainly true that in the immediate background of Barth's work at this point are his sustained disagreement with Emil Brunner on the possibility of natural theology and his absolute opposition to the perverted use of natural theology by Christians supportive of the National Socialist regime in Germany. Yet it is highly doubtful that his view here is simply a product of context.

Barth consistently reiterates throughout *Church Dogmatics* that there is simply no other foundation for knowledge of God than divine revelation. On the one hand, he asserts that there is nothing in creation which cannot be lifted up by God to serve as an instrument of revelation. On the other hand, he posits that nothing in creation *of itself* has the power to reveal God. That noted, there is for Barth no conflict between divine revelation and the creaturely reason that is brought to faith and to conformity with that revelation by the Spirit. Indeed, in the response of faith, human reason finds its true calling. Left to its own devices, then, we can achieve no real knowledge of God, but through the grace of God in divine revelation we are able to know God in spirit and in truth.

## *The limits of the knowledge of God*

Barth proceeds to explore the limits of the knowledge of God in two directions.

First, he considers the point of departure of our knowledge of God. As noted above, human knowledge of God is not formally or technically different to any other human knowledge. Where it does differ is in its unique origin, which means that it is not a knowledge that we can attain for ourselves: God is not simply an Object like any other. Knowing God therefore first requires that we recognize what Barth calls the hiddenness of God. This hiddenness is not some abstract postulate, but a confession of faith based on the witness of Scripture. We recognize that our capacity to know God by faith is one that we can only receive from God, for God cannot be apprehended by our own powers of cognition and would thus remain hidden if God did not intervene. This is not a reason for despair, however, but for gratitude and worship, because recognition of this hiddenness of God is actually the starting point for Barth's affirmation that true knowledge of God can and does exist.

In faith, the God who is and remains hidden becomes apprehensible to us. What happens is that God acts to take into service our thoughts and concepts – which are incapable of apprehending God of themselves – and to direct us and them towards a true apprehension of God. This apprehension is always limited and is never perfect, but it remains true. Thus far from devaluing human words and ideas, Barth asserts that genuine creaturely testimony to God's revelation can arise in faith.

Second, Barth considers the point of arrival of our knowledge of God: the church comes not only *from* the knowledge of God but also comes *to* the knowledge of God. God becomes an Object of our cognition as God causes creaturely reality to witness to God in a miraculous event of grace. The truthfulness and reliability of our resultant knowledge of God is assured, for it directly originates in God and participates in the act of divine Self-knowledge. There is therefore no God behind God or behind God's revelation with whom Christians have to contend – no unknown God or aspect of God that remains obscure and beyond their apprehension in the event of revelation.

The revelation of God not only claims our thoughts and words, but also permits and demands that we should think and speak further about God despite the fact that, on the basis of our own ability, we are unable to do so. Yet what is impossible for us is possible for God: God grants us the ability to participate actively in the revelation of God by way of our human thoughts and speech. This act of grace can only render us humble, and indeed our participation in the revelation of God in this way can only ever occur in prayer, praise and thanksgiving. Where and when this event happens, there arises – by the grace of God – what Barth calls an *analogy of truth* between our discourse about God and God as the Object of our discourse. Human speech about God is raised by God to be able to speak faithfully about God, an ability which lies beyond its usual capacity. This 'analogy' is not static, but dynamic, and it does not fall under our control. Instead, it can only come into being through an act of divine grace as – in faith and obedience – we appropriate 'the promise that we shall speak the truth in the analogy of His truth itself' (II/1, 231).

Both the point of departure and the point of arrival of our knowledge of God are therefore characterized by the grace of revelation. Yet even in revelation, and indeed even in eternity, God remains hidden in revelation. The revelation of God and the hiddenness of God are therefore inseparable, but they do not exist in a static relationship. Rather, they exist in an ordered and teleological dialectic: the veiling of God in a creaturely medium of some sort is the basis of revelation while the unveiling of God to the human being is the goal of revelation. In this ever-renewing movement from the point of departure to the point of arrival, we cannot look to ourselves as reliable indicators of the path along which this knowledge is achieved. Instead, we can only look to and rely upon Jesus Christ, as the One in whose person this movement of divine revelation and human knowledge is true and fulfilled.

The discipline of theology thus remains entirely dependent on grace for its knowledge of God, and thus remains a theology of pilgrims (*theologia viatorum*) that is always underway and never reaches its goal. For this reason, the appropriate disposition of the discipline and its practitioners can only ever be prayerful humility before the miracle and mystery of revelation.

## *Comment*

Knowledge of God in the church is, for Barth, a simple reality. It is not attained by an act of natural reasoning, philosophical speculation or moral postulation: instead, knowledge of God is received in an event of revelation, in which God reveals Godself to us. In this event of unveiling we share in God's true knowledge of Godself, even as God remains veiled in creaturely media. In revelation, then, and only in revelation, we truly *apprehend* God, without ever *comprehending* God. At no point in *Church Dogmatics* does Barth distance himself from this basic epistemological position and its dialectical character.

At the same time, as noted above, this understanding of the knowledge of God has not been without its critics. The forceful rejection of natural theology in particular has been widely disputed, both by Roman Catholic theologians and by other Protestant theologians. The regular rejoinder to Barth at this point is that a particular and true (if delimited) knowledge of God is attainable by reason alone, apart from revelation, and that this is the straightforward witness of Scripture attests. Yet for all such opposition, Barth's rejection of natural theology remained a consistent feature of his theology until the end.

## II  The reality of God

From epistemology, Barth turns to theology, and theology in the narrow sense of the being and the perfections (or attributes) of God. In the course of this section, Barth connects the divine being and the divine action as closely as possible, and outlines his understanding of both through the central concepts of love and freedom. Thereafter, he unfolds a presentation of the divine perfections under the rubric of the same concepts. In each case the method followed – as we would expect from the above – is to follow the revelation of God centred in Jesus Christ as witnessed in Scripture.

### *God: The One who loves in freedom*

Barth begins with the simple statement 'God is', which, he asserts, is the core statement of dogmatics and is not to be hurried over. To know who God is, we must attend to God's Self-revelation: 'God is who He is in His works … in Himself He is not another than He is in His works' (II/1, 260). Though Barth writes here that God's being is not exhausted by God's works, nonetheless these works reveal who God is even beyond God's works. In other words, though there is more to God than what we see in revelation, nevertheless revelation lets us see who God really is. In revelation, we encounter a living God, a God who is free event and free act and free life, and all these things not in some abstract or general way, but in a very concrete and very particular way. Indeed, Barth writes that, far from being mechanically caused or externally conditioned, God's being is 'His own conscious, willed and executed decision' (II/1, 271). God exists uniquely as this personal being, as this being in act, in the nature of the Father, the Son and the Spirit.

From this initial analysis, Barth explores further the divine being and action. The fundamental dimension of the economic activity of God is that it freely seeks and creates communion with humanity: in creation and in reconciliation, God does not will to be without us nor to leave us without God. In the person and work of Jesus Christ, in other words, God makes Godself known to us as the One who loves. Correspondingly, then, the being of God can be described as the One who loves. To understand this 'love', we must not import our own, external conceptions of what love is; rather, we must attend to the act of God itself. When we do, we discover that God seeks communion for its own sake, as an end in itself, irrespective of the worth of the beloved. This divine love for us is of the very essence of God, and it is so without reference to any necessity imposed on God. God's love is an eternal love, and God's love for us is our being taken up into the communion of God's eternal love as Father, Son and Spirit.

When we consider the depth in which God is and lives and loves, Barth posits, we also encounter the concept of the divine freedom. To characterize God as free is to recognize God as the Lord, exercising a lordship of life and love. God lives and loves in freedom in two respects: negatively, God's living and loving are externally unconditioned; positively, they are determined only by God's own will and act, in God's own inner being. In this way, God is *absolute*: first, God and God's attributes cannot be equated or classified with others in a series or in a synthesis, because, second, God is utterly distinct from and independent of everything else. At the same time, the freedom of God allows God to be free even in respect of that freedom, and therefore to *decide* to be conditioned by and to relate to another – as Scripture vividly and repeatedly attests, and as will become pivotal in Barth's doctrine of election which follows in Volume II/2. At the centre of this interaction is Jesus Christ: it is in Jesus Christ that

God has exercised God's freedom, in a way that is not capricious, but faithful to God's own being as love.

## The perfections of God

As the One who loves in freedom, God *lives*, for life is 'the fundamental element in the divine being' (II/1, 322). This life is God's perfect life, for God is the perfect being, perfection itself, and it is a life lived both in Godself and in relation to that which is not God. To know the perfection of God is thus to know not a static or abstract perfection, but the perfection of the living God who loves in freedom. This perfection is lived out in a multitude of various types of perfection. To know God is to know these living perfections, and to come to know them again and again, in ever-new and surprising ways. For Barth, then, the language of the 'perfections' of God is a way of seeking to articulate what are conventionally called the 'attributes' of God.

The perfections of God belong to God, Scripture assures us, not only in revelation but also in eternity, and thus to the very essence of God. Their multiplicity is anchored in the unity of God that is also attested in Scripture. Barth acknowledges that the idea of a multiplicity of perfections may seem to contradict the idea of the simplicity of God. He affirms, however, that God does not just *possess* these perfections; God simply *is* these perfections, in time and in eternity. Moreover, the simplicity of God is a concept that must be derived from and not applied to the divine revelation. The multiplicity of these perfections thus in no way contradicts the simplicity of God, any more than do the three persons of the Trinity: each individual perfection is nothing but the being of God itself, and is thus identical with every other perfection and with the sum of them all.

In his attempt to detail the divine perfections, Barth turns again to the Self-revelation of God in which, as outlined above, God remains veiled in unveiling. This dialectic of revelation must be reflected in the doctrine of the divine perfections: God loves us, and is thus completely knowable to us; yet God is free, so God remains completely unknowable to us; and God is – paradoxically – both at once, in a unity that is dynamic and reciprocal. This dialectical understanding leads Barth to propose two series of divine attributes, fully acknowledging that this particular proposal – indeed, any proposal – can appeal neither to Scripture nor to any other authority for legitimation but can only hope to speak worthily of God. The first series is characterized as the perfections of the divine loving and the second series as the perfections of the divine freedom. The ordering here is important for Barth: even as there is no hierarchy or separation of the two concepts, nevertheless 'God is first of all the One who loves and then and as such the One who is free' (II/1, 351).

To unfold the perfections, Barth turns to the Self-revelation of God as attested in Scripture – both Old and New Testaments. The perfections cannot be explained on the basis of other sources or derived from speculative methods. In particular, Barth rejects any attempt to derive the divine attributes by certain traditional routes such as the way of eminence, the way of negation and the way of causality, or by an analysis of the concepts of finitude and infinity. Instead, he insists that God must define the perfections and the perfections must not define God. In other words, the perfections as predicates are determined in every case by the divine Subject, and not by human conceptions. Hence Barth's description of each divine perfection is won from biblical exegesis, is focused on the revelation of God in Jesus Christ, and is supplemented by lengthy critical engagement with the theological tradition. It is a deeply considered and highly radical account of the divine being.

## *The perfections of the divine loving*

Barth turns first to the perfections of the divine loving. These are: grace and holiness, mercy and righteousness, and patience and wisdom. The perfections are purposefully presented in these co-ordinated pairs, in which the first member specifies a form of the divine love and the second member expresses with particular distinctiveness the relation to the divine freedom in which that form of love is actualized. Each will be briefly considered in turn.

The perfection of grace indicates the way in which God desires and effects communion with another, regardless of the merits (or demerits) of the other. Grace is certainly a gift, but only in so far as God renders Godself the gift: its archetypal form is the Self-giving of God in the incarnation of Jesus Christ. As demonstrated in this unmerited condescension to the creature, grace is of the very essence of the being of God. Precisely as gracious, however, God is also holy. The perfection of holiness indicates that God is the Lord, condemning and overcoming all resistance and opposition to the will of God. This holiness of God, which indicates the judgement of sins, is distinguishable but not separable from the grace of God, which indicates the forgiveness of sins. Holiness is the very essence of God because the grace of God judges and the judgement of God is gracious, as can be paradigmatically seen in the history of Jesus Christ, the Holy One of God. Grace and holiness – just like the related concepts of Gospel and Law, as we will see later – cannot be divorced.

In moving to the perfections of mercy and righteousness, Barth stresses that the grace and holiness of God are not left behind, but afforded greater precision. The divine mercy indicates that God's gracious turning to humanity, as attested in Scripture, presupposes that humanity is in distress and in need. God mercifully wills both to share and to address this self-inflicted human misery, and God's mercy is disclosed above all in the name and history of Jesus Christ. Precisely as merciful, however, God is also righteous. The righteousness of God indicates that when God condescends to overcome the privation and opposition of humanity, God does so in a way which is worthy of God. God is by essence righteous: God is the Judge, the revelation of God is the Law, and the activity of God is the execution of this Law. Yet this divine righteousness is exercised precisely in the divine mercy, for God enters into covenant with sinful humanity in Jesus Christ. Indeed, it is Jesus Christ who is in person the righteousness of God, as revealed paradigmatically on the cross. There is in him no room for any contradiction between righteousness and mercy.

The further perfections of patience and wisdom again illuminate and do not contradict the other perfections. The patience of God indicates that God offers time and space to another and wills to continue with it, to sustain it and to relate to it. The creature, offered this freedom to develop and to respond, thus has a certain independence. Yet the patience of God is not to be confused with inactivity, indifference or neglect in respect of the creature. By contrast, it is a patience whose power and meaning is Jesus Christ, who has already both come to and acted for the creature. Precisely as reflecting the will of God, then, this patience is not capricious: instead, God's patience reflects God's wisdom. That

God is wise indicates that the other perfections of the divine loving are intelligible and purposeful. In God's wisdom, God knows what and why God wills, so that God's whole activity is intelligent, reliable and liberating. For Barth, God's wisdom is the meaning and ground of creation and the instrument of divine providence; it is also identified directly with Jesus Christ, the basis and the goal of all God's activity in creation.

## The perfections of the divine freedom

Barth next turns to the perfections of the divine freedom. These are: unity and omnipresence, constancy and omnipotence, and eternity and glory. Again, they are deliberately presented in co-ordinated pairs, with the first member specifying a form of the divine freedom and the second member expressing with particular distinctiveness the relation to the divine love in which that form of freedom is actualized. Each will again be briefly considered in turn.

The perfection of unity expresses that God is one, and does so in two ways. First, God is unique in terms of who and what God is: God alone is God, and all other gods are false gods. Second, God is simple, meaning that God is not divided or divisible. In God – even in the distinctions of Father, Son and Spirit – there is therefore no separation or opposition. The oneness of God is no idealized or speculative monotheism, but is revealed in the living actuality of the triune God who elects to be for humanity in Jesus Christ. Precisely as one, God is omnipresent, present to everything that is not God in differentiated ways. This perfection means that nothing can exist without God, but only with God and in God's presence. God is thus not non-spatial but, in a unique way, possesses space, God's own particular space, in creation, in the incarnation and in eternity. The meaning and presupposition of God's *general* presence in creation is God's *special* presence in the work of reconciliation; the latter finds its origin, centre and goal in God's incarnation in Jesus Christ.

Turning to the perfections of constancy and omnipotence, Barth offers further specification of the divine freedom. God is constant in that God remains God – without any alteration, diminution or addition – in the constancy of God's knowing, willing and acting. This constancy is not a static or lifeless immutability, but indicates rather that in every change the living God remains the same. At no point in the history of the world with God is the constancy of God's person compromised: at each point, God confirms Godself anew as the same from all eternity. This is true paradigmatically in Jesus Christ, in whom God remains constant even in the condescension of incarnation. Precisely as constant, God is also omnipotent. This omnipotence is not an infinite power in an abstract or neutral sense. By contrast, God's power is personal and specific: it is the omnipotence of God's free knowing and willing, and thus of God's love. The living God knows and wills – in some way – all things, and every sphere of knowing and willing is subject to God. The centre of God's knowing and willing is God's omnipotent Word, Jesus Christ.

The final divine perfections explored by Barth are eternity and glory. The eternity of God indicates not an infinite extension of time, but a simultaneity of past, present and future in pure duration that is the possession and the being of God. This eternity does not negate or oppose creaturely time, but rather grounds and sustains it such that God is present personally at every point of creation's time. Indeed, in Jesus Christ, God submits to creaturely time. The eternity of God is thus neither timeless nor non-temporal, but reflects the *life* of God. God's eternity precedes the beginning of time, accompanies its duration and exists after its consummation. Precisely as eternal, God is also glorious. God's glory refers to the truth and capacity and act in which God witnesses to Godself. In the divine glory, God reaches out to the creature and evokes worship of and pleasure in God. Moreover, this glory is also beautiful, for God is worthy of this creaturely worship and enjoyment. The divine beauty is evident supremely in the person of Jesus Christ. Through him, God not only *is* glorious but *makes* glorious, glorifying those who follow him.

## Comment

In moving from the knowledge of God to the perfections of God, Barth moves his focus decisively away from questions of epistemology, even as the epistemological decisions taken earlier govern the statements of theological ontology which he develops. In the course of this part-volume, then, it is perhaps no accident that reference to the term 'Word of God' progressively fades as reference to the name 'Jesus Christ' steadily increases.

The most important thing to recognize about Barth's understanding of God is perhaps the way in which it represents a *living* God. The description of God as the One who loves in freedom and the twelve perfections of God are all derived from the divine revelation that is centred on Jesus Christ and attested in Scripture. In other words, Barth's account is finally rooted in the dynamic history of encounter between God and the people of God in history. This is as true of the perfections of the divine loving – which are perhaps more immediately discernible in Scripture – as of the perfections of the divine freedom – which are perhaps more often encountered in prayer and liturgy, and more regularly raised in philosophical discussion of the divine being.

It is vital to recognize, however, that Barth's understanding of the divine essence and perfections is not *limited* to the being and action of God in history. Barth insists in the account of each and every perfection that the way God is and acts in the world – in God's economic existence – is not other than the way God is in Godself – in God's immanent life. In other words, in the revelation attested in Scripture, we truly have to do with *God*, and not with a mere appearance or projection of God or with a God that is either limited or reducible to our relationship to God. There is a profound sense of realism evident in Barth's account, which – allied to Barth's dialectical account of our knowledge of God – renders this a *critically realist* account of the divine being.

It is finally worth noting that Barth's treatment of the divine essence and the divine perfections has had a significant influence on the doctrinal work of many subsequent theologians. This influence points to the way in which this part of *Church Dogmatics* has served as an indication and reminder of the importance of the doctrine of God proper in dogmatic work, but also attests that it has – surprisingly – not generated a significant amount of controversy. The same cannot be said of the material which follows.

# III  The election of God

After the doctrines of the knowledge of God and of the reality of God Barth turns to the theme of the divine election, one of the central themes of interest in the works of many Reformed theologians.

His doctrine of election is arguably the most innovative and the most contested writing of his theological career, and another area of dogmatic work in which he found himself rather isolated. In it, drawing inspiration from the work of the French theologian Pierre Maury, Barth offers a radical relocation and reformulation of the doctrine. Central to this revision is his view that the divine election is determinative not merely or even principally of the fate of individual human beings, but primarily and ultimately of the being and action of God. His treatment of the doctrine is in four sections. The introductory section surveys the orientation, foundation and location of the doctrine, outlining Barth's innovative view of each in dialogue with the tradition. The following three sections deal in turn with the election of Jesus Christ, the election of the community and the election of the individual.

## Election in outline

For Barth, the doctrine of election is 'the sum of the Gospel because of all words that can be said or heard it is the best' (II/2, 3). The good news which it communicates is that God has elected to be for humanity the One who loves in freedom. Election as a gracious act relates to the love of God, while as an act of election, it relates to the freedom of God. At its centre is the person of Jesus Christ, who is 'both the electing God and elected man in One' (II/2, 3). This summary is pivotal to Barth's doctrine of election, and will be carefully unpacked over the following pages.

At the outset of his orientation to the doctrine, Barth posits that we must consider that God is revealed as a Subject who 'in virtue of its innermost being, willing and nature does not stand outside all relationships, but stands in a definite relationship *ad extra* to another' (II/2, 6). The *primary* relationship which God elects to enter is with Jesus of Nazareth, together with the people represented in him. For Barth, the decision of election which grounds this relationship and its history – both of Jesus Christ and of the people represented by him – belongs no less to the being of God than all that God is in and for Godself. In other words, God would not be God without this act of election: it represents a divine *Self-determination*. The *secondary* relationship which God elects to enter – solely on the basis of Jesus Christ and the people represented in him – is with creation and history in general. As Barth's doctrine of creation will later echo, this secondary, general relationship exists for the sake of the primary, particular relationship.

Turning to the foundation of the doctrine of election, Barth posits that we must start with the decision of the divine will to be for humanity which is fulfilled in Jesus Christ. The content of the doctrine cannot be determined either by the received tradition of the church, or by the pastoral usefulness of its result, or by the raw data of our Christian experience, or by the philosophical conception of an omnipotent will. Barth explores each of these errant possibilities in turn, in dialogue with classic theological accounts of the divine election, before reasserting that Jesus Christ alone is the basis of the doctrine of election. Barth writes: 'There is no greater depth in God's being and work than that revealed in these happenings and under this name' (II/2, 54).

Barth finally considers his innovative placement of the doctrine of election. He explores in detail some of the alternative positions which this doctrine has historically occupied in works of systematic theology. However, he concludes that the correct place for the doctrine is indeed under the doctrine of God, on the basis that 'God is none other than the One who in His Son or Word elects Himself, and in and with Himself elects His people' (II/2, 76).

At this point, it is worth observing the relationship between Barth's doctrine of election and the received tradition. For the most part, theology historically treated the doctrine of election as referring to the fate of individual human beings: if they were elected by God, they would be saved; otherwise, whether they were explicitly damned or simply passed over, they would not. Barth's position differs from this position in numerous ways.

First, Barth recognizes that the tradition also referred to election as good news; however, he believes that it departed from Scripture in so far as it posited alongside and parallel to God's decree of *election* a decree of *rejection* that was equal and opposite, and could only be bad news. Moreover, it erred even further where it thought that election and rejection were two examples of an otherwise neutral category – divine predestination. By contrast, Barth insists that God's election and rejection are *not* equal and opposite, and that the latter is utterly subordinate to and enclosed in the former. Election, for Barth, is not an equivocal Word of God, but the sum of the Gospel.

Second, Barth admonishes those accounts in the theological tradition which seem to operate with an alternative starting point than Jesus Christ. In contrast to the concrete particularity of God and humanity encountered in his person, Barth finds in these accounts a dangerous recourse to abstract concepts conceived independently of Jesus Christ. This might mean conceiving of a general human experience or person that is not related to Christ or of an absolute divine will that is not determined in him. Among the theologians named here are, in respect of the former, Augustine and John Calvin and, in respect of the latter, Thomas Aquinas, Bonaventure and – again – Calvin. By contrast, Barth insists that to understand the divine election, we must look to Jesus Christ as the concrete revelation of both the divine being and the human being.

Third, Barth recognizes that certain strands of the tradition have explicitly acknowledged that the basis of the doctrine of election is Jesus Christ. Yet the tradition, according to Barth, has departed from Scripture in so far as it has not followed this insight through fully. In this connection, Barth engages particularly with Calvin, Martin Luther and their respective successors. Barth argues that these presentations consider Christ only as the *Object* of election – the elected human, the Mediator through whom we are elected. In this view, however, the *Subject* of election – the One who elects, the electing God – is not determined by Jesus Christ, but remains hidden and inscrutable, a shadowy figure lurking behind Jesus Christ. This means that the divine election is really an absolute decree that determines who is saved and who is not, representing a decision that is independent of Jesus Christ and that stems from an unsearchable and secret divine will. By contrast, as we shall see, Barth insists that Jesus Christ is not only the *Object* of election, but also the *Subject*.

Finally, however, the key difference is that the centre of election for Barth is not the determination of individual people to heaven or hell but the Self-determination of God to be for humanity in Jesus Christ. It is to this election of Jesus Christ, and its implications, that we now turn.

## *The election of Jesus Christ*

In the person of Jesus Christ, according to Barth, God determines Godself to be for sinful humanity and God determines sinful humanity to be for God. This twofold determination of God is the content of the eternal divine decree of election. This act of election is not only an eternal, but also a free and gracious act, and for Barth there is no other work of God that is higher than or prior to this. Election is the most basic and the most essential thing that has to be said about the revelation and activity of God. More specifically, Barth writes, this decree of election takes place in the concrete particularity of Jesus Christ, who is 'the eternal will of God, the eternal decree of God and the eternal beginning of God' (II/2, 99). Not only in time but also in eternity, the being of God is determined by this act of election to be for humanity in Jesus Christ.

Barth first turns to consider what it means to call Jesus Christ the electing God. At the heart of the electing God is not an absolute decree on the basis of which some are foreordained to salvation through Jesus Christ and others are foreordained to reprobation by being passed over, but the *person* of Jesus Christ. Jesus Christ is not only the Reconciler between God and humanity, but also the reconciliation between them, and thus he is not only the Elected, in a passive sense, but the Elector, in an active sense, and the former precisely on the basis of the latter. In other words, Jesus Christ participates, according to Barth, in the divine election from the beginning, together with the Father and the Spirit. Barth insists that 'Jesus Christ reveals to us our election as an election which is made by Him, by His will which is also the will of God' (II/2, 115). If he were merely elected, the Object of election, then we would be back with a hidden divine decree and could not really know or trust our election in him. By contrast, Jesus is truly the Subject of election: 'In the harmony of the triune God He is no less the original Subject of this electing than He is its original object' (II/2, 105). We shall return to this difficult idea later in this chapter.

As electing God, Jesus Christ is also the elected human, and Barth turns next to elucidate this concept. The particular man Jesus of Nazareth is elected in eternity, on the basis of free grace and not of earned merit, in the decree which is the beginning of all God's activity. This man is not elected alone, however, but together with – in him and represented by him – an elect people. He is elected to be the cause and instrument of their election and exaltation. As the elected human, Jesus Christ responds to God by electing God in faith: he obeys God's will, calls upon God's name and believes in God's righteousness. However, his own election is to suffering obedience unto crucifixion and death, in order that we might be spared the rejection that we deserve. His steadfast faithfulness on this path of rejection finds its response in the accompanying steadfast faithfulness of God to him, culminating in resurrection. The appropriate response on our part to our election in Jesus Christ, therefore, can only be our own election of God in faith.

Together, for Barth, these two statements – that Jesus Christ is the electing God and the elected human – not only constitute the doctrine of election but also represent the very centre of the Self-revelation of God. Barth is convinced that previous work on the doctrine erred precisely in separating the two statements. When this happens, Barth suggests, both the doctrine of the electing God and the doctrine of the elected human tend to be posited in abstraction from Jesus Christ. By contrast, Barth asserts that the true election of God is revealed in Jesus Christ.

Moreover, Barth argues that the doctrines of election and salvation must be considered together. In the decree of election, God has elected Godself for communion with sinful humanity, and God has elected sinful humanity for communion with Godself. To bring about this communion with sinful humanity, God has elected to take the rejection which sinful humanity merits (on account of their rejection of God) upon Godself. In Jesus Christ, then, God assumes their reprobation, perdition and death. In the same act of election, however, sinful humanity is elected to participate in the glory of God and in God's blessedness with the promise of eternal life. In other words, election is at the centre of Barth's salvific view of the wonderful exchange: God elects rejection for Godself so that those who deserve rejection might be elected. In this way, according to Barth, Jesus Christ is not only Elector and Elected, but also Rejector and Rejected. Here, for Barth, is the only place where we can speak of double predestination – in the person of Jesus Christ.

This decision of election is the very will and being of the living God: Barth writes that 'the eternal will of God which is the predestination of all things is God's life in the form of the history, encounter and decision between Himself and man … willed and known from all eternity' (II/2, 175). At the same time, precisely this divine Self-determination in election also determines the being and autonomy of the human being, recognizing its individuality and freedom in covenant relationship with God. As we will see in Chapter 7, this is the foundation of Barth's theological ethics: as

God elects the creature to covenant relationship, so responsibility and obedience are commanded of the creature.

## The election of the community

The election of Jesus Christ is simultaneously and secondarily the election of the community of Jesus Christ in and together with him. The focus of Barth switches now from Jesus Christ to the community elected in him to respond to God in faithful service. In turning to this corporate aspect of election, rather than to the individual elect person or persons, Barth considers himself to be following the witness of Scripture, which speaks in the first place of the election of the community and only then of the individuals who are elect in it. Barth proceeds to identify two 'circles' of election: the 'inner circle' of those actively called to witness to the world on behalf of Jesus Christ, and the 'outer circle' which comprises the wider world in which Jesus Christ is proclaimed. Both circles are elect, but the focus here is on the 'inner circle'.

Barth posits that just as the election of God had a twofold determination in respect of Jesus Christ – election and rejection – so too the 'inner circle' of the community has a dual aspect. Corresponding to Jesus Christ as the crucified Messiah are the people of Israel, who resist their election and therefore attest the divine judgement. Corresponding to Jesus Christ as the risen Lord of the church is the Christian community of Jews and Gentiles, recognizing and confessing the mercy of God in Jesus Christ.

Barth insists that we do *not* have to do here with two communities, one elect and one rejected; rather, we have to do with one community *in two forms*, elected together in their unity. In the first form, the community evidences the human turning away from the electing God; in the second form, it evidences the electing God turning towards humanity. The two cannot be separated, but form a unity in distinction, and within the divine election, both forms of the community fulfil a role. In the exploration of these roles, Barth offers a series of sustained exegetical reflections, focused on the difficult text of Romans 9–11.

First, in the form of Israel, the community has to attest the divine judgement which God elects for Godself in Jesus Christ, the crucified Messiah. Israel is charged with the hearing, reception and acceptance of the promise of God. It is consequently commanded to set aside the old human who resists the divine election and represents human vanity and helplessness. On each count, however, Israel as such and on the whole fails to obey its calling. According to Barth, however, precisely in this failure it nevertheless serves God: it attests the divine judgement, demonstrates that the Word has been heard and exhibits the powerlessness of humanity. And precisely in this failure, Barth insists, Israel cannot abrogate or abolish its election in Jesus Christ.

Second, in the form of the church, the community has to attest the divine mercy in which God elects to be for humanity in Jesus Christ, its risen Lord. It is charged not only with the hearing, reception and acceptance of the promise, but with responding to it in faith and in witness. And it thereby has to attest the coming both of the new human who grasps the divine election and of eternal life in the kingdom of God. On each count, the church takes up the witness of Israel in auxiliary service, witnessing to its existence as the *fulfilment* of the election of Israel in so far as it arises from Israel and Israel too lives in it. At the same time, however, on each count the church also exists in hidden form within Israel from the beginning, and thus represents also the *foundation* of the election of Israel.

## The election of the individual

Following his treatment of the election of Jesus Christ and the election of the community, Barth finally turns to the topic which usually dominated previous presentations of the doctrine – the election of the individual. This ordering is important for Barth: the election of the individual is mediated and conditioned by the election of the community, and both are in turn determined by the election of Jesus Christ. At all points in this section, Barth's theological exposition is accompanied by sustained and detailed attention to a wide variety of passages of Scripture.

Barth states right at the beginning that the community must witness that every person 'belongs eternally to Jesus Christ and is therefore not rejected, but elected by God in Jesus Christ' (II/2, 306). Already, then, Barth has left much traditional doctrine far behind. The proclamation of the Christian community is not that just some people, but that *all* people are elect in Jesus Christ. Thus people need no longer worry and fear that they are not elect, for he has assumed the sinful self-determination of all, their rejection of the grace and relationship offered by God and their lives of sinful and fatal isolation, and has suffered and overcome this on the cross. The result is that they do not receive the rejection that they deserve but are appointed to eternal life. In this respect again, election is the sum of the Gospel, and – as such – not a general theory of salvation but an evangelical address to every person.

Individuals demonstrate that they are elect as they respond to the calling of the Spirit and believe in and correspond to their election in Jesus Christ. Election thus takes place with a definite goal: in and with the community, the individual is called to live as a covenant partner of God. They are called to receive the love and the blessing of God, and to respond to it with gratitude and service. In fulfilling this calling, they become a witness of Jesus Christ and share in the ongoing ministry of reconciliation. There are, of course, those who reject their calling and lie against the truth of their election. Yet Barth affirms that precisely this rejection, which merits the rejection of God, has *already* been removed by the work of Jesus Christ, who elected to become the Rejected in their place. Thus not even the sinful rejection of God can reverse the election of an individual in Jesus Christ: our sinful self-determination is no match for our determination in Jesus Christ in the divine election.

The opposition between these two groups – those who respond and those who do not – can therefore only ever be relative, for both remain in the sphere of grace. Those who fail to respond serve to remind those who do that the rejection of both has been taken away in Jesus Christ; those who respond serve to remind those who do not that the election of Jesus Christ triumphs over all human rejection. Indeed, the true contrast between election and rejection does not lie between these two groups, but only in the one person Jesus Christ, who is both elected and rejected. For this reason, though Barth denies that all will *necessarily* be saved (the doctrine of *apokatastasis*), he is unwilling to state that there is *anyone* who will *not* be saved.

## Comment

Barth's doctrine of election represents one of the most radical portions of *Church Dogmatics* and one of his most significant contributions to recent theology. Some of its most innovative features have been explored above – the understanding of the doctrine as primarily about the divine determination of the divine being, the corresponding location of the doctrine of election in the doctrine of God, the desire to ground all statements concerning election both noetically and ontically in Jesus Christ, and the view that all humanity is elect in Jesus Christ and that none are rejected. In his Christocentric reconception of the doctrine, Barth has reformulated or overcome many of the issues that troubled his theological predecessors, from double predestination to Christian assurance. In the wake of such theological innovation, however, has come great theological controversy. Three particular issues are worthy of brief mention.

First, there is the question of the extent of salvation. Barth states that all people are elect in Jesus Christ, yet denies that this necessarily means that all will be saved. For some commentators, Barth is simply being inconsistent here: universal election must imply universal salvation. And belief in universal salvation has often been seen as heretical in the church and in direct conflict with certain passages of Scripture. Barth is clearly aware of all this, yet he refuses to be moved from his position. He writes: 'If we are to respect the freedom of divine grace, we cannot venture the statement that [the final extent of the circle of election] must and will finally be coincident with the world of man as such (as in the doctrine of the so-called *apokatastasis*)' (II/2, 417). This unwillingness to turn the free gift of salvation into a metaphysical principle remained Barth's position to the end.

Second, there is the question of what it means to call Jesus Christ, together with the Father and the Spirit, the 'Subject of election'. On one reading of Barth, the Subject of election is the triune God – Father, Son and Spirit – ontologically existing prior to and apart from the act of election. The immanent Trinity is thus the presupposition of the divine election in Jesus Christ, and God would be a Trinity whether or not the world had been created. On this reading, the eternal Son as eternal Son is necessarily defined without reference to the incarnation: only contingently is the eternal Son determined with reference to the incarnation. To call Jesus Christ the 'Subject of election' is a figure of speech, for the eternal Son in himself and the eternal Son as determined for incarnation are not identical but form a unity in distinction. However, a very different reading of Barth posits that God is Lord even over God's being such that God has determined Godself in God's second mode of being to be for humanity in Jesus Christ without qualification. The decision of election is thus the presupposition – or co-supposition – of the Trinitarian being of God. There is therefore no eternal Son who is not determined for incarnation, and no room for a doctrine of the immanent Trinity that is not determined by the divine election. To call Jesus Christ the 'Subject of election' is thus again a figure of speech, but now reflecting the fact that the decision of election rests on the singularity of the Person of God, who is both the Father who begets and the Son – Jesus Christ – who is begotten. The debate between these two readings of Barth is lively, with much to be said on both sides, and shows no sign of diminishing.

Finally, there is the question of Barth's theological presentation of Israel. Given the time at which Barth was writing, in the period of the Second World War, this material has added retrospective significance. On the one hand, Barth posits that the community in its form as Israel has to serve the representation of the divine judgement. On the other hand, Barth also asserts that the community in its form as Israel also witnesses to the divine mercy and that it remains irrevocably elect in Jesus Christ. Underlying Barth's careful attempt to exposit this aporetic matter is his exegesis of Romans 9–11, a passage which has proven immensely difficult to Christians of all ages – and perhaps particularly the present age – to understand. Given this background, it is no surprise that some have read Barth's work sympathetically at this point, while others have not been sparing in their criticism.

# CHAPTER FOUR

# The doctrine of creation

In volume III of *Church Dogmatics*, Barth unfolds his doctrine of creation. The turn to this theme involved Barth writing on a topic for which he felt far less prepared, yet the result remains insightful and challenging. The material was written in the later years and immediate aftermath of the Second World War, at a time when many parts of the world, not least much of Europe, lay in ruins. Despite this context, and on the basis of extensive engagement with and reflection upon Scripture, Barth presents a doctrine of creation which unremittingly affirms the goodness of creation, the love of God for it, and the potential of humanity within it, and he does so without ever lapsing into facile optimism or losing sight of the gravity of sin and evil. Volume III contains four part-volumes, covering the work of creation; the creature; the Creator and the creature; and the ethics of creation. The first three will be explored below; the final part-volume – on ethics – will be explored in Chapter 7.

## I  The work of creation

In volume III/1 of *Church Dogmatics*, Barth explores the divine act of creation. Underlying his work here, as throughout volume III, is Barth's consistent principle that all theological knowledge must be derived from the revelation of God in Jesus Christ attested in Scripture. This part-volume consists of three sections. The first section explores the divine creation of the world as a confession of faith which rests on the divine Self-revelation. The second section explores the relationship between the divine act of creation and the history of the covenant of grace. Finally, the third section considers creation as divine benefit, exploring the way in which creation is both actualized and justified by God.

## Faith in God the Creator

In this brief section, Barth investigates the nature of the core statements of the doctrine of creation and the basis on which we can utter them.

For Barth, to believe that God is the Creator and that the world is created is 'no less than the whole remaining content of Christian confession … an article of faith' (III/1, 3). When we state that God created heaven and earth and all that is in them, and that the reality distinct from God is willed and established by God, we are thus not dealing with self-evident truths. By contrast, we are dealing with statements of *faith*, made in response to the Self-revelation of God attested in Scripture. This has two immediate consequences. First, we should not unfold the meaning of these statements by means of general concepts or abstract speculations; instead we should unfold them by way of the *particular content* of God's revelation. Second, when we attend to God's revelation attested in Scripture, we find that the primary and central Object of its witness is Jesus Christ; hence it is in light of him that we must consider and understand what Scripture attests about creation.

In Jesus Christ, Barth posits, we find assurance both of the reality of God as Creator, and of our own reality as creatures. We learn, first, that God is not alone, but is Lord of a realm distinct from God, and that the reality of this realm is confirmed by the existence of the man Jesus. And we learn that the creature is not alone: in this man Jesus, the eternal Son of God becomes human and calls God Father, encountering God the Creator from below, in the form of a creature. In Jesus Christ, moreover, we find the integration of all that Scripture has to teach about creation. We learn that God is an eternal Father who graciously determines to be for humanity in Jesus Christ by the Spirit; that creation is a free and loving divine event which bestows on creation once and for all its essence and existence as a gift; and that the centre of the creation of heaven and earth is the humanity of Jesus Christ and the covenant of grace.

Barth concludes that 'from every angle Jesus Christ is the key to the secret of creation' (III/1, 28). He is the foundation of our knowledge of creation, and faith in him is the basis of the belief that God is the Creator of heaven and earth and of the knowledge of God's power over all things, God's right over all things, and God's benevolence to all things.

In this short section we see a number of elements that are significant for the further elaboration of Barth's doctrine of creation. To speak *theologically* about creation, we can only attend to the witness of Scripture and, in particular, to the person and work of *Jesus Christ*. This means, formally, that the doctrine of creation cannot be treated in isolation, without reference to both the foregoing doctrine of God and the following doctrine of reconciliation. And this means, materially, that when we attend to God as Creator, we do not have to do with a speculative or impersonal world-cause, but with the Father of Jesus Christ, and that when we attend to the human as created, we do not have to with an abstract or general creature, but with one which is elect from eternity in Jesus Christ. The implications of this Christ-centred approach will emerge clearly in what follows.

## *Creation and covenant*

This important section lays out Barth's views of creation and covenant. The first subsection attends to the relationship between creation and history, while the following subsections explore in more detail the relationship between creation and covenant.

In the first subsection, Barth begins by positing that the act of creation is the beginning of all things and of all history distinct from God. Creation thus has a unique status: it is the first external work of God, the first event in history. Yet creation is also inextricably connected with the further series of God's works within creation. These later works have in common that they institute, preserve and execute the covenant partnership into which God calls humanity in Jesus Christ. As a result, Barth writes, 'Creation sets the stage for the story of the covenant of grace' (III/1, 44). This is perhaps the central claim of this whole part-volume: that creation must be considered together with this covenant, and thus with the divine act of election which is the foundation of both.

In the covenant of grace, as we saw in the previous chapter, God freely elected lowliness and humiliation for Godself in Jesus Christ in order that sinful humanity might be raised and exalted. This gracious election took place in eternity – *before* creation. Precisely as a result, however, Barth contends that it renders creation *necessary*: if it is God's eternal will to be for humanity in Jesus Christ, then the man Jesus and the rest of creation have to be created for that will to be realized. To claim that Jesus Christ is the genuine basis of creation, then, is not only true in a *noetic* way, such that, as we saw above, he is the One through whom we can know and understand the event. It is also true in an *ontic* way, because he is the necessary foundation of its existence, in the eternal will of God.

What this means is that, for Barth, nothing in creation exists in and for itself, but only with reference to the covenant of grace in Jesus Christ and its purpose. The aim of creation as a whole, and of the history of creation in all its diversity, is thus the covenant of grace and the specific history of that covenant. It is not the case that the realm of nature (creation) and the realm of grace (covenant) are seen by Barth to be identical. Rather, Barth contends that there is nothing in the former which does not already both point towards and emerge from the latter, and nothing in the latter which does not also belong within the former.

The event of creation itself – like the covenant of grace which is its aim – belongs to history. It is not a timeless truth in an eternal sphere, but a concrete act of God that takes place as the foundation of time. It is, then, a historical event. At this point, Barth turns to consider the two accounts of creation that are found in Genesis, and confronts the problem of how to approach these ancient texts in light of the modern discipline of history.

Barth first observes that the act of creation, as a divine action, is not a historical event that we can see or comprehend, nor is it the kind of historical event which is the object of study of the discipline of history as such. Barth therefore calls the history of creation 'non-historical' or 'pre-historical': the narratives of this history found in Genesis are not 'history' in the modern, technical sense. Instead, Barth describes the form of the Genesis narratives as 'saga' – as 'an intuitive and poetic picture of a pre-historical reality of history which is enacted once and for all within the confines of time and space' (III/1, 81). Yet far from rendering the creation accounts untrustworthy or worthless, their form as 'saga' matches perfectly their 'pre-historical' content, and they are as worthy of attention as material in Scripture which takes other non-historical forms such as poetry or meditation.

At this point, Barth carefully distinguishes between 'saga' and 'myth'. Mythical narratives, he avers, attempt to communicate the fundamental principles of general events and characters that are true across time and space. When they speak of creation, then, myths correspondingly evade precisely the concrete particularity, the divine otherness and the historical continuity that the biblical 'saga' accounts attest. The Genesis narratives, then, offer not creation myth, but real creation history. As such, and in all their human limitation, they are able by the power of the Spirit to offer a true witness to God.

What Barth has done here is to reject an understanding of the Genesis accounts as scientific records of history, but without compromising their theological significance and truth. This middle position does not read the creation narratives as a literal account of what actually happened, but nor does it discard them as totally uninstructive or as mere myth. Instead, Barth wants to attend carefully to the lessons which these creation sagas have for us as witnessing to the divine revelation.

This conception of the Genesis accounts as pre-historical history plays a central role in the two subsections that follow, as Barth explores more closely the relationship between creation and covenant. He proceeds by way of sustained and detailed exegesis of the two Genesis narratives – Genesis 1.1–2.4a and Genesis 2.4b–25. In the process, Barth seeks rigorously to contrast the creation sagas found in Genesis with the creation myths found in the ancient cultures of Mesopotamia, Greece, Egypt, Babylon, Canaan and Persia. Though he is keenly aware of the many material resonances involved, Barth carefully highlights the significant theological differences. In particular, he suggests that the texts of Genesis in distinct ways point forward to the concrete relationship between God and humanity in the history of the covenant, whereas the mythical accounts lack this concrete historicity and continuity.

However, Barth makes no attempt in these two subsections to engage with science and its view of cosmic origins. On the one hand, this reflects his view that theological truth can only come from the Self-revelation of God and not from science. Barth observes that the Genesis accounts themselves are not particularly interested in matters scientific but only in the Word of God. On the other hand, this indicates Barth's perception of the limitations of science, and his contention that if science and theology respect their boundaries, they will not come to contradiction. He asserts, indeed, that there is free scope for the work of science *beyond* what Christian doctrine has to say about creation. Instead, the dialogue partners with whom Barth does engage here represent a wide range of biblical commentators and a great variety of theologians.

The second subsection considers creation as the external basis of the covenant. This indicates, for Barth, that while creation is a freely willed act of God, it does not take place for its own sake. Rather, it has in view a goal beyond the creation of the creature – covenant partnership with the creature, as fulfilled in the person of Jesus Christ. The outer basis of the covenant is therefore the divine act of creation. The inner basis of the covenant is the divine love manifest in the eternal election of God to be for humanity in Jesus Christ.

The exegesis in this section focuses on the first Genesis creation account, which narrates the different days of creation. Barth carefully links the divine activities on each day – together comprising the first work of God – to the subsequent events of the covenant of grace – covering the further works of God. Just as humanity – in Jesus Christ – is the focus of the covenant, so, too, humanity is ultimately the focus of this creation narrative. Barth concludes: 'the cosmos is prepared to make possible the existence and continuance of man as God's partner in this covenant' (III/1, 207–8).

In this connection, Barth carefully analyses the biblical assertion that humanity is created by God 'in our image'. For Barth, drawing here on the language of the Jewish philosopher Martin Buber, the creation of humanity gives rise to a relationship between an 'I' (God) and a 'Thou' (the human), and so a true and unique counterpart to God in creation. There also arises an 'I'–'Thou' relationship *within* creation, in the co-existence and encounter of human beings with each other, the most fundamental form of which, for Barth, is the relationship between man and woman. Humanity, according to Barth, is thus not primarily differentiated by race, nation, class or belief, but by gender: humanity exists as man and woman, with the latter ordained to be the glory and the helper of the former.

Barth posits that these two new relationships arising from the act of creation (God–creature and man–woman) ultimately correspond to the eternal 'I'–'Thou' relationship that exists between the Father and the Son in the Trinity. There exists, therefore, what Barth calls an analogy of relations (*analogia relationis*). To be created in correspondence with the image of God means to be created in correspondence with the 'I'–'Thou' relationship at the heart of God. In the case of the human being, then, this means being created *both* 'as a Thou that can be addressed by God but also as an I responsible to God' (III/1, 198), *and* in the 'I'–'Thou' relationship of man and woman.

In other words, the biblical 'in our image' does not refer to a quality, attribute, possession or attitude of the creature. Indeed, Barth rejects views which locate the image of God in the capacity of reason or the exercise of dominion, in the possession of a soul or of a body, or in the presence of certain moral or intellectual talents. By contrast, for Barth, to be created in correspondence with the divine image means to be called by God into relationships of attentiveness and responsibility. At the centre of Barth's conception of the image of God is Jesus Christ, a theme which will re-emerge in volume III/2. For the present, we simply observe that, precisely as the true and basic creaturely image of God, Jesus Christ does not appear alone, but together with – indeed as the Head of – his community, the church, with whom he exists in precisely such a relationship of attentiveness and responsibility.

The third subsection considers the covenant as the internal basis of creation. It is not the case, for Barth, that creation serves merely as the presupposition or promise of the covenant. Rather, from the very beginning, creation is also characterized and determined by the covenant of grace. While the outer basis of creation is the divine wisdom and omnipotence of God, then, the inner basis of creation is the covenant of grace for which God determines Godself in love and freedom.

The exegesis in this section focuses on the second creation narrative in Genesis – of the creation (in turn) of man, the Garden of Eden and woman. For Barth, this whole narrative is directed towards the commencement of the history of the covenant between God and humanity which will begin once creation has ended. At each point, Barth highlights the ways in which the creation narrative anticipates and prefigures covenant history, drawing out a series of detailed typological connections between them. In particular, as in the previous subsection, Barth highlights the fact that 'God did not create man alone, as a single human being, but in the unequal duality of male and female' (III/1, 288). Barth considers this association and communion of man and woman to be not only the essence of humanity and the consummation of the history of creation, but also a prototype of the history of the covenant of God with Israel that is ultimately fulfilled in Jesus Christ and the church.

Throughout this subsection, Barth explores the basis, meaning and goal of the divine work of creation as grounded in the gracious covenant of God with humanity in Jesus Christ. His exegetical consideration of Genesis resources this exploration, not by way of providing historical or scientific data, but rather by illuminating the theological issues in view. From these 'saga' accounts in Genesis, Barth consistently discerns that creation is both a prefiguration and a determination of the covenant, with man and woman together in Jesus Christ at the centre of both.

## *The Yes of God the Creator*

In the final section of this part-volume, Barth considers creation as a finished work. He develops the idea that creation is a benefit: it is willed, executed and approved by God, and God rejoices in it. Indeed, Barth affirms, God's good pleasure is 'the root, the foundation and the end of divine creation' (III/1, 331). Thinkers such as Marcion and Arthur Schopenhauer who fail to see creation in this way have, according to Barth, simply failed to consider creation and covenant together.

Creation as benefit has, for Barth, two corollaries: creation exists as God actualizes it and creation exists as good as God justifies it.

The first benefit – existence – indicates that creation is real, and not a matter of appearance, illusion or dreaming. For Barth, this affirmation is neither self-evident, nor possible on the basis of religious self-consciousness or philosophical speculation. Rather, it is only possible on the basis of the Self-revelation of God as Creator in Jesus Christ. As such, this affirmation is a matter of faith. Here, Barth engages with the work of René Descartes, positing that his failure to persuade stems from his lack of attention to God's Self-revelation.

The second benefit – justification – indicates that the creation is well pleasing to God: it is elected, accepted and justified by God, and God is beneficent to it. In other words, creation not only *is*; it is also *good*. Again, this statement is only possible on the basis of God's Self-revelation, and – specifically – in view of the covenant with humanity which is the divinely willed purpose of creation. When Barth affirms the goodness of creation, he does not proceed from an idealistic or superficial optimism that is blind to the sadness and misery of creation. Rather, he posits a goodness that fully encompasses this aspect of creation, taking seriously the issues of sin and suffering. However, Barth believes that in the humiliation and exaltation of Jesus Christ, God has entered into our human contradictions of joy and sorrow, suffering and triumph. Jesus Christ shares our perils and guarantees our hope, with the result that 'in Him the created world is already perfect in spite of its imperfection' (III/1, 385). Here, Barth criticizes the eighteenth-century optimism of figures such as Gottfried Leibniz and Christian Wolff, whose responses to theodicy were not grounded in Jesus Christ and thus failed to take seriously the problems of sin, evil and death.

## *Comment*

Barth's account of the work of creation is unapologetically theological and theologically unapologetic. The most significant move that he makes is to link the event of creation with the history of the covenant such that creation in general exists for the sake of the covenant in particular. This immediately distances Barth formally from all theological accounts which attempt to treat the doctrine of creation independently of Jesus Christ or to elaborate its contours on the basis of natural theology or philosophical speculation. And this also dictates that Barth is neither beholden to nor threatened by scientific explorations of the universe's origins: if each discipline and its limits are properly construed, there need be no conflict between them. Barth correspondingly affords little attention at this point, or indeed anywhere at all in his doctrine of creation, to the findings of natural science.

For Barth, the God of creation is not an 'unmoved mover', 'first principle' or 'ultimate cause' without further specification, but the *Father* of Jesus Christ, who in eternity determines God's being to be for humanity and who in time actualizes this determination in the midst of creation in the life, death and resurrection of Jesus

Christ. The divine election to be for humanity in Jesus Christ is thus both the originating dynamic and also the historical purpose of the event of creation. The human creature is neither an unreal apparition, nor an independent semi-deity, nor an overflowing emanation of God, but is created in Jesus Christ to be the covenant partner of God, corresponding to the divine image as a creature in the ordered duality of man and woman and attending to the divine will in freedom and responsibility. The human capacity for relationality is thus no abstract capacity for relationship in general but a particular capacity for ordered relations with God and other people.

Hovering in the background throughout Barth's doctrine of creation is the doctrine of nothingness – Barth's attempt to describe the emergence and existence of sin and evil in the world. This will be covered in more detail in volume III/3, but it should be noted in passing that the evident presence of sin and evil in the world does not deter Barth from an unequivocal assertion of the *goodness* of creation. As Barth writes, 'In creation as such no sin takes place and no sin is envisaged' (III/1, 211). This message is as radical now as it must have been originally, in the immediate aftermath of the Second World War.

Two criticisms have featured prominently in evaluations of Barth's doctrine of creation. The first is that it is unashamedly anthropocentric, and the second is that it is explicitly patriarchal. In respect of the first charge, the centring of creation on the covenant of God with humanity does indeed render Barth's presentation anthropocentric. Yet one might note that the Scripture in general – the fount of dogmatics – and Genesis in particular are unapologetically focused on the human dimension of creation. And we must also consider that Barth's understanding of the dominion of humanity over creation is characterized not by sentiments of disrespect or devaluation but by awareness of connectedness and accountability. In respect of the second critique, Barth does indeed find the clear order of Father and Son, mirrored in that of Jesus and the church, to be analogously present in the order of man and woman. And one might again observe that Scripture itself has been interpreted to endorse this particular view of the inequality of the sexes in certain passages. For all Barth's attempts to limit and circumscribe the hierarchy between male and female which he here indicates, the basic move remains highly contentious.

## II  The creature

In volume III/2 of *Church Dogmatics*, Barth turns from the work of creation in general to the creature in particular. This part-volume represents Barth's most extended treatment of theological anthropology, of what it is to be a human creature, and it echoes many of the themes from the previous part-volume. In particular, Barth's methodology, in which theological knowledge must derive from the Self-revelation of God in Jesus Christ, is again prominent. There are five sections in this work, each exploring a different dimension of human being: as a problem of dogmatics, as a creature of God, as determined as the covenant partner of God, as soul and body, and as a creature in time.

### *The human as a problem of dogmatics*

When Barth turns to consider matters of anthropology, there is no sense in which he leaves either the Creator or the rest of creation behind. Just as there can be no independent doctrine of creation, as we noted above, so there can be no independent doctrine of the creature. However, Barth has *no* desire to offer a comprehensive cosmology or world-view, for Scripture itself is largely silent on the relation between the rest of creation and God. Hence Barth remains focused on *humanity*, which – as we saw above – is the centre and goal of creation.

Barth's sole source for his understanding of the human creature is the Word of God – the divine Self-revelation attested in Scripture. The problem for dogmatics that Barth finds here, however, is that 'the revelation of God does not show us man as we wish to see him, in the wholeness of his created being, but in its perversion and corruption' (III/2, 26). Though still the creature of God, of course, humanity is radically and completely corrupted; and so there arises the question of how we can discover its essential created nature.

Barth's answer to this problem is that the very same Word of God which shows us real sinfulness also shows us real creatureliness. The real creaturely nature of humanity is preserved by God in spite of our wickedness, and it is revealed to us in the man Jesus and in his relationship to God. Jesus is therefore the way we come to know what true humanity is, for in his human nature we can recognize what is the true nature of our own humanity and that of others. In Jesus, we see that the grace and determination of God are primary for understanding humanity, while the sin and self-determination of humanity itself are secondary, and therefore that our wilful disobedience cannot undermine *either* the covenant grace of God *or* our status as covenant partners.

What Barth is doing here is to found his theological anthropology on Christology, and thus to base his understanding of human nature solely on the man Jesus. Of course, Barth acknowledges that Jesus is qualitatively different to us – that the human nature of Jesus is without sin, contradicting and judging our own sinfulness, and that the man Jesus alone is one with God, the Word of God incarnate. Nevertheless, it is in the man Jesus that God knows us and our nature. Correspondingly, it is to Jesus that we must look to discover true human nature as it was originally willed and created by God.

## *The human as creature of God*

When we turn to Jesus to understand human nature, we are confronted not by a static idea or a fixed image, but by a concrete man who performs specific acts in a particular history. Indeed, his person and his activity and his history must not be separated, for the New Testament 'knows this man only in His work and history' (III/2, 59). This history is absolutely unique to him alone, and in it we recognize the presence of God to us and the deliverance of God for us. Indeed, Jesus has no other existence beside or beyond accomplishing this salvific work.

The nature of our humanity cannot be directly read off the history of Jesus: we share neither his sinlessness nor his direct identity with God. However, as Jesus' work takes place for all people, and as a decision about them is eternally taken in and by him, it belongs to the essence of *every* human that Jesus was destined to become and then became one of us. As Barth summarizes, 'The ontological determination of humanity is grounded in the fact that one man among all others is the man Jesus' (III/2, 132). In other words, we learn from Jesus that humanity cannot be seen or understood apart from God and the divine deliverance accomplished in him. To be human is thus, in Barth's words, 'to be in the sphere where the first and merciful will of God towards His creatures, His will to save and keep them from the power of nothingness, is revealed in action' (III/2, 145). This crucial point resonates with Barth's earlier doctrine of election and its position that we are all elect in Jesus Christ.

Barth observes that other disciplines provide knowledge of humanity through analysis of natural, ethical and existential phenomena, and here he engages in turn the work of evolutionary theorists, of Johann Fichte and of Karl Jaspers. But in so far as none of these consider humanity in relation to God, they do not address true human nature. By contrast, Christian theology posits on the basis of Jesus that the real human is a being which – in Barth's words – 'belongs to God, to which God turns as Saviour, the determination of which is God's glory, which exists under the lordship of God and is set in the service of God' (III/2, 121).

To be human, then, for Barth, simply means to be with Jesus and therefore with God. Not only our person but also our work and our history can consist only in participating in what God signifies and does for us. Genuine godlessness and sinfulness are simply *contrary* to our human nature: they are, to use Barth's term 'an ontological impossibility'. We cannot escape our divine determination, which is unique in the sphere of creation. More precisely, to be with God means – first – that we are from God, that our being is absolutely dependent on God. This dependence rests on the gracious election of Jesus, in whom we are chosen from all eternity such that we share in the salvation found in him. But it also means – second – that we are called by God, that we are summoned to hear the Word of God. The divine address is the person of Jesus at the centre of creation, who not only speaks but is *himself* the divine speech. Gathering these two ideas together, Barth writes: 'Summoned because chosen – here we have a first definition of real man' (III/2, 150). And just as the being of Jesus is a history, so too this existence of humanity as with God, chosen and summoned by God, is not a mere state of affairs but takes place as a dynamic history.

In this dynamic history – determined in and by Jesus Christ – God is for humanity and humanity may be for God. Hearing the gracious divine call, humanity expresses its gratitude to God and takes on responsibility before God. In this way, we fulfil our true being in our living response to the grace of God: we correspond to God's Word in our knowledge of God, in our obedience to God, and in our invocation of God. Barth summarizes this response under the rubric of freedom, describing this as 'the most profound and comprehensive aspect of the real man' (III/2, 195). Human freedom is evidently not, then, a neutral capacity but has only one positive meaning – correspondence to the divine Word. Any other use of freedom would be to choose non-being and *un*-freedom – to choose our own impossibility. As Barth earlier notes, 'sin itself is only man's irrational and inexplicable affirmation of the nothingness which God as Creator has negated' (III/2, 143).

Perhaps the best way to understand Barth's depiction of human being is as a history involving a twofold movement. First, there is a movement from God to the human, in which God determines the being and history of the creature in Jesus Christ, creating it and calling it for the purpose of covenant partnership. And second, there is a movement from the human to God, in which the creature determines their own history in correspondence with this divine initiative, responding to the divine summons in true freedom. Barth writes of this double pattern that 'the being of man is the creature which, as it is this history, shows itself capable of being this history' (III/2, 199). These movements of divine call and human response – corresponding to Barth's use elsewhere of Gospel and Law – represent the fundamental pattern of Barth's ethics, as we will see in Chapter 7. What is crucial to note at this juncture is simply that the two movements are not equal and opposite: the first, divine movement entirely initiates, circumscribes and directs the second, creaturely movement. Even when we are lost to ourselves and fail to respond to God, then, we are not lost to God.

## The human as covenant partner

God has created humanity with the purpose of being God's covenant partner. This purpose is eternally determined in the divine act of election and is primarily realized in the person of the man Jesus, rendering him the starting point for Barth's investigation. Jesus is unique: even though he remains fully human, God exists immediately in him and he lives – as we saw above – completely *for God*. Barth refers to this as the *divinity* of the man Jesus. At the same time, however, Barth posits that there is a corresponding *humanity* of the man Jesus, such that 'He is man for man, for other men, His fellows' (III/2, 208). As well as living completely for God, then, he also lives completely *for humanity*, with no other purpose than the salvation of humanity. There is no competition between these two orientations: it is precisely as the man Jesus is *for humanity* that he is *for God*, and precisely as he is *for God* that he is *for humanity*. Correspondingly, Barth posits that 'His humanity is in the closest correspondence with His divinity … [and] His divinity has its correspondence and image in the humanity in which it is mirrored' (III/2, 216). This formal parallel is no accident: it is grounded materially in the eternal divine election of God to be for humanity in Jesus Christ. The man Jesus is for others as he is for God *because* God first is for humanity.

Barth here takes a further step. He asserts that the relationship that the divine election creates – between the Creator God and the man Jesus – corresponds to the prior relationship between Father and Son in the Trinity. Barth posits that there exists between these two relationships an analogy of relations, an *analogia relationis*, such as we encountered above in volume III/1. There is certainly no question of an *analogia entis*, an analogy of being, between God and the man Jesus. But there is an analogy of relations between (a) the created relationship between God and humanity in the man Jesus and (b) the intra-Trinitarian relationship between the Father and the Son. The pattern of *both* relationships is elucidated by Barth through the divine perfections of freedom and love.

Turning to our human nature, Barth begins by observing once again that the difference between Jesus and ourselves is fundamental. Yet we are elect in him, and therefore as his history takes place for God and for us, we too are directly implicated, being determined by God for life with God as covenant partners. Though we can deny God and break the covenant from our side, we cannot defeat or efface this determination.

An immediate consequence of this Christological determination of humanity, in light of the fact that Jesus is *for others*, is that we cannot treat of individuals in and of themselves, but only in so far as we see them *with others*. Barth writes: 'Every supposed humanity which is not radically and from the very first fellow-humanity is inhumanity' (III/2, 228). Barth thus sternly rejects Friedrich Nietzsche's idea of the 'superhuman' who is isolated from other humans, opposing to it the Christian ideas of Jesus as the Neighbour and of recognizing him in our neighbours. Our true humanity consists, then, not in being *for* others without qualification, which would usurp the role of Jesus, but in being *with* others and thus *for* them in our own way.

Central here is Barth's focus once again on an 'I'–'Thou' relationship, this time of one person with another person. Barth describes carefully the different elements of this relationship – encounter, communication, assistance and gladness. To exist in such relationships, he argues, is not an accidental feature of our creaturely human being, but an inescapable one. The freedom with which we embrace this existence in co-humanity is for Barth the 'secret of being in encounter and therefore the secret of humanity' (III/2, 273). Finally, in a passage echoing material from volume III/1, Barth offers further precision to the definition of humanity as co-humanity, positing that the original and proper form of co-humanity is the co-existence of man and woman in a relationship which is ordered and hierarchical, though without superiority or inferiority.

It is important to recognize that Barth does not claim that we are covenant partners of God by virtue of our created nature, as if it were our own possibility. Although covenant partnership with God may be our divine *determination*, its *actualization* is always and everywhere a matter of free and unmerited divine grace – of divine election. However, Barth does assert that it is by virtue of our created nature that we are covenant partners of other humans. In other words, we inescapably exist together as 'I' and 'Thou', and the basic form of this co-existence is as man and woman. Indeed, it is precisely this temporal relationship with other humans that indicates the further possibility that we are created to be in relationship with God. Indeed, Barth posits, the first relationship offers an image of the second, despite all the dissimilarities.

We have here a further example of the analogy of relations. More specifically, the relationships between human beings, and between man and woman in particular, offer in their own way an analogy not only to the relationship between the man Jesus and humanity but also to the relationship between God and the man Jesus and ultimately to that between Father and Son. This series or ladder of analogous relations lies behind Barth's statement – reiterating his finding from volume III/1 – that 'God created man in His own image, in correspondence with His own being and essence' (III/2, 324).

What Barth is attempting to delineate in this section is the form of our created existence which renders us capable of the covenant partnership which is its aim. He does this formally by way of a series of analogies of relation, spanning from the inner life of the Trinity to the encounter of man and woman. And he does this materially by way of highlighting the dimensions of freedom and love, call and response, and – ultimately – joy which are common to the truthful forms of all of these relationships. At the centre – both formally and materially – of Barth's presentation is the person of Jesus Christ, the man existing *for* others. In this light, Barth characterizes our created existence as a life in encounter *with* others. We can, of course, attempt to contradict this orientation, but Barth denies that we can ultimately succeed: we can no more undo our existence as covenant partners in co-humanity than we can our calling to be covenant partners of God.

## The human as soul and body

In this section, Barth explores the structure of the human creature as body and soul. He draws extensively at this point on a wide range of texts from Scripture, and engages various philosophical accounts along the way. His starting point is, as ever, the man Jesus, whom he describes as 'one whole man, embodied soul and besouled body' (III/2, 327). There is an irreversible order to this relationship of soul and body in Jesus, for Barth: the former is primary and the latter is secondary. Indeed, in Jesus' ordered existence as soul and body, Barth finds a mirror image of the ordered relationship between Jesus and his community – another example, Barth suggests, of the analogy of relations.

For Barth, human creatures are – similarly to Jesus – 'wholly and simultaneously both soul and body, always and in every relation soulful, and always and in every relation bodily' (III/2, 372). Any dualistic conception of humanity, in which body and soul are seen as self-contained substances, or any monistic conception, in which the distinction between the two is elided, results in a disastrous separation of body and soul. By contrast, the human creature is soul and body in a differentiated unity, and thus 'capable of meeting God, of being a person for and in relation to Him, and of being one as God is one' (III/2, 395). Our creaturely existence, however, is not simply a matter of body and soul, but also of spirit. For Barth, to have spirit is to be grounded, constituted and maintained by God in our existence as soul and body. In other words, in our creaturely existence, we are absolutely dependent on God being with us.

To have spirit, then, is not a human possession or attribute, but depends utterly on the activity of God, the One who is Spirit, the principle of our creaturely reality.

The goal of our creaturely existence as soul and body in ordered duality is covenant relationship with God. It is our existence as soul and body, according to Barth, which gives us the ability both to perceive God in God's revelation – by the powers of awareness and thought – and to respond to God in our action – by the powers of desire and volition. Barth posits that in this order, as we are addressed by God, we are rational creatures.

## The human in time

In the final section of this part-volume, Barth explores the form of the human creature as temporal. Again, the starting point is the history of the man Jesus. The life of Jesus marks a fixed timespan, but with his resurrection from the dead there begins a new and eternal chapter. This post-resurrection history sheds light back on his earlier history, revealing that the time of the man Jesus is also the time of the appearance and presence of God. Moreover, it reveals both that God has a different time from our time and that God wills to grant us a share in this time, in his eternity. There is a connection here to Barth's treatment of the divine eternity in volume II/1: God's eternity does not exclude but includes time and temporality. Barth therefore writes that the life of Jesus is 'at once the centre and the beginning and end of all the times of all the lifetimes of all men' (III/2, 440). It is the time God willed to have for humanity – to establish the covenant as the goal of creation. Consequently, it is the hidden meaning and the ultimate fulfilment of all times. The being of Jesus thus not only exists as a being in the present, but also extends back beyond creation and forward beyond the eschaton, the end of time, thereby embracing all times. In light of this, Barth describes Jesus as the Lord of time.

Clearly, as human creatures, we are not lords of time. We live in the flow of past, present and future, and we are not in possession of time at all, moving only from the 'no longer' to the 'not yet'. In the grace of election, however, Barth writes that God 'places our being in time in the light and under the promise of the true and genuine being in time actualised in [Jesus]' (III/2, 519). In the man Jesus, we see that God wills and creates and guarantees our time, giving it to us as the creaturely form of our existence, and we also see that God negates our lost and fallen time, restoring our true and genuine being in time. Indeed, for Barth, we are only in time as we are with God: God is the guarantee of the reality of our being in the past, the present and the future.

In light of its determination for divine covenant, creaturely human life has duration, but this duration is finite: God grants us all our allotted time. Yet we see in Jesus that this limitation is not a restriction or a threat; by contrast, it indicates a time given *by* God and spent *with* God, and God is a gracious God. As finite, our existence has a beginning and an end. Before we were, however, God was; indeed we were elect in Jesus Christ from all eternity. For this reason, our beginning stands not under a threat of dissolution, but under the promise of grace. And our end is not simply an event of divine judgement; in view of the crucifixion and resurrection of Jesus, we see that God is Lord even over death, and thus gracious and for us even in our death. Our allotted time is thus embedded in and surrounded by God's time, leading Barth to see the human being's temporal finitude as 'a powerful invitation and direction to throw himself upon God's free grace' (III/2, 569).

## *Comment*

Barth's whole account of the human being as creature addresses the question 'Given that the purposed destiny of the human being is to be a covenant partner of God, what can we say about the human being *as creature*?' To answer this question, Barth turns to the man Jesus, whose history is attested in Scripture. He does so in the belief that theological truth about human beings as creatures can only be gained when they are considered in their relation to God, which means looking to their election, creation and reconciliation in Jesus Christ. Barth does not seek to disparage the wisdom and insight available from other disciplines, but insists that their contributions be considered in light of the real human as revealed in Jesus. There is then, for Barth, no value theologically in starting with or seeking a general or abstract concept of human nature. Instead, knowledge of humanity is grounded noetically and ontically in Jesus: noetically, in that he is the source of this knowledge, and ontically, in that our humanity is grounded in his.

Each of the four material subsections explored above therefore begins with a characterization of Jesus – as 'man for God', 'man for other men', 'whole man' and 'Lord of time', respectively. Each then moves, with explicit recognition of the relevant differences, to a characterization of the human creature – as 'being with God', 'being with others', 'being as body and soul' and 'being in time'. In the process, Barth discerns and invokes a series of 'analogies of relations', allowing him to connect a series of Trinitarian, Christological and anthropological 'I'–'Thou' relationships characterized by freedom and love.

Two further points deserve mention at this stage. First, it is important to recognize that Barth conceives of the being of the man Jesus and the being of the human creature as histories. In Jesus, it is seen that his person, essence, work and history are inseparable. Similarly, then, human nature is not some static or quantifiable essence; instead, it indicates a lived history of encounter with God and other humans within creation and stands under the determination of the divine election in Jesus Christ. This dynamic conception of the inseparability of nature and history will recur prominently in volume IV/1. Second, once again we find sin present in the background of Barth's presentation but not at its centre. His treatment of the nothingness that threatens creation and the creature will feature below, and a full presentation of his understanding of sin will appear in the following chapter. In the meantime, it is worth noting simply that Barth is cognisant of sin and its consequences at each relevant juncture. And it is worth emphasizing that Barth nevertheless holds steadfastly both to the original goodness of the creature and to the divine determination of this goodness which cannot be undone by creaturely sin.

## III  The Creator and the creature

Barth turns in volume III/3 to the doctrine of the divine providence. Having considered in turn the divine creation and the human creature, he now moves to consider the foundation, the sphere and the parameters of the relationship between God and the creature. This relationship in all of its dimensions is posited as being grounded in the relationship between God and the creature as it takes place in Jesus Christ. The part-volume contains four sections. The first section introduces the basis and form of the doctrine of providence, while the second considers its content under the rubric of God as Lord of the creature. The third section offers Barth's account of the nothingness which threatens the divine creation but is overcome in Jesus Christ. Finally, the fourth section considers the created realm of heaven, and its angelic inhabitants.

## *The basis and form of providence*

For Barth, providence means 'the superior dealings of the Creator with His creation, the wisdom, omnipotence and goodness with which He maintains and governs in time this distinct reality according to the counsel of His own will' (III/3, 3). The statement that God rules over all things providentially is – along with the statement of God's creation of all things – a confession of faith. God's presence and rule in world occurrence is not something empirically visible or provable, nor is it to be confused with a general philosophy of history or a conception of cosmic processes. By contrast, for Barth, the divine rule of providence is 'a hidden history, which is neither felt, seen, known, nor dialectically perceived by man, but can only be believed on the basis of [the] Word of God' (III/3, 19). Because of this, it must be conceived in light of the gracious election of God to be for humanity in Jesus Christ.

When the divine act of creation is completed, the divine rule of providence begins, guaranteeing and confirming creation and providing the necessary background for the covenant of grace which takes place within it. Providence is thus not itself the covenant, but its presupposition. Barth explains: 'The faithfulness of God is that He co-ordinates creaturely occurrence under His lordship with the occurrence of the covenant, grace and salvation, that He subordinates the former to the latter and makes it serve it' (III/3, 41). Again, then, we see how creaturely history in general exists for the sake of covenant history in particular, with the former as a subordinate reflection of the latter. Creaturely occurrence serves to provide time, space and opportunity not only for God to be present and active in the covenant of grace, but also for the creature to exist and to do so to the divine glory. This service is not possible by dint of its own power, but only as it is called and enabled by God.

The crucial step which Barth takes here is to posit belief in providence as being possible only on the basis of the Self-revelation of God in Jesus Christ. This has three ramifications. First, it leads Barth to criticize those conceptions of providence which are based on natural theology, philosophical worldviews or phenomenological assumptions. These views are, for him, theologically invalid as they are not based on revelation. Second, it means that God does not create the world and then withdraw; rather, in the divine freedom of election God chooses to continue in relationship with creation as the Lord of its history. Hence no thing and no event in creation can escape or avoid the providence of God. And third, it indicates that God's providential rule is a gracious lordship, determined by God's election to be for humanity in Jesus Christ. Correspondingly, Barth criticizes theologies of providence – including some from his own, Reformed tradition – which have insufficiently recognized this Christ-centred dimension.

## *God as Lord of the creature*

Having outlined the parameters of his doctrine of providence, Barth turns to address its details. He structures the main part of this section under three headings derived from traditional Protestant theologies of providence – the divine preserving, the divine accompanying and the divine ruling. He then concludes with a final subsection on the Christian under the lordship of God.

The divine *preserving* refers to the way in which God exercises lordship by upholding and sustaining the creature in its existence and activity. For Barth, God freely and graciously wills to be faithful to the creature which God has elected in Jesus Christ in eternity and created in time. However, unlike creation, preservation is not an *immediate* action of God upon the creature, but takes place *mediately*, by way of the context of creation.

This divine preservation is necessary for two reasons. First, the creature is created out of nothing, in an act – as we will see below – in which God distinguished what God did will from the nothingness that God did not will. Though God is superior to nothingness, nothingness is superior to the creature. Consequently, if the divine preservation were withdrawn, the creature would be 'overwhelmed by chaos and fall into nothingness' (III/3, 74). This first, negative delimitation, however, is not the basic reason for preservation. Second, then, the deeper reason for the preservation of the creature is its eternal election in Jesus Christ to participate in the covenant of grace, to live in and by the grace of God. Because God fundamentally wills us to live in and by the grace of God, so God wills the continuation of our created existence and activity which allows for this covenant relationship. And just as our existence as covenant partners is possible only by the divine grace, so too our continuing existence as creatures is possible only by the divine grace. In both cases, we are referred to Jesus Christ, who both fulfilled the covenant of grace by overcoming sin and nothingness and did so from within the perilous limitations of creaturely existence. As Barth concludes, 'Because the creature is saved by Him, because it partakes of this salvation by Him, the creature is sustained and preserved by Him' (III/3, 85).

The divine *accompanying* refers to the divine lordship over the creature in its autonomous activity. As God preserves us, so we are given time and space for our own history, our own being in action. This does not mean that the divine action ceases at the point where ours begins; rather, for Barth, God's action inescapably accompanies our action, affirming and respecting its integrity. The key to understanding this relationship between divine action and human action is Jesus Christ. In him, Barth writes, 'The preceding action of the Creator and the following of the creature ... are seen in action: the fatherly lordship of the Creator; the childlike obedience of the creature; and the Spirit in whom both take place together' (III/3, 94).

In Jesus, we see that the divine action accompanies the creaturely action with absolute superiority: there is an absolute qualitative distinction between the divine action and the human action. Correspondingly, in the divine accompanying, it is the divine will which is – without exception – accomplished, as it precedes, accompanies and follows the creature. At this point, it may seem that the emphasis upon the supremacy of the divine action jeopardizes the integrity and reality of creaturely action. But precisely here, Barth insists that the conceptual elements of the divine accompanying – the will of God, the freedom of the creature and so on – are not merely empty ciphers or abstract ideas, but are to be filled out with what Barth calls 'Christian meaning' (III/3, 117). And what this fundamentally implies is that because the divine activity is the activity of grace, God does not in any sense threaten or destroy the free activity of the creature. Instead, as we will see repeatedly below, it is precisely the majesty of the divine activity which affirms and confirms the autonomy and the integrity of our creaturely action. Barth acknowledges that this appears to be something of a paradox, and suggests that to understand it, we must be willing to overcome our fear-complex that God might be an enemy of our freedom and that we would be better as completely autonomous beings. In truth, Barth argues, there is nothing better for the creature than to be ruled by the divine grace, for the gracious and omnipotent activity of God 'not merely leaves the activity of the creature free, but continually makes it free' (III/3, 150).

There are three elements of the one divine act of accompanying.

First, the activity of God precedes our action. God does so eternally, in the divine decree to be for us in Jesus Christ that precedes both creaturely action and creation itself. And God does so temporally, in the ongoing divine determination of the totality of creaturely activity which precedes our act. Again, however, this divine precedence – including God's foreknowledge and foreordination – does not mean a weakening or suppression of our power and responsibility. Instead, when seen in light of the covenant in Jesus Christ, it indicates that in God we live and move and have our being and that our genuine freedom is given by God.

Second, the activity of God concurs with our action, as the divine activity proceeds simultaneously with the creaturely activity. As it does so, it determines our action completely, as it 'takes place in and with and over the activity of the creature' (III/3, 132). Again, however, this divine action is not an oppressive or imperious determination of our action, but is instead the activity of God's Word, moving us by the power, wisdom and goodness that is God's Spirit. It is by Word and Spirit that God works in the incarnation, posits Barth, and by the same Word and Spirit that God works in us. As such, the divine action occurs in an entirely different order than the creaturely action, just as God and the creature fall within an entirely different order of being. God's activity is thus not a despotic work of tyranny, but a fatherly work of grace. It does not prejudice but preserves the freedom and responsibility of the individual and its action according to its own nature and limits. The irresistible lordship of God is thus not the enemy of creaturely freedom but its guarantee.

Third, the activity of God follows our action, for God will still be, and be at work, even when the creature and its work have reached their end. God will ordain the ongoing effects of each creaturely action in God's ongoing rule and government of the world. At this point, Barth is already consciously infringing upon the final aspect of the divine providence – the divine ruling.

The divine *ruling* refers to the power of God over God's creation in general and God's creature in particular, and God's power to arrange the course of the history of both. This is not a blind or arbitrary power, but has a definite purpose – the glory of God in the salvation and glorification of the creature. Expressed from the other side, God wills that the goal of the creature who proceeds from and is accompanied by God is to return to God. God achieves this purpose by ordering creaturely occurrence, determining not only its execution but also its results. And God accomplishes this in respect of both the totality of creation and its individual parts. Again, however, this directionality of the divine activity does not abrogate the activity of the creature, but rather safeguards it. Barth therefore avers that 'Between the sovereignty of God and the freedom of the creature there is no contradiction' (III/3, 166). As long as we keep in mind who and what we mean by God, remaining attentive to Scripture, there is no problem in affirming both the divine rule and the creaturely freedom.

The God who orders and rules the world as its Lord is not an abstract supreme deity but the King of Israel and the Father of Jesus Christ. And just as the covenant of grace is the internal basis of creation, so world events are not an end in themselves but are to be viewed in light of the events of the covenant attested in Scripture. It is in God's rule over the covenant of grace in particular that we see the original and pattern of God's rule over world history in general. The former rule is revealed in the covenant, while the latter rule takes place in hidden form: if we did not know the former, we could not perceive the latter. At the same time, Barth posits that there are certain constant features within world occurrence which offer a testimony to the divine rule over creation: the history of Scripture, the history of the church, the history of the Jews, the limitation of human life and the existence of angels. All of these are signs and witnesses of the divine rule over creation, though none can prove or reveal it.

In a final subsection here, Barth turns to consider the Christian who exists under this universal lordship of God. All creatures live under the providential preserving, accompanying and ruling; however, it is the Christian alone who knows this. They see at the centre of world history Jesus Christ, in whom the lordship of God and the subjection of the creature is a paradigmatic reality. In him, they see that to be a creature who is subject to the divine lordship is a position of freedom and happiness. And – crucially – they allow this knowledge of God's gracious providence actively to shape their life in the Christian attitudes of faith, obedience and prayer. In this way – in belief, conformity and petition – their creaturely activity acquires in Christ a share in the universal lordship of God and co-operates in the work of the kingdom of God. At such times, by the grace of God, God's lordship is actualized and God's will is done in the life of the Christian and of the community.

What Barth has done in this dense section on God as Lord of the creature is to offer an account of the relationship between divine action and human action. His account affirms both the complete sovereignty of God and the genuine freedom of the creature, and – as such – may appear somewhat paradoxical. But instead of trying to satisfy the criteria of formal analysis or philosophical logic, Barth's purpose here is to offer a richly descriptive account of this relationship as it is attested in Scripture. More specifically, Barth sketches its contours with central attention to the person of Jesus Christ, in whom we see what it means for divine action to take place in, with and over creaturely action *without* jeopardizing human integrity. The result is a non-competitive construal of the relationship between God and humanity, which celebrates rather than fears creaturely life under the lordship of God and which affirms yet circumscribes the freedom of human action under the divine providence. This, then, is Barth's model for how we should understand our existence in the covenant of grace in particular, and human history and interaction in the world in general.

## *Nothingness*

At various previous points in Barth's doctrine of creation, we have already encountered the concept of nothingness. Nothingness is Barth's way of referring to the resistance which exists in opposition to God's universal lordship and rule, threatening and corrupting the creation of God and its inhabitants. In this short, but important, section, Barth attempts in greater detail to describe what nothingness is and does.

Barth begins by outlining the problematic nature of conceiving of nothingness. Nothingness cannot be the result of the positive will of God, for this would compromise the divine holiness, but nor can it be the result of the simple activity of the creature, for this would compromise the divine omnicausality. The power of nothingness cannot be pessimistically overestimated, for this would compromise the efficacy of the work of Jesus Christ, but nor can it be optimistically underestimated, as if it were merely a principle at our disposal. It is little wonder that Barth writes of facing here 'an extraordinarily clear demonstration of the necessary brokenness of all theological thought and utterance' (III/3, 293). The result is that theology can neither systematize nor explain nothingness, but only seek to offer a report.

For Barth, if we wish to learn what nothingness is, we must look beyond the merely negative aspects of creation – such as darkness, failure, sadness and death, all of which in truth belong to the original perfection of creation – and look instead to Jesus Christ. In him, Barth writes, is revealed 'not only the goodness of God's creation in its twofold [positive and negative] form, but also the true nothingness ..., the adversary with whom no compromise is possible' (III/3, 302). In the incarnation, Barth asserts, God encountered and engaged the hostile threat and assault of this nothingness, taking up the cause of the creature. In doing so, God demonstrated that nothingness not only challenges the *work* of God – creation and the creature – but also, and therefore, challenges *God*. In the crucifixion, however, God exposed nothingness as the adversary and defeated it in its entirety, thereby liberating the creature and the creation. This victory over nothingness is the work of God alone, and can be ours only through hope in Jesus Christ, in whom it is overcome.

Though human sin will not be Barth's focus until volume IV, he mentions it in passing here, noting that, in the light of Jesus Christ, we see the concrete form of nothingness to be *human sin*. As such, Barth writes, 'we ourselves ... have become the victims and servants of nothingness, sharing its nature and producing and extending it' (III/3, 306). In this way, we become and are responsible for it, as we disobey the gracious God who is for us in Jesus Christ and fall under the harmful sway of evil and death. We will return to this theme in Chapter 5.

In view of the history of Jesus Christ, Barth proceeds to a more comprehensive series of statements about nothingness. First, nothingness 'is', but not in the same way that God 'is' or the creature 'is'; in other words, it has its own, *particular*, third way of being. Second, nothingness does not constitute an essential or original determination of either God or the creature; instead it rather represents the *frontier* of the positive will and activity of God. Third, nothingness is not an empirically observable phenomenon, but can only be known as God *reveals* to us that God has opposed it in Jesus Christ. Fourth, nothingness is defined by Barth as 'that from which God separates Himself and in face of which He asserts Himself and exerts His positive will' (III/3, 351). Nothingness is thus ontically determined in the divine act of election to be for humanity in Jesus Christ, or – more specifically – in the divine act of *rejection* which is its immediate corollary. Fifth, the peculiar character of nothingness is that it is *evil*, opposed both to the grace of God and to everything created. Consequently, it cannot be explained or systematized, let alone synthesized with any aspect of God or creation.

All these insights depend for Barth upon the fact that the conflict with nothingness is primarily the affair, not of the creature, but of God. It is in the decisive act of the covenant of grace, in the crucifixion of Jesus Christ, that there takes place the true conflict between God and nothingness. As a result of this final victory, nothingness – in contrast with the Creator and even (by divine grace) the creature – has no duration or perpetuity: it is already past and destroyed. Correspondingly, the threat of nothingness which still faces us today has no true or ultimate power; its existence is, in Barth's words, 'only an echo, a shadow, of what it was but is no longer, of what it could do but can do no longer' (III/3, 367). Indeed, even this ongoing semblance of significance is only possible through divine permission. As such, nothingness functions only under the divine lordship and can only serve the will and work of God.

This corner of the doctrine of creation is one of the most difficult sections of *Church Dogmatics*. In it, Barth seeks to offer an account of nothingness as that which threatens and corrupts the good creation of God. In the process, he engages in sustained conversation on this theme with a series of important thinkers – Friedrich Schleiermacher, Martin Heidegger and Jean-Paul Sartre. The defining particularity of his own presentation is that its explicit ontic and noetic ground – as we would expect – is Jesus Christ. Correspondingly, Barth does not start his work with abstract conceptions of God, creation or evil, nor does he operate with abstract ideas of divine omnipotence and goodness or human incapacity and fallenness. Instead, he starts from the lived history of Jesus Christ, at the culmination of which nothingness is once and for all destroyed on the cross. In this light, Barth sees nothingness as that which God from the start rejects and at this point defeats in order to safeguard the creature. Though this destruction remains hidden to the world for now, its final and definitive revelation for and to all creation will occur in the return of Jesus Christ.

What Barth provides in this section is therefore not a systematic account of the origin and course of nothingness, let alone a metaphysical explanation of it. Instead, he offers a descriptive narrative which is utterly dependent for its content on the covenant of grace as it is actualized in Jesus Christ. In him, it is revealed that nothingness is a genuine paradox: Barth at one point describes its existence 'as inherent contradiction, as impossible possibility' (III/3, 351). Perhaps correspondingly, his account has been criticized *both* for taking evil too seriously *and* for not taking it seriously enough. On the one hand, his account describes nothingness as definitely *existing* (albeit in a very particular way), thereby according it an ontic status denied it in accounts of evil which speak of evil simply as privation. On the other hand, his account describes nothingness as utterly *defeated* (on the cross of Jesus Christ), therewith affirming that present-day manifestations of evil lack genuine power or substance and serve the divine will. Such conflicting interpretations perhaps indicate more the immense difficulty facing theologians in dogmatic enquiry at this point and the corresponding fragmentariness of their theological utterances than any desperate failings of Barth's account of nothingness.

## The kingdom of heaven and the angels

In this last section of the doctrine of providence, Barth turns to that part of creation which is the kingdom of heaven, and to the angels who inhabit it and who thereby contribute to the divine providence. Barth recognizes immediately the manifold difficulties in theological thinking here, acknowledging that we are once again dealing with the realm of saga – events within the real, spatio-temporal history of the covenant which are historically non-verifiable. Yet he argues strongly that the content of Scripture *demands* such thinking and, moreover, that it must *determine* such thinking.

Barth begins as ever with Jesus Christ and the covenant of grace. In the revelation of this covenant, heaven is seen – in an inconceivable way – as the distinctive sphere within creation *in which* both God and the ascended Jesus Christ are present. It is thus a realm subject to the preservation and governance of God, a realm of obedience in which the will of God is fulfilled. Moreover, for Barth, heaven is also seen as the place *from which* the kingdom of God comes to us – not only in spiritual benefits and divine judgements, but also, and essentially, in Jesus Christ. Wherever in creation God is present and active, and thus the will of God is done, there too the kingdom of heaven is present.

The creatures of heaven – angels – similarly exist at the disposal of God, and wherever God is present and active in creation, they surround and accompany and serve the divine will. As God eternally elects in Jesus Christ to take up the cause of earthly creatures, so angels too serve them and their cause. Indeed, angels belong *essentially* to this movement of the kingdom of God from God to humanity, and in it their fundamental task is to *witness*: Barth calls them God's 'primary, authentic, constant, inflexible and infallible witnesses' (III/3, 462–3). The lordship of God over the creature is thus always accompanied by the message of the angels – heralding God, indicating God and glorifying God.

In a coda to this section, Barth explores the adversary of the kingdom of heaven and the angels – the demonic sphere and its inhabitants. He writes that theologians are 'commanded merely to give it a passing glance and then to turn our backs upon it' (III/3, 522). Scripture never alludes to this sphere independently, but only with reference to God's conflict against it. Barth therefore insists that the two kingdoms and their inhabitants are not to be considered as equal and opposite. The demonic sphere has its origin not in the divine election of creation but in the rejection of nothingness which this act of election implies. Thus it exists in the same way that nothingness exists: illegitimately, improperly and unnaturally, continuing only under the divine sovereignty and in the divine service. For Barth, we must correspondingly neither ignore nor absolutize this sphere; instead, we must simply and steadfastly oppose to it the truth of God who has triumphed over it in Jesus Christ.

At each stage of this section, what Barth is doing is trying to avoid any *speculation* concerning heaven and its inhabitants and to follow instead the (rather modest) material that is attested in Scripture. For this reason, he criticises the more abstract, elaborate and imaginative accounts of heaven – and its circles, hierarchies, inhabitants and ministries – that have regularly appeared in the history of theology. His own approach recognizes by contrast the almost *incidental* role that the angels have in the history of the covenant, and seeks to understand their work accordingly as self-effacing messengers whose life and work are utterly bound to God. It is by way of this sort of theological description that Barth traverses this scriptural yet difficult material.

## *Comment*

This part-volume of *Church Dogmatics* traverses a vast range of theological material within the doctrine of creation, from the divine providence to the divine lordship, and from the kingdom of heaven to the role of nothingness. At each stage, Barth attempts to ground his theological knowledge *noetically* in the Self-revelation of God in Jesus Christ and the covenant of grace. And, in the process, he attempts to allow the content of his theological knowledge to be *ontically* determined by the same Jesus Christ. What this means in practice is that in respect of the rather difficult subject matter in view Barth is particularly invested in careful reading and deep contemplation of Scripture.

In this twofold Christ-centred grounding of his understanding of the sphere and parameters of the relationship between God and the creature, Barth substantiates his view that the covenant is the inner basis of creation and that there can correspondingly be no independent doctrine of creation.

Such a Christ-centred construal of the relationship between Creator and creation is certainly not a traditional way of proceeding in dogmatics. Precisely at this point, according to Barth, elements of natural theology or of speculative abstraction have often arisen in doctrinal accounts. Correspondingly, concepts such as divine omnipotence, human freedom and demonic power have been developed without sufficient attention to the God who reveals Godself – and therewith the pinnacle of the relationship between

Creator and relation – in Jesus Christ. For Barth, such accounts can correspondingly only stumble; the only alternative is to describe the way things are in light of God's revelation.

It may be objected that Barth offers an account of the relationship of humanity to God which does inadequate justice to the freedom and independence of the creature. Yet, for Barth, to wish to do this is precisely where the problem lies – in an effort to remove ourselves from the divine providence. By contrast, for Barth, true creaturely freedom *includes* the fact that God creates, limits and directs it; freedom apart from this would be the freedom of a second god. It may also be objected that Barth does not take sufficiently seriously the reality, power and success of the work of evil within creation. Yet, for Barth, to view evil in isolation is just where the problem lies – in the temptation to see nothingness and its servants as a force opposing God and the angels which exists outwith the lordship of God and is not already entirely defeated. By contrast, for Barth, nothingness may be real, but it is so only in its futility, in its transitoriness and in its final overthrow by God in Jesus Christ.

What Barth is in effect doing in both these cases, and indeed throughout this part-volume, is to draw out the implications for the doctrine of creation of the innovative doctrine of election that was advanced in volume II. It is in light of God's eternal decision to be for the creature in Jesus Christ that the ongoing relationship of the Creator to the creation is to be seen and understood. For Barth, creation is never simply creation, and this is the case even and before we formally consider doctrine of reconciliation. It is this doctrine of reconciliation to which we now turn in Chapter 5.

# CHAPTER FIVE

# The doctrine of reconciliation – I

Barth turns in volume IV of *Church Dogmatics* to what he considered to be the centre of all Christian knowledge – 'the vast territory of the doctrine of reconciliation' (IV/1, ix). He began writing this volume in the early 1950s, in the context of the ruins of post-war Europe and of the rise of the Cold War, and continued the work steadfastly over the rest of the decade. Thereafter, however, his capacity to work diminished, and the final sections of the volume were uncompleted on his death in 1968. Even so, this volume represents a majestic achievement, running to almost three thousand pages. Under the rubric of the doctrine of reconciliation, it gives us Barth's mature work on the doctrines of Christology, sin, soteriology and pneumatology – including the work of the Spirit both in the church and in the individual, together with his (part-finished) ethics of reconciliation. Given this scope, it is not possible to treat the doctrine of reconciliation in one chapter. This chapter, then, begins with an orientation to Barth's doctrine of reconciliation, followed by explorations of its detailed work in Christology and in the doctrine of sin. In what follows in Chapter 6, there is an investigation of the other doctrines treated under reconciliation – pneumatology, soteriology, ecclesiology and the Christian life – while Chapter 7 below includes consideration of the ethics of reconciliation which concludes the volume.

# I The content and structure of the doctrine of reconciliation

In the introductory part of the doctrine of reconciliation, there are two sections: first, Barth introduces the work of God the Reconciler – the central subject matter of the doctrine; and second, Barth surveys the way in which he treats the doctrine in the volumes ahead.

## *The work of God the Reconciler*

Barth asserts that we stand here at the centre of Christian dogmatics – the covenant of grace fulfilled in the act of reconciliation in which God stands for humanity in Jesus Christ. Barth begins with the claim that '"God with us" is the centre of the Christian message' (IV/1, 5). This message indicates the dynamic reality in history of the presence of God with us: in the divine being and life and act, in time and in eternity, God does not will to be God without humanity but wills to have a common history with us. Moreover, this common history is not limited to God's gracious eternal will to create and to sustain us, but it also includes – indeed first and fundamentally so – God's gracious eternal will to act for our salvation once and for all in Jesus Christ. This salvation, it is revealed in Jesus Christ, is something that sinful humanity had refused and forfeited. The Christian message, however, is that God takes up our cause and effects our salvation, in spite of our sin, by becoming human for us in Jesus Christ.

The event of reconciliation in Jesus Christ is the fulfilment of the covenant – the communion between God and humanity which, as we saw in Chapter 4, was freely and graciously purposed as the goal of creation, but which was jeopardized by the sinfulness of humanity. The fulfilment of the covenant takes place as the first and basic and eternal will of God – that God be God *for us* and that we be creatures *for God*, as we saw in Chapter 3 – is revealed and accomplished in time as sin and death are defeated in the history of Jesus Christ. This means, first, that this fulfilment is not a chance or arbitrary event but is eternally purposed by God. Barth correspondingly writes of 'the unconditional, eternal and divine validity and scope of the atonement accomplished in Jesus Christ' (IV/1, 46). And it means, second, that this fulfilment takes place within a context of human disobedience and thus can come only from God. Hence the human response that is rendered possible – yet also demanded – by this unmerited act of divine grace can only be one of gratitude and faith that witnesses to this event.

What Barth emphasizes above all in this introductory section is that Jesus Christ is the centre of the doctrine of reconciliation. But Barth does not conceive this centre in static terms; instead, Barth conceives of the history of God with us in Jesus Christ as an *act* or *event* in which the divine being, life and history are united with ours in the person of the Mediator. Thus, the event of reconciliation encompasses the whole life-act of Jesus Christ. However, as was noted in Chapter 3 in the doctrine of election and in Chapter 4 in Barth's theological anthropology, it is not simply the history of one human being which is united with the history of God; as all humanity is elect in Jesus Christ, so the history of all human beings is determined by the events of his history, and thus becomes part of the event of reconciliation. In the doctrine of reconciliation, then, everything stands or falls by the name of Jesus Christ. Jesus Christ is its centre both noetically, as the divine act of reconciliation *is revealed* in him, and ontically, in that he – in the history of his person – simply *is* the reconciliation.

## *A survey of the doctrine of reconciliation*

Barth's survey of the doctrine of reconciliation falls into four subsections. The first three subsections each contemplate one particular aspect of the doctrine: the first explores the grace of God in Jesus Christ, the second considers the being of humanity in Jesus Christ and the third examines Jesus Christ the Mediator. For Barth, attending to these three aspects allows for three perspectives to be brought to bear on the attempt to understand the event of reconciliation. Correspondingly, they lead to the three distinct but inseparable explorations of the doctrine in volumes IV/1, IV/2 and IV/3 of *Church Dogmatics*. With this tripartite structure, Barth offers a radical departure from the traditional pattern of presentation which structures Christology under the headings of first the person and then the work of Jesus Christ.

Each of the three explorations of the doctrine of reconciliation not only contains a section on the theme of Christology proper, but also sections on other topics pertaining to the doctrine of reconciliation – namely the doctrines of sin, soteriology, pneumatology, ecclesiology and the Christian life. The reason is that, as we saw in Chapters 3 and 4, it is of the very essence of the history of Jesus Christ to be *for humanity*. Correspondingly, we cannot consider Christology itself without considering also the implications of Jesus Christ for human existence, and – conversely – we cannot consider human existence in reconciliation without considering Jesus Christ. To fail to connect these other doctrines rigorously with the person and work and history of Jesus Christ is an error which, according to Barth, many previous theological undertakings have committed. By contrast, Barth asserts that in his doctrine of reconciliation Christology will both take its place 'as the necessary beginning' *and* 'work itself out in the whole' (IV/1, 128).

The material briefly outlined in each of these first three subsections is unfolded extensively in the course of Barth's doctrine of reconciliation, and will be considered in more detail in due course. For the present, we turn to the fourth subsection, in which Barth offers a concise account of how his presentation of the doctrine will proceed both materially and formally. Again, we will delay treatment of the material features of this account until we examine its full treatment in these volumes. However, it is highly instructive here to examine the *form* in which the doctrine will be presented. This allows us to gain an overview of the contents of each of the volumes of the doctrine of reconciliation and of their connections.

On the following page, the structure of Barth's doctrine of reconciliation is represented in diagrammatic form, drawing on the traditional Christological language of 'natures', 'states' and 'offices' in order to indicate where and how these topics will be approached. The diagram shows the way in which the three distinct perspectives on the doctrine of reconciliation that Barth explores – based on the three Christological aspects or perspectives noted above, and related to the three Messianic offices of priest, king and prophet – govern the structure of the work as a whole. Moreover, it evidences the way in which the treatment of each of the theological doctrines considered within this volume – including Christology – is *divided* between these three perspectives on the doctrine.

## Content of the Doctrine of Reconciliation

| *volume* | IV/1 | IV/2 | IV/3 |
|---|---|---|---|
| *title* | The Lord as Servant | The Servant as Lord | Jesus Christ, true Witness |
| *aspect of doctrine* | divine grace in Jesus Christ | human being in Jesus Christ | Jesus Christ the Mediator |
| *Christology* | §59 obedience of Son of God | §64 exaltation of Son of Man | §69 glory of the Mediator |
| *- nature* | divine | human | [union] |
| *- state* | humiliation | exaltation | [union] |
| *- office* | priest | king | prophet |
| *doctrine of sin* | §60 pride | §65 sloth | §70 falsehood |
| *- result* | fall | misery | condemnation |
| *soteriology* | §61 justification | §66 sanctification | §71 vocation |
| *work of the Spirit in the church* | §62 gathering of the community | §67 upbuilding of the community | §72 sending of the community |
| *work of the Spirit in the Christian* | §63 faith | §68 love | §73 hope |

| IV/4 | | | |
|---|---|---|---|
| *ethics of reconciliation* | §75 baptism | §§76– Lord's Prayer | Lord's Supper |
| | | ['Lord's Prayer' and 'Lord's Supper' not completed] | |

In what follows in this and the next chapter, the exploration of Barth's doctrine of reconciliation will proceed, not by working in turn *through* each part-volume and its doctrines, but by working in turn through each doctrine *across* the three part-volumes, thereby *reuniting* the doctrines. This allows for certain connections to be made between the part-volumes which are sometimes overlooked.

Hence the rest of this chapter considers Christology and the doctrine of sin; the remaining doctrines are considered in Chapter 6.

## II Christology

Christology stands at the beginning of Barth's doctrine of reconciliation, and he addresses the subject in three ways. His first treatment, in volume IV/1, considers that in Jesus Christ we have to do with God and the action of God. In Jesus Christ, we see that the Godness of God includes the will and the ability to condescend and become human for our salvation: in him, then, the Lord humbles himself to be a servant. Barth's second treatment, in volume IV/2, considers that in Jesus Christ we have to do with a human creature. As such, Jesus Christ is exposed to creatureliness and sinfulness, yet as a result of his union with God his humanity is superior to his creatureliness and free from its sinfulness: in him, then, this servant is exalted to be the Lord.

To consider the reconciling work of Jesus Christ from the two perspectives outlined so far is not uncommon, but Barth proceeds to offer an innovative view on how the two perspectives *relate*. In older dogmatic works, the humiliation and exaltation of Jesus Christ were often considered to be two temporal 'states' within the life of Jesus Christ – first there was humiliation (beginning in incarnation and culminating in crucifixion), and then there was exaltation (beginning in resurrection and culminating in ascension). For Barth, however, the one work of Jesus Christ that constitutes his existence embraces both humiliation and exaltation *simultaneously*. Instead of humiliation and exaltation being two successive 'states' of the person of Jesus Christ, then, Barth considers them to be two simultaneous *movements* within the life of Jesus Christ. The movement of humiliation pertains to his divine nature and the movement of exaltation pertains to his human nature, and together they constitute the reconciling of work of Christ. These two movements within the doctrine of reconciliation are therefore to be seen *together*. How this works out in practice will be seen below.

In Barth's third treatment, in volume IV/3, he once again moves beyond traditional theological presentations of the doctrine of rec-onciliation by considering Jesus Christ not only in the duality of his two natures and states, but also under a third aspect – the *unity* of his person, work and history. In this perspective, Barth acknowledges, nothing *material* is added to the discussion of the first two perspectives. Instead, what is new for Barth here is that 'Jesus Christ is the actuality of the atonement, and as such the truth of it which speaks for itself' (IV/1, 136). Jesus Christ thus *reveals* to us true God and true humanity, along with the true relationship between them, and *calls* us into life in this true relationship. This perspective on the doctrine of reconciliation is therefore to be seen *together* with, and not apart from, the first two perspectives.

In the case of each of these discourses on Christology, it should be noted at the start that Barth's text is saturated with references to and exegesis of Scripture. Nowhere in *Church Dogmatics* is his work so closely patterned and shaped by the narrative of the biblical witness pertaining to Jesus Christ, and nowhere is Barth's insistence on the reality, the historicity and the truth of Jesus Christ so evident as here. In the analysis below, some of the passages exegeted in detail will be referenced, but there is little space for a full investigation.

The three different perspectives are now explored in order.

## IV/1: The obedience of the Son of God

In this first perspective on Christology, we have to do with that aspect of the work of Jesus Christ in which, as very God, 'He willed to be obedient to the Father, and to become the servant of all and therefore man and therefore the One who fulfilled in His death the reconciling will of God' (IV/1, 159). Barth orders this work to the *priestly* office of Jesus Christ, and unfolds the corresponding material in three main sections, each of which will be considered in turn.

In the first main section, Barth considers 'The Way of the Son of God into the Far Country'. The title alludes to the parable of the prodigal son, and in this section, Barth focuses particularly on the deity of Jesus Christ as it is humbled. As Scripture indicates, from the beginning Christians have recognized that in the person of Jesus Christ we have to do with One who is not only a true human being, but also the Son or Word of God. But Scripture also attests that, precisely as this unique person, Jesus Christ wills to be an obedient servant – both of God and of the world – and that he does this not accidentally or capriciously, but necessarily and essentially. This revelation leads Barth to the difficult statement that 'The true God – if the man Jesus is the true God – is obedient' (IV/1, 164).

Barth emphasizes at this point that Jesus Christ was born a Jew, and thus within the history of God's elect people, Israel. As such, Jesus Christ cannot be viewed docetically: he is not some ideal figure or mythical archetype, but instead lives in a concrete time and context. Moreover, for Barth, this historical particularity is not a matter of chance but of necessity. In his work, Jesus Christ confirms and fulfils God's eternal election of Israel despite its manifest disobedience as the chosen people. Furthermore, the fact that Son of God becomes Jewish flesh, and thus lives in solidarity with this sinful people, indicates for Barth that Jesus Christ exists together with Israel under the divine wrath, judgement and rejection. This, for Barth, is the lowliest of positions. It indicates precisely what it means for Jesus Christ to become flesh and highlights the humiliation which the Son of God obediently undergoes in the incarnation. Barth correspondingly writes that in Jesus Christ, 'God, the electing eternal God, willed Himself to be rejected and therefore perishing man' (IV/1, 175).

Barth finds in this Self-humiliation of God in the incarnation the mystery of the deity of Christ. This mystery has an outer moment – in relation to the incarnation. Although God humbles Godself in Jesus Christ, God in Christ does not cease to be God, nor is there any opposition or contradiction between God in Christ and God in Godself. Instead, Barth contends, we must learn what God is and does from the incarnation. If we do this, we see that the incarnate humiliation and obedience of God is an act of the divine love and freedom, willed for and by Jesus Christ in the eternal and gracious divine act of election. Thus in Barth's view it is just as natural for God to be lowly as it is for God to be exalted. But this mystery also has an inner moment – in relation to the eternal being of God. For Barth, if the obedience in humiliation of the incarnate Jesus is God's own work, then it cannot be alien to God. In other words, there must also be an obedience *within* the divine being, an obedience of the Son to the Father. Hence Barth writes, 'there is in God Himself an above and a below, a *prius* (before) and a *posterius* (after), a superiority and a subordination' (IV/1, 200–1). This may seem a shocking statement, but Barth counsels that if we attend carefully to the revelation of God in Jesus Christ then this is what we learn. There is, for Barth, nothing unworthy of God in such a conception of the divine being: we only *think* that there is when we adopt an all-too-human mode of thought.

At every point in this discussion of reconciliation, Barth has in view the doctrine of election that we examined in Chapter 3. Barth insists that the history of Jesus Christ in all its dimensions – its incarnation in Jewish flesh, its obedient humiliation in time, and its eternal foundation in obedience – results from the eternal and gracious will of God to be for humanity in Jesus Christ. Thus none of these dimensions of his life and work and history are coincidental or arbitrary; rather, in the concrete determination of the eternal will of God in the event of election, they are all necessary. Indeed, so intrinsic to the being of God is this event of reconciliation that – as was seen in the doctrine of election – there can for Barth be no reference to the Son of God other than as the One who in eternity is determined for and identified with this event.

In the second main section, Barth considers 'The Judge Judged in Our Place'. The way of the Son of God into the 'far country' explored above has a particular purpose and end in view: the reconciliation of the world with God. However, Barth argues, we cannot move too quickly to this positive outcome, for 'the grace of God is not a cheap grace' (IV/1, 216). In this section, then, Barth focuses on the culmination of the priestly work of Jesus Christ on the cross.

Barth begins with the observation that the coming of the Saviour into the world is also the coming of the Judge of the world. As the world in hostility to God seeks to be its own judge and justification, it stands condemned and rejected by the judgement of God in Jesus Christ. At the same time, however, in passing this judgement, God demonstrates the divine grace by pronouncing us free and offering us life. And as we are redeemed in this pronouncement, Jesus Christ takes the place of sinful humanity and undergoes the righteous judgement of God for us. Concisely rendered: in the event of the atonement, the Son came as our Judge, but in the resultant judgement, he was judged in our place. In this event, Barth writes, the One 'who is in the one person the electing God and the one elect man is as the rejecting God, the God who judges sin in the flesh, in His own person the one rejected man' (IV/1, 237). The atonement is therefore once again rooted in the eternal election of God.

Barth posits that in the event of the atonement Jesus Christ is for us in a unique way that is not at all dependent upon our response. First, he is for us as the One who is the true Judge, the One who vitiates our all-too-human attempts to be judges of others and, even more tragically, of ourselves. Second, he is for us as the One who is judged, who – in his sinlessness – takes the place of us sinners. As Jesus Christ obediently takes our evil case upon himself, for Barth, our sin no longer belongs to us but becomes his alone. Third, he is for us as the One who freely submits to judgement in suffering, crucifixion and death. As this act of passion is the act of the incarnate Son of God, Barth writes, it is 'the radical divine action which attacks and destroys at its very root the primary evil in the world' (IV/1, 254). And finally, he is for us as the One who does what is right before God and therefore stands for us as the obedient and free covenant partner of God. In his person, and on our behalf, the Fall of humanity is reversed. In light of this fourfold 'for us' of Jesus Christ, Barth contends that there is nothing that we can contribute to his life-act beyond a simple 'Amen'.

There are three things worth observing about this account of the crucifixion. First, the account is unhesitatingly a *substitutionary* account: Jesus Christ takes our place on the cross. For Barth, we are sinners who are simply unable to redeem ourselves, hence Jesus Christ takes our place to enable our salvation. This feature of the account has been criticized by some for emphasizing human incapacity and human replaceability. Barth would certainly assert that humanity is *incapable* of effecting its own salvation, but would not assert that their substitution by Jesus Christ renders them *replaceable*. Indeed, for Barth, the work of Jesus Christ for us actually *establishes* us as free, responsible and irreplaceable human beings. Second, this account is framed as a *penal* account in the sense that in our place Jesus Christ suffers judgement and punishment. However, it is crucial to recognize that Barth's account is not *primarily* focused on the idea of punishment. It is not for Barth that the punishment of Jesus Christ satisfies the wrath of God or spares us from any future punishment that awaits us; punishment is simply not the focus. The important thing for Barth is rather that in and through the suffering of the cross, Jesus Christ accomplishes what is necessary to put an end to us as sinners and to sin itself. Finally, this account is certainly framed in *legal* terms: the ideas of Judge, Judged and judgement are prominent. However, Barth indicates clearly that his theology is not bound to this particular scriptural framework. He contends here that his entire presentation could just as well be framed in the equally scriptural language of priesthood and sacrifice without material loss. And to demonstrate this, he offers some brief indications as to how precisely this might be done in closing this section.

In the third main section, Barth turns to 'The Verdict of the Father', in which he addresses what he calls the 'transitional problem': 'How does [Jesus Christ] come to us or we to Him?' (IV/1, 284). In view here is not only the structural transition from Christology to the other topics in the doctrine of reconciliation, but also the issue of the relationship between faith and history more generally. For Barth, however, to focus on the latter issue is simply to avoid the real *scandal* of the crucifixion – 'that we have died in and with [Jesus Christ], that as the people we were we have been done away with and destroyed' (IV/1, 295). The real question is not of faith and history, but of whether, in light of this destructive event, there is anything more to be said of us *sinners*.

For Barth, there is indeed more to be said, and the reason for this lies in the resurrection of Jesus Christ – an act of God which has implications for all humanity. Barth writes that the resurrection represents God's acknowledgement and approval of the obedient life of Jesus Christ in his action and his passion for us. The event of the resurrection is therefore the *verdict* of the Father – and indeed, Barth writes, of the Spirit – upon Jesus Christ, and therefore both the *justification* of Jesus Christ as the One who obediently wills to suffer on the cross and the *justification* (in a rather different sense) of God as the One who eternally purposes this event. However, in the power of the resurrection, Barth explains, the event of the cross is lifted out of its historical particularity to become an event that took place once but for all times. The resurrection is therefore also the *justification* of us as sinners, as those who – in Jesus Christ – are crucified on the cross but then raised to new life. In this threefold justification, then, Barth writes that the crucifixion and the resurrection are 'the two basic events of the one history of God with a sinful and corrupt world' (IV/1, 310).

What this means is that just as we as sinners are put to death in the crucifixion of Jesus Christ, so too in the resurrection of Jesus Christ we are raised to new life. Our status before God is altered by these events, from alienation to reconciliation, and this is true *regardless* of our attitude or response to it. We can therefore recognize this reconciliation only by faith and not by sight.

Barth acknowledges that we live in 'a time between the times' (IV/1, 323). Jesus Christ is no longer with his community in the same way as he was prior to his ascension, nor is he present in the same way as he will be at the end of time. There are many people who fail to hear or to recognize this good news, who live as if they were still unreconciled to God. And the transformation of the human situation and the presence of Jesus Christ are not yet visibly and finally revealed. However, for Barth, the Christian perspective should not be 'the minus-sign of an anxious "Not yet," ... but the plus-sign of an "Already"' (IV/1, 327). We are thus not only to look *forward* in hope to the final manifestation of the reconciliation to come, but also to look *back* in faith to the reconciliation already achieved. Even here and now, Jesus Christ is present and active in the work of his Spirit, being in his person the origin, sustainer and goal of the Christian community. Hence we are called to witness with confidence – in all our life and proclamation – to the reconciliation of all people to God in him.

What Barth achieves in this transitional section is to highlight the *objectivity* of our reconciliation with God on the basis of the resurrection. The resurrection is, for Barth, not only the *noetic* basis of this reconciliation, in that it *reveals* this reconciliation to us; it is also – together with the crucifixion – the *ontic* basis of this reconciliation, in that in the resurrection of Jesus, we are *also* and *already* raised to new life. Together, the distinct events of crucifixion and resurrection exist in a profound unity: it is the one God who acts in the one Jesus Christ to effect the one divine goal of reconciliation on the basis of the one divine decree of election. As this event takes place in history, we are objectively included in it by virtue of our election in Jesus Christ. At this point, as in the doctrine of election, concerns may arise concerning the possibly universalist implications of this doctrine, but Barth does not consider this issue further here: it will arise again later in the doctrine of reconciliation, and will thus reappear in Chapter 6 below.

At the same time, and correspondingly, Barth is keen in this section to highlight the *historicity* of the resurrection. On the one hand, he acknowledges that the resurrection, as an act of God, is not subject to investigation by modern historical scholarship. The event is therefore genuinely inscrutable, though of course the events subsequent to it are not. On the other hand, Barth asserts that the resurrection of Jesus Christ is an event – like the crucifixion – which really happened in human history, time and space. Consequently, he contends, the resurrection confronted the early disciples as an incontrovertible fact that led to faith in Jesus Christ. Barth therefore fiercely, if implicitly, opposes the ideas of figures such as Rudolf Bultmann, who, in their primary focus on the rise of faith in the early Christian community, risk occluding or deny outright the historicity of the resurrection. For Barth, echoing Paul, it would be the case that if the resurrection did not actually take place, then all else would be in vain.

## IV/2: The exaltation of the Son of Man

In this second perspective on Christology, we have to do with that aspect of the work of Jesus Christ in which, as very human, he is 'exalted as this servant to be the Lord, the new and true and royal man who participates in the being and life and lordship and act of God' (IV/2, 3). While in volume IV/1 Barth explored the divine Self-condescension in Jesus Christ, here, in volume IV/2, Barth considers the exaltation of humanity in Jesus Christ, which he orders to the *kingly* or royal office of Jesus Christ. Again, in parallel with volume IV/1, the material is divided into three sections.

In the first main section, Barth considers 'The Homecoming of the Son of Man'. The title alludes again to the parable of the prodigal son, and in this section, Barth focuses on the humanity of Jesus Christ as it is exalted. On the one hand, this humanity is similar to ours, being 'like us in our creaturely form, but also in its determination by sin and death' (IV/2, 27). On the other hand, this humanity is dissimilar to ours: in his history, in its union with God the Son, there takes place uniquely the exaltation of humanity – the translation of humanity from the (humanly chosen) place of corruption, death and alienation from God to the (divinely elected) place of freedom, peace and life with God.

Barth opens by indicating the eternal grounds for this exaltation of humanity in the divine election of grace. Here, he recapitulates by way of summary some of the material from volume II/2, explored above in Chapter 3: Jesus Christ is not only the electing God, but also the elected human, and the rest of humanity is elect in him.

Thereafter, however, he moves to consider what is here the central theme: the historical fulfilment of the divine election of grace in the incarnation. Central to this event is the free act of divine love in which 'God assumed a being as man into His being as God' (IV/2, 41). This assumption – the Word becoming flesh – is, for Barth, both the *ontic* basis of the incarnation, that is, the ground of the *being* of Jesus Christ, and also the *noetic* basis of the incarnation, that is, the ground of our *knowledge* of Jesus Christ.

In the material which follows, Barth explores this *work* of the Son – and thus the manner of the incarnation – from a number of different angles. At each point, he engages at length with traditional presentations of the *person* of Jesus Christ, drawing particularly on the insights of patristic, Lutheran and Reformed writings, even as he seeks to outline his own constructive view.

Barth affirms, first, that what God assumes into unity with Godself is not *simply* an individual human being, but what he calls 'the *humanum*, the being and essence, the nature and kind, which is that of all men' (IV/2, 48). In other words, the concrete humanity of Jesus Christ has direct relevance for all other people, but has no independent existence outwith its assumption by God. Here, he affirms the historic doctrine of the *anhypostasis–enhypostasis* existence of the human nature of Jesus Christ. Moreover, Barth asserts that the existence of the Son of God becomes and is the existence of a human being without ceasing to be God, such that when we have to do with this individual, we truly have to do with God. Here, Barth affirms the historic doctrine of the *hypostatic union* of God and humanity in Jesus Christ.

In a further step, Barth affirms that in the act in which the one Subject, Jesus Christ, takes on human form, divine essence and human essence are united. There takes place in his history an indivisible *union* of the two essences, and thus a *communion* between them, yet the divine essence and the human essence remain *distinct*. Here, Barth affirms the historic Chalcedonian doctrine of the *two natures* of Jesus Christ. And finally, Barth affirms that in the union of divine essence and human essence in Jesus Christ, 'we have to do with the exaltation of the essence common to all men' (IV/2, 69). In the *communication* that takes place between the two natures in the history of Jesus Christ, Barth writes, the Son of God has a part in the human essence which is assumed, and the human essence receives a part in the divine essence which assumes it. The order here – first the humiliation of the divine essence, then the exaltation of the human essence – is important and irreversible.

The exaltation of Jesus Christ means, for Barth, the perfect communion of the human essence with the divine essence, a life utterly by and from the grace of God, and thus an existence 'in and with God, ... adopted and controlled and sanctified and ruled by Him' (IV/2, 88). This exaltation must not be misconstrued as divinization, as if the humanity assumed by the Word of God became divine. Rather, even and precisely in its exaltation, the humanity of Jesus remains *truly* human, just as (as noted above) even and precisely in its humiliation, the Son of God remains *truly* divine. In the history of Jesus Christ, the ordered determination of the divine essence for humiliation and of the human essence for exaltation are concretely and commonly *actualized*, as his work takes place in the *unity* of his divinity and his humanity. As Barth writes, then, 'it is the act of the humiliation of the Son of God as such which is the exaltation of the Son of Man, and in Him of human essence' (IV/2, 100). This last reference reminds us that in the exaltation of the humanity of Jesus Christ, all humanity is included.

The theological significance of this discussion of the incarnation is that Barth has taken the traditional language of Christology – of union, communion and communication; of person and natures – and has both derived these from and related them to the single, *dynamic* event of the incarnation which is the lived *history* of Jesus Christ. Barth concludes: 'We have "actualised" the doctrine of the incarnation' (IV/2, 105). We see here once again Barth's desire to speak of the existence of Jesus Christ as a *history*, of his life as an *event*, of his person as a *being in action*, in a way that goes radically beyond the insights of the historic tradition.

Central to this 'actualisation' of the incarnation is Barth's move – discussed above – to posit the two 'states' of humiliation and exaltation *not* as states but as *movements*, and *not* as sequential but as *simultaneous*. In ascribing the former history to the divine essence and the latter history to the human essence, against the background of the *unity* of Jesus Christ, Barth posits that the *history* of Jesus Christ is the event in which the eternal will of God to be gracious to humanity is fulfilled. At the same time, there is no conceptual gap between the person and the work of Jesus Christ: these concepts have both been integrated into a theological framework rooted in the category of history.

Barth moves thereafter to consider the revelation of the exaltation of humanity in Jesus Christ. Our knowledge of the incarnation, and of the exaltation of humanity in it, depends on the divine Self-revelation. And that means that our knowledge of Jesus Christ takes place as an event of grace in the work of the Spirit. The Spirit accomplishes the Self-witness of Jesus Christ: in the present time between the times, the Spirit witnesses to the truth of the history of Jesus Christ and to the exaltation and freedom of our humanity in him. It is here, Barth posits, that we find the true significance of the resurrection and ascension as marking the event of the Self-declaration of Jesus Christ. As the passion and crucifixion *constitute* the fulfilment of the incarnation of Jesus Christ (and of the exaltation of humanity in him), so the resurrection and ascension *reveal* the secret of the incarnation (including its exaltation of humanity). And like the resurrection, so too our knowledge of God is only possible by virtue of the grace and activity of God.

In the second main section, Barth examines the new and true human being who is constituted in Jesus Christ, in a section entitled 'The Royal Man'. This section, which draws heavily on exegesis of a variety of passages from the Gospels, considers directly the kingly work of Jesus Christ.

Barth begins by considering the way in which the Gospels portray the unique existence of Jesus. For Barth, these texts present Jesus Christ as One who genuinely *encountered* people, and, more than this, who in encountering them called forth from them a *decision* in response to his person. Moreover, Jesus Christ – in light of the resurrection appearances – appears in the Gospels as someone *unforgettable*, as the witness of God who fulfilled the covenant and brought the kingdom of God. Finally, the writers of the Gospels also depict Jesus Christ as someone *irrevocable*, in the sense that his presence becomes for those who encounter him not only a past event, but also a present reality.

Barth deepens this initial exploration by moving to consider what it means for Jesus Christ to be the 'new human'. The central point which Barth makes is that 'as a man [Jesus Christ] exists analogously to the mode of existence of God' (IV/2, 166). In other words, for Barth, when we see Jesus, we see an image, a similitude, a parallel in creaturely form, of the purpose and work and attitude of God. We have already seen the Christological concept of *correspondence* which is in view at this point in Chapter 4. Here, what it means is expanded in material terms in respect of the life of Jesus. For Barth, it means that Jesus exists as One who is ignored and forgotten in the world, who consorts with the lowly and sinful, and who calls existing value systems and social structures into question. Beyond all this, however, is the fundamental fact that Jesus, like God, is not against sinful humanity but in obedience and freedom he is *for humanity* – not only *with* humanity, but *for* humanity – on the way which leads to his crucifixion. To the eternal 'Yes' of God to humanity and the creation, then, there corresponds the incarnate 'Yes' of Jesus, imaging and reflecting the divine love in its compassion for lost humanity.

In the corresponding history of Jesus Christ, the kingdom of God irrupts on earth. In his complete life-act, across his words and his deeds, Jesus Christ not only proclaims but also effects the inbreaking of the kingdom of God. And yet the way of this human Jesus in his kingly office is characterized from start to finish by the cross. This is not a matter of caprice, but reflects the obedience of Jesus to follow to the bitter end the path determined for him in eternity by the divine election. Correspondingly, for Barth, the crucifixion represents not the *contradiction* of the royal human Jesus, but his *coronation*. It is not only the temporal end but also the eternal purpose of his life, and it provides the basis of Christian hope and the shape of Christian discipleship.

The material throughout this section on 'The Royal Man' is saturated with references to Scripture in a compelling way. Through careful exegesis, primarily drawn from the Gospels, Barth presents an engaging and engaged scriptural picture of Jesus through which he explores the relationship of his life and work both to the being of God and to the coming of the kingdom of God. This attention to the humanity of Jesus offers at least an initial rebuke to those who find in *Church Dogmatics* little place for genuine human action.

In the third main section, Barth turns to 'The Direction of the Son', in which he once again addresses what he calls the 'transitional problem': 'To what extent is there a way from the one to the other, from [Jesus Christ] to us?' (IV/2, 265). In answering, Barth starts from the concrete reality that there is such a way – that, by virtue of the reconciliation of God and humanity in Jesus Christ, 'There is no one … who does not participate in Him in this turning to God' (IV/2, 271). We saw above that this means for Barth that Jesus Christ is our *justification*, such that we are righteous and acceptable to God. Here, Barth adds that Jesus Christ is also our *sanctification*, in that God now addresses us as those who are reconciled and converted to God and thus free and holy before God. Both of these claims will be considered further in Chapter 6. Of course, we do not achieve our justification or sanctification for ourselves, but in Jesus Christ, these statements become necessary as the very truth of our being and history. The truth of our existence is therefore once again *eccentric* – lying outside ourselves in Jesus Christ.

When we speak of our sanctification in Jesus Christ, we speak of something that is *hidden* to humanity. It is hidden, not only because knowledge of Jesus Christ as Lord is not within our capabilities, but also because in Jesus Christ the exaltation of humanity is concealed in the event of his crucifixion. The truth of our exaltation in the crucifixion of Jesus Christ is *revealed* to us, however, by the Spirit of Jesus Christ. As the presence and activity of Jesus Christ in the power of his resurrection, the Spirit reveals both our election to grace in the history of his crucifixion and resurrection and our transition in him from imprisonment, death and sin to freedom, life and righteousness. Consequently, Barth describes the character of the Spirit as light, liberation, knowledge, and peace, and – ultimately – as life. The Spirit is, Barth writes, 'the Alpha and Omega, the beginning and continuance, the principle and power of the Christian life' (IV/2, 320). As the Spirit must always come again as sheer gift, so Barth observes that though we are already Christians in Jesus Christ, of ourselves we are only ever in the process of becoming Christians – our status as Christians is gift, not possession.

The mediation of the Spirit between Jesus Christ and the community is not alien to the Spirit, for the Spirit also and originally mediates the unity of the Father and the Son in the Trinity. And as God makes possible and actual the existence of the Christian community by the presence and action of the Spirit, so, Barth writes, the will of God is done on earth. As the Spirit of Jesus Christ, the Spirit operates by providing concrete *direction* – *indicating* to us our true situation, *warning* us to accept our new freedom, and *instructing* us in obedience. In this way, God is as fully and unreservedly at work in the existence of the community as in the existence of Jesus of Nazareth. Correspondingly, the history of this community – as we already noted in Chapter 4 – is not one history among many, but represents the true meaning of world history at large.

In this transitional section, then, Barth once again explores how the work of Jesus Christ comes to have relevance for us. For Barth, the secret lies in the operation of the Spirit, who is the power in which Jesus Christ is present today. There is a real emphasis here on the dynamic, historical activity of the Spirit: the Spirit *reveals* to us our exaltation in the history of Jesus Christ, *creates* the Christian community where this knowledge of our new existence in Jesus Christ is shared, and *directs* our subsequent thought and action in witness to Jesus Christ. This section is thus dominated by attention to *pneumatology*, though Barth continues to insist – in parallel with the transitional section in volume IV/1 – on the objective and universal relevance of the work of Jesus Christ. It is only in the Christian community, however, and by the power of the Spirit of Jesus Christ, that this work is recognized and confessed.

## *IV/3: The glory of the Mediator*

In the first two perspectives on Christology, Barth has considered the history of Jesus Christ as consisting of two great movements, grounded in the unity of his person as fully divine and fully human. As noted above, in this third perspective on Christology in volume IV/3 Barth does not seek to add anything new to this foregoing *material* presentation. However, he now attends to the *formal* dimension of Christology, to the way in which reconciliation is not only *achieved* but also *revealed* in Jesus Christ. This Christological chapter is entitled 'The Glory of the Mediator' and attends to the *prophetic* office of Jesus Christ. Its title reflects the fact that Jesus Christ is not only the One who *effects* the reconciliation of God with humanity but also the One who is *revealed* and who *reveals* himself as such. After an initial excursus on the importance of this theme, Barth pursues its Christological content in three main sections.

In the first main section, Barth considers Jesus Christ as 'The Light of Life'. Here, Barth is keen to show that the life of Jesus Christ, in whom God and humanity are reconciled, is one which shines out – Jesus Christ is a Word who *speaks* so that reconciliation is not a mute but an eloquent event. What this means is that the living God who acts for our reconciliation also speaks of our reconciliation, and does so in the person of the Reconciler, Jesus Christ, who is revealed to be the one Mediator between God and humanity.

Barth begins by affirming the belief that Jesus Christ truly *lives*. This confession of faith is not without support in the present, for precisely as he lives, Jesus Christ speaks. And so Barth posits that '[Jesus Christ] is His own authentic Witness ... He grounds and summons and creates knowledge of Himself and His life, making it actual and therefore possible' (IV/3, 46). This construal of his work lies at the heart of the *prophetic* office of Jesus Christ, within which Barth references the glorious life of Jesus Christ under descriptors such as light, name, revelation, truth and Logos. Of course, Jesus Christ is not merely a prophet comparable to the Old Testament prophets, even if the history of prophecy in Israel prefigures his own prophetic work. By stark contrast, Jesus Christ is unique in his prophetic work as the one and universal Mediator between God and humanity.

The *basis* on which this prophetic office can be ascribed to Jesus Christ can only consist, for Barth, in the Self-revelation of God in Jesus Christ. This Christocentric approach is fully consistent with Barth's method throughout *Church Dogmatics*, and while Barth recognizes the evident circularity of such a procedure, he considers it to be *virtuous* rather than *vicious*, noting that it follows Anselm's procedure of believing in order to understand. Indeed, he writes, the real question which confronts us here is not one of the *basis* of the prophecy but one of *obedience* to the Prophet, and thus of the extent to which our lives in free gratitude respond and correspond to the life of Jesus Christ as prophecy.

Jesus Christ is not, for Barth, simply a light of life, but *the* light of life. Barth writes that 'Jesus Christ as attested to us in Holy Scripture is the one Word of God whom we must hear' (IV/3, 86), a statement repeated from volume II/1 and the Barmen Declaration. As the one Word of God, Jesus Christ is, in Barth's words, 'the total and complete declaration of God concerning Himself and the people whom He addresses in His Word' (IV/3, 99). For Barth, this means that Jesus Christ stands alone above all the other words of God spoken within creation, and serves to empower and delimit those other words. The true Word requires no completion by other words, has no serious competition from other words, and suffers no combination with other words.

Barth at this point considers the relationship between the Word of Jesus Christ and other words in creation which are not identical to him but which may be or become true words. Included in this category are the testimony of Scripture and the proclamation of the church, the two secondary forms of the Word of God detailed in volumes I/1 and I/2. However, Barth also includes in this category the possibility of true words of God spoken and heard *outwith* the church, in the secular sphere. His reason for this is that 'in the world reconciled by God in Jesus Christ there is no secular sphere abandoned by Him or withdrawn from His control' (IV/3, 119). This is explicitly not a retreat to natural theology, however: precisely here, we still have to do with Jesus Christ, as he employs creaturely media in the secular realm to serve in his Self-attestation.

To the frustration of some readers, Barth deliberately avoids offering any concrete examples of this phenomenon. However, he offers criteria to help identify such words: they must conform materially to the one Word, they can seek only to correspond to and confirm that one Word, and they can function as true words only in the service and by the will of that one Word. Their limitation is thus that they can only ever witness to their origin in the one Word of Jesus Christ; but as they do this, by the power of the Spirit, they are words which will lead the listening church more deeply than before back to Scripture. For that reason, the church must be ready and willing to hear such words, even as it must always test them for authenticity against the one Word.

Famously, Barth also considers in this section what he calls the 'little lights of creation', those features of the creaturely world which relate to its role as the external basis of the covenant. In this category, Barth identifies the existence, the rhythm, the contrariety, the laws, the freedom and the mystery of the cosmos. Together, these indicate that 'the self-declaration of God in Jesus Christ does not take place in a dark and empty and indefinite sphere, but in one which has real existence, fullness, form and brightness' (IV/3, 151). These little lights are thus not strictly matters of faith or of reconciliation, but attest the fact that the world is created by God to be the theatre of reconciliation.

Thus far, Barth has highlighted that the reconciliation that takes place in the priestly and kingly work of Jesus Christ does not go unheralded but is revealed through his prophetic work. Jesus Christ is unequivocally the one Word of God and light of life, speaking forth the one Word of reconciliation. He is thus alive and present today and provides the one criterion against which all the words within creation must be tested. To recognize that God can speak words in unexpected places is not to displace Jesus Christ in favour of natural theology, but rather to assert his supreme lordship over the created world in its entirety.

In the second main section, Barth considers the theme 'Jesus is Victor', a phrase Barth borrows from Johann Blumhardt. Here, Barth considers that the prophetic work of Jesus Christ – as his priestly and royal work – takes place as a *history*. Indeed, Barth writes that the event of reconciliation 'is a drama which can only be followed, or rather experienced and recounted' (IV/3, 166).

The historical nature of the prophetic work of Jesus Christ in revelation is evidenced by the presence in history of opposition to the revealed light of Jesus Christ. Even if such rebellion will not ultimately prevail, it is nevertheless to be taken seriously. Correspondingly, for Barth, there is no easy 'triumph of grace' in which the principle of good eternally triumphs over the principle of evil, contrary to the criticism of scholars such as G. C. Berkouwer. Instead, Barth explains, there is a *history*, the history of Jesus Christ, in which war is waged – ultimately victoriously – against the powers of sin, death and the devil.

The historical nature of the prophetic work of Jesus Christ is further evidenced as it reveals to us that we are directly implicated in the event of reconciliation as an event which is for us and to us. The history of reconciliation is thus, in Barth's words, 'history in which we have a share whether we realise and like it or not, history in which our own history takes place' (IV/3, 183). Both Christians and non-Christians are implicated in the antithesis between the light of the reconciling work of Jesus Christ and the darkness of human opposition and ignorance which results. Though this conflict is ongoing, however, its final outcome is never in doubt – a point Barth illustrates by way of a detailed exegesis of the conversion of Paul as it is recounted in Acts.

This history of reconciliation is also, as mentioned above, a *productive* history. Barth writes that it 'evokes its own reflection … in the form of Christian knowledge of what has taken place in Jesus Christ' (IV/3, 212). This means that a relationship is established between the event of reconciliation objectively achieved in Jesus Christ and the Christian knowledge subjectively gained of this event. Though these events are clearly to be distinguished, Barth emphasizes that they are not to be separated. True Christian knowledge of reconciliation involves encounter with Jesus Christ;

in this encounter the Christian is subjectively awakened to their reality as one who is objectively reconciled in Jesus Christ and is given a share in the event of salvation. In other words, Christian *knowledge* of reconciliation, for Barth, simply *is* reconciliation. The prophetic dimension of the history of Jesus Christ is therefore not simply a past event but an ongoing reality. Barth writes that 'although this history … took place once, in its very singularity it really takes place … for all times and in many other times' (IV/3, 224). The event of reconciliation – through the prophetic office of Jesus Christ – continues to be present and effective today.

Throughout this exploration of the revelation of reconciliation, Barth is at all points keen to emphasize its *historicity*. Over against those who would see Jesus Christ as an ideal rather than a historical figure and those who would see his existence as continuing today only in the lives of believers and the church, Barth posits the ongoing presence and work of Jesus Christ and thus the ongoing import of his prophetic history. It is a prophetic history which *begins* with Jesus Christ, the One who from all eternity, as we saw in Chapter 3, is elected to be the one Mediator of grace between God and humanity. It is a prophetic history which *unfolds*, as noted, in the face of human resistance, overcoming this through the proclamation of reconciliation. And, finally, it is a prophetic history which will *end* with his return, at which point the victory of Jesus Christ which is already assured and certain will be manifest to all creation.

In the third main section, entitled 'The Promise of the Spirit', Barth turns one final time to the 'transitional problem': 'To what extent is there a real and conceivable way … from [Jesus Christ] to us?' (IV/3, 276). In answering, Barth begins once again with the inclusive view that, both in time and in eternity, Jesus Christ is never alone but is always to be considered together with all humanity. This inclusive truth – grounded in the eternal election of God – is revealed in the prophetic work of Jesus Christ, as the reconciliation that has taken place in him makes itself known. The primal form of this revelation, of the glorification of the Mediator, is the historic and irrevocable event of the resurrection. It is in the power of this event that Jesus Christ exercises his prophetic office today and that the way from him to us is actual and possible. And in this time between the resurrection of Jesus Christ and his final return, this power is the power of the Spirit.

Barth turns first, and once again, to the resurrection of Jesus Christ. This event intimates that in the event of reconciliation, in Barth's words, 'the world and every man has ... received a new and positive determination' (IV/3, 300). This transformation is not simply possible but actual and underway, and forms the basis of the mission of the Christian community. *De facto* (in fact), only Christians actually and effectively belong to Jesus Christ; but the resurrection message is that *de iure* (by right), *all people* belong to him. This new reality is currently only fulfilled in Jesus Christ, however, and in the rest of the world it is concealed, being revealed only to faith. Nevertheless, Barth posits, the reconciliation of God and humanity is sure and certain even in the present, and it awaits only its final and consummate revelation in the return of Jesus Christ.

Second, Barth explores the very existence of this time between the times, and posits it to be a function of the good will of Jesus Christ. It has the aim, Barth writes, of 'granting to and procuring for the creation reconciled to God in Him both time and space ... to share in the harvest which follows from the sowing of reconciliation' (IV/3, 331). God thus offers humanity time and space to respond freely and responsibly to reconciliation. While Barth clearly has Christians in view here, those able actively to acknowledge the revelation of Jesus Christ and to affirm their reconciliation in him, there is nevertheless for Barth no *qualitative* distinction between Christians and non-Christians. The reason is, as Barth has noted before, that Christians constantly regress to non-Christian modes of thought and action and thus – with the exception of Jesus Christ – never fully embody the truth of their new reality. Barth posits that it is not possible that we can be both Christians and non-Christians at the same time, yet – paradoxically – that is precisely what we are, living in impossible possibility.

Barth lastly returns to matters pneumatological, noting that the Spirit is '[Jesus Christ's] direct and immediate presence and action among and with and in us' (IV/3, 350). It is the Spirit who promises to Christians not only the sure and final return of Jesus Christ but also his ongoing presence and help in their lives. By the power and promise of the Spirit, Christians are awakened and empowered to true knowledge, confession and freedom. However, the Spirit is also the promise to *non-Christians* that they too are reconciled to God in Jesus Christ, even if they have not heard or accepted this good news yet. Regardless of their attitude and action, then, to them also the promise of the Spirit avails and applies, albeit this promise is not yet fulfilled.

In this transitional section, Barth once again explores how the work of Jesus Christ comes to affect us, and answers once again that it is the operation of the Spirit which renders this actual and possible. In view, then, is not an abstract or theoretical relationship between faith and history, but the incomprehensible reality of the presence of Jesus Christ today in the power of the Spirit. For Barth, this is a real, historical and objective event, not a merely subjective or existential motif. Correspondingly, Barth emphasizes the *historical* dimension not only of the foundational events of reconciliation – the crucifixion and resurrection – but also of the present work of Jesus Christ through the Spirit. In light of the perfection of this work, Barth does not overplay the distinction between Christians and non-Christians: he observes that both groups are objectively reconciled in Jesus Christ and that the promise of the Spirit applies objectively to all. However, Barth does affirm that only the Christian may live under the sign of reconciliation in freedom, gratitude and joy, becoming a responsible subject who not only hears but repeats the Word of God.

## *Comment*

Taken together, these three major sections of the doctrine of reconciliation present a Christology of breath-taking vision and scope. As has already been indicated in the introduction to this section, Barth formally integrates the person and the work of Jesus Christ, the two states of humiliation and exaltation, and the three offices of prophet, priest and king. He remains throughout consistent with his methodological principle of deriving knowledge of God and of humanity only from Jesus Christ. His presentation of the person of Jesus Christ abandons potentially abstract and static modes of discourse for a conceptuality characterized by the narrative of history, and by discourse of event and encounter. And in his 'transitional sections', he creates space for a deep consideration of the work of the Spirit in reconciliation.

Materially speaking, Barth grounds his whole understanding of the person and work of Jesus Christ in the eternal election of

God to be for humanity: as indicated previously, for Barth, there is no Son of God who is not from the very beginning determined for incarnation and obedience in Jesus Christ. Barth affirms the unique, objective and historic efficacy of the work of Jesus Christ, denying that Jesus Christ is merely a symbolic or ideal figure. And Barth affirms the inclusion of all people within the scope of the redemption from the power of sin and death which Jesus Christ effects and reveals. Finally, Barth affirms not only the past but also the ongoing and future dimensions of the work of Jesus Christ in the power of the Spirit, offering a powerful statement of the *current* reality of reconciliation, even as the *full* consummation of the covenant of grace is yet to come.

Barth is well aware that different methods of investigation and different forms of presentation might be pursued in Christology. His Christocentric method of deriving knowledge of God (and of humanity) exclusively from Jesus Christ has already been seen in Chapter 1 to be a matter of disagreement. And the objective inclusion of all humanity in the person of Jesus Christ, an inclusion that reaches its zenith here in the work of Jesus Christ, has already been discussed in Chapter 3. Particular features of the Christological material presented here have also given rise to dissent, notably the move to consider the states of humiliation and exaltation as simultaneous and not successive, and the move to order particular offices to particular states and natures. In both cases, some have feared an elision of Christological content; yet one can perhaps just as easily point to the theological insights gained by this procedure.

Criticism aside, it remains the case that in ambition, insight and complexity, the Christology presented in volume IV of *Church Dogmatics* remains one of the towering achievements of recent theology. It remains a starting point and central partner for ongoing constructive conversation in the field.

# III  The doctrine of sin

Thus far, Barth has considered the positive side of the reconciliation of humanity with God as it is grounded and enclosed in Jesus Christ. However, in so far as this fulfilment of the covenant takes place in the context of our hostility to God, the doctrine of reconciliation must also consider this negative dimension of the matter – the sin in respect of which all of us are both author and victim. Barth turns at this point, therefore, to consider the unreconciled sinner who is the negative presupposition of the event of reconciliation.

It is essential to note immediately that, for Barth, the doctrine of sin is not an autonomous area of enquiry in theology. First, as we saw in Chapter 4, sin has no independent reality of its own. It belongs properly neither to the will of God nor to the creation of God, and is present within creation only as an interloper and usurper that is subject to God. Second, sin is not defined in Scripture as the transgression of an abstract or natural law. By contrast, sin refers to opposition to the will of God revealed in the history of Jesus Christ. Hence Barth posits that 'only when we know Jesus Christ do we really know that man is the man of sin, and what sin is, and what it means for man' (IV/1, 389).

It is also important to recognize that Barth rejects the category of 'original sin' in the traditional sense of the biological inheritance of sin. He writes that in such an account, original sin becomes 'my fate which I may acknowledge but for which I cannot acknowledge or regard myself responsible' (IV/1, 500). However, he retains the term 'original sin' to indicate the way in which God treats all humanity alike in view of its radical and universal disobedience. And so, following Scripture, Barth writes that in Adam, 'God has sentenced and condemned all mankind and human history, concluding it in disobedience' (IV/1, 512).

Barth presents his material doctrine of sin under three headings – pride, sloth and falsehood. These three characterizations of sin are complementary rather than mutually exclusive: in some way, for Barth, sin is always pride, always sloth and always falsehood. Each characterization shall be considered in turn.

## IV/1: Pride and Fall

The first mode of human sin that Barth considers is human *pride*. In Jesus Christ, as we have seen, there is effected and revealed the divine obedience and humility, as the Son of God becomes a servant for our sake without ceasing to be the Lord. However, we see in the light of his history that our own attitude does not correspond to this obedience and humility of God, but rather both contradicts and opposes it. At every point, then, our human attitude is one of pride. Barth defines pride as a form of the disobedience of humanity and, more specifically, of the unbelief of humanity that rejects Jesus Christ.

Barth considers this trait of human pride in four different ways, linking each one to an aspect of the story of the Fall from Genesis 3. First, the decision of God to condescend to become human in Jesus Christ is not met by a corresponding humility on our part, but instead by our desire to be gods. Second, the decision of God to exercise rule as a servant in Jesus Christ is not met by a corresponding servitude on our part, but instead by our desire to be lords. Third, the decision of God to be the Judge of humanity in Jesus Christ is not met by a corresponding penitence on our part, but instead by our desire to be our own judges. And fourth, the decision of God to be judged in our place in the passion of Jesus Christ is not met by a corresponding acceptance of this gracious help on our part, but instead by our desire to help ourselves. Beyond carefully relating each aspect of pride to Genesis 3, Barth also illuminates each by way of an extended exegesis of apposite Old Testament passages.

The presence of human pride means that we are creatures of the *Fall*. The humility of faith and obedience which God demands of us as the creatures and covenant partners of God is replaced by its corrupt opposite. Our corruption is both radical and complete: Barth writes that 'in the whole sphere of human activities there are no exceptions to the sin and corruption of man' (IV/1, 496). At the same time, however, because of our eternal election in Jesus Christ, we remain irrevocably the object of the electing grace of God such that no matter how far we have fallen or will fall, we never cease to be the creature and covenant partner of God. Barth explains that the human being cannot fall 'lower than the depth to which God humbled Himself for him in Jesus Christ' (IV/1, 480–1).

We live therefore under two contradicting determinations. The key move that Barth makes here is to *dynamize* our view of these determinations. Instead of seeing ourselves as locked in stasis between the old life and the new life, we are to see ourselves as a history in motion – *retrospectively* determined by our sin and *prospectively* determined in Jesus Christ. In other words, the person of pride and sinfulness has no future for God because that person has been put to death in Jesus Christ on the cross. Conversely, through the resurrection of Jesus Christ to new life, the only life that is open to us now is life in the kingdom of God. And as each person continues to sin despite this translation, Barth asserts, so there is demonstrated 'the real paradox and absurdity of his being' (IV/1, 502).

## IV/2: Sloth and misery

The second mode of human sin that Barth considers is human *sloth*. In Jesus Christ, as we have seen, there is effected and revealed the exaltation of humanity, as the Son of Man becomes the Lord. However, our own life-act does not correspond to the royal humanity elevated and unveiled in him or to the resultant direction given to us by his Spirit. Instead, it is revealed in Jesus Christ that we are guilty of sloth – 'the evil inaction which is absolutely forbidden and reprehensible' (IV/2, 403). Not only do we fail to do God's will; we actively do what God does not will. At issue here is not only, once again, human disobedience and unbelief, but also human ingratitude towards God, culminating in our rejection of Jesus Christ.

When in sloth we refuse to use the freedom that is won for us in Jesus Christ, this has mortal implications for our existence. Barth unfolds these consequences in terms of the four dimensions of humanity outlined in Chapter 4 – human beings as related to God, as co-humanity, as body and soul, and as finite creatures. Barth notes, first, that in our sloth we ignore and disobey God and thereby demonstrate our *stupidity* by way of 'a culpable relapse into self-contradiction; into incoherent, confused and corrupt thought and speech and action' (IV/2, 412). We thus deny our true being as addressed by God in Jesus Christ. Barth then observes that in our sloth we isolate ourselves from other human beings and manifest only *inhumanity* to our neighbours; we thus deny our true being as elected and created in our co-humanity. Barth posits next that in our sloth we allow body and soul to go separate ways and that in the disobedient indiscipline which results we manifest our *dissipation*; we thus deny our true being as the unity of soul and body. And finally, Barth asserts that in our sloth we refuse to accept the limitations of our existence; we thus deny our true being as finite creatures before God who are given the hope of eternal life in Jesus Christ. In the *human anxiety* which results, there lies, for Barth, the root cause of all our stupidity, inhumanity and dissipation.

At each point in this analysis of sloth, it is emphasized that we choose our own self-contradiction, in acts of sin that have been made impossible by the crucifixion of Jesus Christ. Moreover, at each point it is highlighted that humanity excels at concealing this self-contradiction under the veil of hypocrisy. Finally, once again, at each point Barth illuminates his view by way of an extended exegetical treatment of an episode from the Old Testament.

The result of the sloth of humanity is simply *misery*. Instead of corresponding to our exaltation in Jesus Christ, we live a false existence in exile from communion with God in which we are unable to help ourselves. In Jesus Christ, however, we are rescued from the misery of sloth as the bondage of our will is broken by the event of the crucifixion. The result is that the human being is liberated to live in true freedom, which means, for Barth, 'in the election, corresponding to his own election and creation and determination, of faith and obedience and gratitude and loyalty to God' (IV/2, 494). In reality, however, this new freedom in Jesus Christ and the impossible bondage of the old will continue to co-exist in antithesis in the ongoing dynamic struggle of the Christian life.

## IV/3: Falsehood and condemnation

The final mode of human sin that Barth considers is human *falsehood*. If pride and sloth represent the sinful works of humanity, for Barth, then falsehood represents the sinful word of humanity. In Jesus Christ, as we have seen, there is revealed the glory of the Mediator and of the reconciliation achieved for all humanity in him. In encounter with the truth of this prophetic work of Jesus Christ, however, we offer merely a negative reflection of his glory, a darkness resisting his light, and a contradiction of his truth. Living under the shadow of the denial, perversion and falsification of this truth, for Barth, means that we are necessarily found on the road to condemnation. At regular intervals throughout the ensuing section, Barth engages in an extended and remarkable exegesis of the book of Job, on the basis that Job provides a strange yet unmistakable witness to the true witness of Jesus Christ.

The truth against which our falsehood becomes evident is not, for Barth, a mere idea or principle, nor is it a truth which is either comfortable or comforting. Instead, it is the truth of the concrete presence of the living Jesus Christ in the power of the Spirit, and it is a truth which in the first instance contradicts us. Jesus Christ is the actualization and reconciliation of both God and humanity in genuine freedom, the One who both *is* and *speaks* the Truth of reconciliation, and who in the power of the Spirit both reveals and condemns our falsehood.

It is our falsehood which is, in Barth's words, 'the great enemy which resists the divine promise declared in the prophetic work of Jesus Christ' (IV/3, 434). Even though it is ultimately impotent in face of the victory won in Jesus Christ, our falsehood opposes the truth of reconciliation and asserts a false and sinful freedom over and against the true freedom achieved and granted in him. It may do this simply by evading and avoiding the truth of Jesus Christ. However, Barth notes, it may also do this by domesticating or accommodating the truth of Jesus Christ such that while it yet appears Christian, it has in fact become untruth. Indeed, precisely here Barth discerns the primary form of falsehood – *Christian* falsehood. As we lie in respect of Jesus Christ, so we become liars in respect of all things. Barth affirms, however, that in all situations 'Jesus Christ as the true Witness infallibly differentiates falsehood from the truth' (IV/3, 439).

Our falsehood can only lead, according to Barth, to our *condemnation*. Just as we are guilty in our pride and enslaved in our sloth, so too we are judged in our falsehood. As we evade the Word of truth, we evade precisely the forgiveness and freedom which it contains and effects, and we stand instead under the threat of damnation. This is not only a distant, future prospect, but also means that even today, in Barth's words, our 'whole being is given an aspect which deforms, distorts and corrupts its true reality' (IV/3, 468). Nevertheless, Barth notes, it is not within human power to change the truth of Jesus Christ into falsehood: the truth of the living Jesus Christ remains valid and effective. For this reason, Barth holds open the possibility that in the truth of this reality, there might be contained the promise of the salvation of all people. We must certainly not expect such; but we can nevertheless hope and pray for it.

## Comment

In its scriptural foundation, material unfolding and dogmatic provocation, the doctrine of sin presented across the doctrine of reconciliation in *Church Dogmatics* provides an important voice in theological conversation. It presents a clear vision of the intensity and extensity of the power of sin in human lives; but it presents an even clearer vision of the majesty and glory of the unequivocal victory of God over sin in the history of Jesus Christ. There are two significant features of this account of human sin which deserve identification and comment, as both have proven controversial among readers of Barth.

The first is the way in which Barth derives his account of sin in a manner consistent with his overall methodology – that is, from the revelation of the will of God in the history of Jesus Christ. The corollary of this Christocentric move, however, is that Barth denies any space for (true) knowledge of sin in the absence of knowledge of Jesus Christ. This point is reflected in the *location* of the sections of the doctrine of sin in *Church Dogmatics*, in each case following a section on Christology. The result is that there is no positive account in Barth's theology of natural law, or of the creaturely conscience which would appropriate a natural law. Here, Barth's theological method leads him – as it did in the case of natural theology, investigated in Chapter 3 – to a position simply at odds with much of the Christian tradition, and it is thus no surprise that many have disputed his fundamental method at this point.

The second is the way in which this account of human sin is paradoxical. On the one hand, sin is condemned, broken and rejected by God, overcome in the crucifixion and resurrection of Jesus Christ. On the other hand, sin remains at work in human lives such that at every point we continue to choose the impossible possibility of sin. Such an account closely follows the contours of Barth's doctrine of nothingness, treated in Chapter 4. And given its paradoxical character, it may be no surprise that Barth has been criticized both for taking sin too seriously, and for not taking sin seriously enough. However, the paradox has dynamic and purposive character: the sin of the old person is daily crucified and left behind; the freedom of new life in Jesus Christ is daily received. And the final resolution of the paradox will come at the eschaton. This view of Christian existence will be explored further as we move to consider soteriology in Chapter 6.

# CHAPTER SIX

# The doctrine of reconciliation – II

In this chapter, we continue with the exploration of volume IV of *Church Dogmatics*. Following the investigation of the structure, Christology and doctrine of sin of Barth's doctrine of reconciliation in Chapter 5 above, we now continue by attending in this chapter to its accounts of soteriology, pneumatology and ecclesiology, and the Christian life. A consideration of the ethics which conclude the doctrine of reconciliation will follow as part of Chapter 7.

## I Soteriology

In the crucifixion and the resurrection, as we saw in Chapter 5, there takes place in Jesus Christ both the rejection of the elected human being and the election of the rejected human being. In his doctrine of sin, also explored in Chapter 5, Barth addressed particularly the negative aspect of these events – the destruction of the sinful human being on the cross of Jesus Christ that is revealed in the resurrection. At this point, however, Barth turns to soteriology, to investigate the positive implications *for us* of the fact that the gracious 'Yes' of God is more powerful than the sinful 'No' of humanity.

Barth considers these positive implications under the different forms in which there takes place the objective conversion of humanity to God in Jesus Christ. Particularly since the time of the Reformation, it has been common to identify these forms as justification and sanctification: justification speaks of the *verdict* pronounced on humanity by God in Jesus Christ and sanctification speaks of the *direction* set for humanity by God in Jesus Christ. Barth considers this practice to have been both correct and indispensable, but asserts that these two forms do not exhaust the truth of the new human being established and revealed in Jesus Christ. Consequently, Barth adds a further, third form which indicates that the justification and sanctification of humanity have a purpose and a goal – the *vocation* of humanity. By this, Barth wishes to indicate the content of the *promise* given to humanity by God in Jesus Christ: an eternal future of participation in the being and life of God. In what follows, each of these three forms of soteriology will be considered in sequence.

## *IV/1: Justification*

As we saw in Chapter 5, Barth posits that the sinful human being has been put to death in Jesus Christ. Yet in the same judgement in which this occurs, Barth writes, God 'pardons us and places us in a new life before Him and with Him' (IV/1, 516). This translation of our being from sinfulness to righteousness, which takes place in the history of Jesus Christ, is at the heart of the doctrine of justification. It is therefore understandable, to Barth, that it has been taken by some, notably Martin Luther, to be *the* Word of the Gospel. Yet while Barth acknowledges that there can be no true church *without* this doctrine, he resists the idea that it must always be the *centre* of Christian faith and doctrine. For Barth, this centre can only be the confession of Jesus Christ.

Barth turns first to the *verdict* of God in justification. In the divine judgement upon humanity, God acts to defend and maintain God's right and justice in face of the wrong and sin of humanity. Yet even, indeed precisely, in this righteous judgement executed in Jesus Christ, Barth insists that God remains gracious and true to Godself because – as Chapter 3 indicated – there is no contradiction between the divine righteousness and the divine grace. Thus concealed under the righteous divine 'No' of the cross there is, for Barth, the gracious divine 'Yes' of God's eternal election to take up the cause of sinful humanity. In this way, there takes place in Jesus Christ not only the divine justification of humanity, but also (albeit in a rather different sense) the Self-justification of God, who in the event of justification in Jesus Christ demonstrates God's gracious righteousness in liberating us from sin and restoring us to righteousness.

In view of our justification, we exist paradoxically as both condemned and rejected in judgement because of our sin, and pardoned and restored in Jesus Christ despite our sin. On both sides of this conception, Barth maintains, God acts graciously and righteously. The key to understanding the relationship between them, as we saw in Chapter 5, is to recognize that Barth construes the two determinations as existing not in a lifeless stasis, but in a dynamic history – 'the history of God with man' (IV/1, 545). What this means is that we live in a *movement* from our past in sinfulness under God's judgement to our future in righteousness under God's forgiveness. We are both sinners and righteous at the same time, as Luther rightly observed with his famous '*simul iustus et peccator*', but we live as such only in the movement from the one to the other. In other words, there can be no peace or complacency in the life of the justified sinner, as if one could rest content with the idea of being under both determinations; instead, there must always be an active impulse and movement away from the old life of sin and towards a new life of righteousness.

The trouble, for Barth, is that we cannot experience or perceive this dynamic and progressive history. If we look at ourselves empirically, we remain mired in sin and far from righteousness. And yet, for Barth, our justification does not belong to some ideal or abstract world of natural religion or speculative philosophy. Instead, Barth asserts, our justification is real for us (and revealed to us) only in Jesus Christ. It is in the history of Jesus Christ that there takes place definitively the clash of human wrong and divine righteousness. It is in him that the judgement and the forgiveness of God are both pronounced and revealed. And because we are from all eternity elect in him, so his history is the truth of our history. Indeed, the history of Jesus Christ is the truth of all human history such that *all* human beings are justified in him, regardless of whether they are Christians or not. It is thus in him, in Barth's words, 'there takes place that transition of man from his wrong to his right, from death to life' (IV/1, 557).

Barth is clear that, even after our forgiveness, in and of ourselves we remain totally unrighteous, and thus always compelled to confession. Correspondingly, he writes, 'There is no present in which the justification of man is not still this beginning of justification' (IV/1, 575). There is thus no place for human confidence or arrogance in justification, as Barth illustrates clearly from Scripture. At the same time, Barth is clear that, precisely in justification, there is set forth the affirmation of God and the goal of humanity as we are irresistibly set in motion from our past to our future. And there is thus no room in justification for human uncertainty or defeatism either. In justification, God forgives our past sins, accords us a new righteousness, and sets us in new hope: while we must certainly still confess our sin, so too we must grasp hold of God's promise of grace.

For Barth, our justification is hidden to us, but it is revealed in Jesus Christ. Therefore all that we can do in response is to know of it and to witness to it in humility and gratitude. This response marks, for Barth, the human situation of *faith*, in which we recognize the reality of justification in spite of empirical appearances. Barth writes that faith is 'the humility of obedience' (IV/1, 620) and 'the obedience of humility' (IV/1, 626). Justifying faith is thus an encounter with the living Jesus Christ, in which we correspond in faith to the faithfulness of God in him. Negatively, for Barth, faith recognizes that no human works – including faith – can contribute to our justification, and that there is no place here for pride or self-justification. Barth thus sees himself to be opposed to the traditional Roman Catholic view of justification as completed in human works. Positively, for Barth, faith recognizes and accepts that the justification achieved in Jesus Christ is concrete and valid for *all* people, whether they have come to faith or not.

## IV/2: Sanctification

The reconciliation of God with humanity in Jesus Christ achieves not only our justification but also our sanctification. If justification represents the divine turning of God to humanity in spite of our sin, then sanctification represents the divine turning of humanity to God in spite of our sin. The task of sanctification is to speak of the exaltation of humanity, of the introduction by God of 'a faithful covenant-partner who is well-pleasing to Him and blessed by Him' (IV/2, 499). Sanctification thus indicates the way in which the holiness of God effects and demands the corresponding holiness of the people of God.

Barth begins with an account of sanctification as a *participation* in Christ. As all humanity is already elect and justified in Jesus Christ *de iure* (by right), so too is all humanity already sanctified *de iure* (by right) in Jesus Christ. As with justification, then, sanctification is true in respect of all human beings, regardless of whether they are Christians or not. This is a corollary of the *objective* nature of the reconciliation accomplished by Jesus Christ, as described in Chapter 5. However, Barth continues, it is only those who *de facto* (in fact) acknowledge and confess their justification in Jesus Christ who are able to *recognize* the sanctification of all humanity in him. And in this recognition, their whole life is set under the direction of Jesus Christ by the power of the Spirit. Of course, they remain creatures of sloth; but under this direction they now become, in Barth's memorable phrase, 'disturbed sinners' (IV/2, 524).

This means that, in sanctification, our old life as sinners is compromised as we are set in sovereign antithesis to it: sin may persist, but we are now liberated from its enslavement and are no longer compelled to disobedience. As new and sanctified creatures, we are instead freed and called by Jesus Christ to gather with the community of those who know of their sanctification, and to enact a life of obedience and love that witnesses to the sanctification of all humanity in him. The obedience which results is fragmentary and unsatisfactory, Barth acknowledges, but it is obedience nonetheless, the true and free human response of those called to be covenant partners of God. As such, for all its paradoxical limitations, it can offer a creaturely reflection of the holiness of God.

Barth proceeds to relate sanctification to the *call* to discipleship. As we encounter Jesus Christ in revelation, we encounter not only the grace of God, but also the command of God. We will return to this point when we explore Barth's theological ethics in Chapter 7. For now, Barth draws attention to the fact that the call to discipleship is a call not only to obey a command, but also to obey a person – Jesus Christ. This call demands a break with our sinful past and a denial of our sinful being, in order to follow the call to discipleship and the practice of simple obedience. When we do this, Barth asserts, our action will always 'set forth the kingdom of God drawn near' (IV/2, 543), such that the world will see a sign of what has taken place in Jesus Christ. Barth outlines the prominent directions for action which the command of Jesus Christ in the Gospels always indicates, culminating in the call to take up one's cross.

This notion of a break with the past brings Barth to the topic of *conversion*. Conversion is, for Barth, a divine activity, and perhaps his crucial insight in what follows is that conversion is not completed in one act or even in a series of acts; rather, it is for everyone a *process* or a *movement* and 'becomes and is the content and character of the whole act of his life as such' (IV/2, 566). The reason is that, as we saw already in Chapter 5, we exist in a history of conflicting determinations – of sin and of grace. So, for Barth, we are not only simultaneously justified and sinners, as Luther rightly observed, but we are also simultaneously sanctified and sinners, existing in the constant *movement* from past sinful action to future liberated action. And again, though the resultant conversion may empirically seem rather halting and illusory, Barth assures us that the true and original and complete conversion of humanity to God has already taken place for us in Jesus Christ.

Following their conversion, Christians cannot be Christians to no purpose: the radical alteration of the human situation in Jesus Christ demands good human *works* if it is to be meaningful. Of course, such works are not relevant for justification, nor are they immune to divine judgement. Nevertheless, even though we remain sinners and all our acts are sinful, precisely our obedience as sanctified sinners can be taken into the service of God and render good works.

To close, Barth revisits the theme of the cross in sanctification. The cross is, for Barth, 'the most concrete form of the fellowship between Christ and the Christian' (IV/2, 599): as the exaltation of the humanity of Jesus Christ led to his crucifixion, so our exaltation and sanctification in him commands us to bear and suffer our own cross. Of course, we do not experience the judgement and rejection of God as did Jesus Christ, nor do we contribute to the reconciliation achieved in him. Instead, as we are sanctified in him, our existence *corresponds* to his in so far as it is characterized by the cross. And, as Barth notes, the cross involves 'hardship, anguish, grief, pain and finally death' (IV/2, 602). Life under the cross is thus a humble, provisional existence. Yet precisely this is existence in communion with Jesus Christ, pointing beyond its limitations to the gracious eternal will of God in Jesus Christ, and the future revelation of God's victory.

# *IV/3: Vocation*

As the prophetic light of Jesus Christ shines in the world, it can and does shine on, in and through us. This leads Barth to consider in an innovative way the doctrine of vocation alongside justification and sanctification. In vocation, the promise of the event of reconciliation is fulfilled, and the Christian is 'set and instituted in actual fellowship with Jesus Christ, namely, in the service of His prophecy, … and therefore in the service of God and his fellow-men' (IV/3, 482).

Barth begins by considering the wider *context* within which the vocation of the Christian takes place. The ultimate foundation of vocation is the eternal divine election, discussed in Chapter 3, by dint of which all humanity stands already in the light of the history of Jesus Christ in time, discussed in Chapter 5, in which that election is revealed and accomplished. Barth again distinguishes between our objective situation, in which we are already called *de iure* (by right), and our subjective situation *de facto* (in fact), in which we must be called – and called ever anew – in our own lives. The result is twofold. First, Barth *relativizes* any *absolute* distinction between Christians and non-Christians in respect of vocation. And second, Barth posits that those *already* called are responsible for witnessing to Jesus Christ to those *not* (yet) called in the same way.

For all that vocation has an eternal foundation, Barth does not deny that 'something comes to pass when it really becomes an event' (IV/3, 499). When we are called by Jesus Christ in the power of the Spirit to active participation in the truth of reconciliation, there takes place in *our* time and in *our* history a spiritual event which begins a new epoch in *our* lives. Previous theologians sought to formulate a framework or system to capture the different elements or stages of this event – a so-called 'order of salvation' (*ordo salutis*). However, Barth writes, this risks abstracting from the one work of Jesus Christ to 'the very dubious ways in which it is reflected in human existence' (IV/3, 507–8). By contrast, the dynamic *process* of vocation, of our 'illumination' or 'awakening', includes the *totality* of what makes one a Christian, and therefore refers to the *whole* person encountered and transformed.

The goal of our vocation, for Barth, is that we become and remain Christians. Barth thereby emphasizes the necessity of a *genuine* calling to Christian life. The power of this calling does not overwhelm or compel; rather, it is the power of liberation, as Jesus Christ calls us in such a way that we freely respond in faith and obedience and freely begin to live a new form of existence centred on him. The resultant distinction between a Christian and a non-Christian is thus never grounded in the Christian but is always a gift from Jesus Christ. In their new existence, by the grace and power of the Spirit, Christians become what they truly are: children of God, analogous – despite all the dissimilarity – to Jesus Christ, and disciples of Jesus Christ.

At this point, Barth states that the ultimate goal of vocation is 'union with Christ', the perfect communion of the believer and the Reconciler. This union involves neither the dissolution of the Christian or Jesus Christ, nor their absolute identification. Instead, Barth writes, Jesus Christ refreshes Christians from above 'by offering and giving Himself to them and making them His own' (IV/3, 542). Jesus Christ becomes Lord of their thought, speech and action, living in them without in any way compromising their freedom. Christians respond to him in faith, obedience and freedom such that they live in him, and such that their thinking, speaking and acting is ruled and determined by him. On both sides, the union is one of action within a covenant history of free encounter, rather than a static arrangement or coercive relationship.

In a final step, Barth considers what it means to be a Christian. What makes a Christian, for Barth, is not a denial of the world or an obedience to the commandments, nor is it an experience of grace or an assurance of salvation. Beyond all this, Barth argues, what truly makes a Christian is that God calls and makes them to be God's *witnesses*. As witnesses, Christians will inevitably encounter *affliction* that arises from the reaction of a sinful world to the message of Jesus Christ. The root cause of this affliction, however, is their union with Christ, and thus their being brought under the shadow of the cross. Yet precisely in affliction, the witness is already determined by and moving towards the final revelation of the victory of the resurrected Jesus Christ. In all this, the vocation of the Christian is a liberation – reconciliation with God is no longer concealed from us, and we are freed to recognize, accept and witness to it. Vocation thus involves, in Barth's words, 'a distinction and alteration of the being of the man who is called' (IV/3, 650). This transformation is not a past event or a secure possession, but continues in the present and throughout the journey of discipleship.

# Comment

In his soteriology, Barth sets out a vision of how the reconciliation achieved in the person and work of Jesus Christ effects the conversion of humanity to God under the forms of justification, sanctification and vocation. In considering the grace of vocation alongside the double grace of justification and sanctification, Barth effects a clear advance on most expositions by illuminating the distinctive future-oriented purpose of the Christian life. Yet through his realization of the humility, provisionality and vulnerability of Christian life, Barth draws attention to the fact that the true centre of the Christian life can only be Jesus Christ.

Four features of Barth's presentation of this topic are worthy of particular comment at this juncture.

First, there is the way in which Jesus Christ is once again posited as the ontic and noetic foundation of the divinely effected conversion of humanity to God. Each of the three forms of conversion is *objectively* accomplished (the ontic dimension) and revealed (the noetic dimension) in Jesus Christ. As a result of the eternal election of God to be for humanity in Jesus Christ, not only our justification – as in the broad Protestant tradition – but also our sanctification and our vocation are *de iure* (by right) both realized and announced *in him*. And this is true – against the broad Protestant tradition – regardless of whether or not we have faith in Jesus Christ. In this way, for Barth, not only our justification, but also our sanctification and our vocation are basically *alien* and *extrinsic* to us, as they are not to be seen in our works or persons but are primarily achieved for us *already* in Jesus Christ. In another sense, however, our justification, sanctification and vocation are radically *proper* and *intrinsic* to us, in that they are true precisely at the most foundational level of our existence – in our history as covenant partners elected in Jesus Christ. It is not surprising that this radical proposal has not found universal acceptance.

Second, there is the way in which the divinely effected conversion of humanity to God which has objectively taken place *de iure* (by right) outwith us in Jesus Christ is distinguished from its *de facto* (in fact) outworking in our subjective existence. For all the objectivity in which our history is taken up and becomes a part of the history of Jesus Christ, it is no less true, Barth indicates, that Jesus Christ in his history condescends to become the meaning and the truth of our history, that God is at work in our lives by the power of the Spirit. In soteriology, we are never to be considered apart from Jesus Christ and his work; but nor is Jesus Christ to be considered apart from us and our lives. Thus our justification, sanctification and vocation are irreversible truths not only for us but also in us, as we come to know and accept them. And this is true even as the empirical evidence may be ambiguous at best: for Barth, the old life of sin is truly finished, while the new life of the Christian is truly hidden with Jesus Christ in God.

Third, there is the way in which the divinely effected conversion of humanity to God in our lives takes place as a history. Just as the original humiliation of the Son of God and exaltation of the Son of Man takes place in a dynamic event of reconciliation in history, so too its image in our own justification, sanctification and vocation is an event within the history of our conversion to God. For Barth, then, the three forms of soteriology pertain neither to any static nature or essence of humanity, nor to any secure possession or achievement of humanity, but to the new life ascribed to us in the dynamic of our lived covenant relationship with God. In Barth's view, we can only ever be at the beginning of our journey with God, and that journey is never complete in time. It is correspondingly difficult for Barth to think of *progress* in the Christian life, and on this point his work has encountered significant resistance. For Barth, our relationship with God and its history are possible only by virtue of divine grace, a grace on which we constantly depend but for which we can only pray.

Finally, there is the way in which the divinely effected conversion of humanity to God has significant implications for our human action. In the history of our reconciliation with God in Jesus Christ, the being of sin that was ours yesterday and still lingers today is vanquished, destroyed in the verdict pronounced in Jesus Christ. At the same time, the liberated being of righteousness and new life that will be ours tomorrow is already ours today, set under the direction given by Jesus Christ. Even though we are still sinners, then, we are disturbed sinners, called and liberated for good works in union with Christ. And the primary form which these obedient works take in the Christian life, by the grace of God, is that of witness. The justified and sanctified Christian is thus called to attest across their life to the reconciliation that has already taken place not only for them but for all humanity in Jesus Christ. And however questionable and fragmentary the resultant human response to Jesus Christ may be, it is nonetheless a real and important response of human obedience, called forth by the Spirit and of service as a witness to the kingdom of God.

Two broader aspects of Barth's presentation of soteriology which have been found to be rather controversial deserve further note at this juncture. First, there is the way in which, for Barth, all humanity is directly and necessarily implicated in the reconciliation of God with humanity in the history of Jesus Christ. It has been noted already that Barth has been accused of proffering a universalist theology, and this presentation of soteriology – in which all humanity is *by right* justified, sanctified and called in him – seems to offer little comfort to Barth's critics. At this point, one can only refer back to Chapter 4, and reiterate both Barth's explicit denial of universalism and his fervent hope that it may nonetheless turn out to be true. Second, there is the (corresponding) fear that, for Barth, the achievement of our conversion to God in Jesus Christ leaves human history with little enduring significance. In particular, there is a concern that Barth's emphasis on the prophetic work of Jesus Christ in announcing reconciliation – not to mention his hesitancy about human moral progress – jeopardizes the need for and integrity of the demanded human witness. In response, however, one might note that Barth's theology of union with Christ seeks to articulate not only a meaningful role for human activity but also a specific place for it within the divine economy. Our human witness may be provisional, yet it remains significant. This theme will be revisited in Chapter 7.

## II  Pneumatology and ecclesiology

Barth moves at this point from a focus on the *ascription* to humanity of the salvation won in the work of Jesus Christ to a focus on the *appropriation* by humanity of that same salvation. Barth writes, 'The one reality of the atonement has both an objective and a subjective side in so far as … it is both a divine act and offer and also an active human participation in it' (IV/1, 643). Here, then, Barth turns to the *subjective* side of reconciliation. That there is such a side at all – that there are people who recognize and confess their reconciliation with God – is absolutely dependent on the divine grace that has its basis and power in the work of Jesus Christ. We thus remain at this point firmly within the sphere of his history. At the same time, in entering the sphere of active human participation in the reality of that reconciliation, we move to a new dimension of that history – a dimension only possible and actual as a result of the being and work of the Spirit. It is the Spirit who is, in Barth's words, 'God in this particular address and gift, God in this awakening power, God as the Creator of this other man' (IV/1, 645).

The treatment of pneumatology in Barth's doctrine of reconciliation is articulated in two distinct but inseparable trajectories: the first treats of the work of the Spirit in the Christian community, and the second attends to the work of the Spirit in Christian individuals. The *ordering* here is important. Barth is anxious to avoid the pitfalls of certain previous Protestant treatments of the experience of grace, which in his view tended primarily to address the matter of *individual* salvation in a way which marginalized the importance of the church in the reception and work of reconciliation. By contrast, by virtue of his order Barth seeks to emphasize the importance of the *corporate*, ecclesial dimension of salvation – the ordering here thus echoes the consideration of the election of the community before that of the individual described in Chapter 3.

In what follows, then, we consider first the three *ecclesial* dimensions of the work of the Spirit – in gathering, upbuilding and sending the Christian community. The work of the Spirit in individuals will be treated thereafter.

## IV/1: The gathering of the community

The church, Barth observes, 'exists only as a definite history takes place, … only as it is gathered and lets itself be gathered and gathers itself by the living Jesus Christ through the Holy Spirit' (IV/1, 650). This statement makes clear already that Barth prefers to conceive of the church not primarily as an *institution* but as an *event*. For Barth, the church simply *is* or *takes place* as God calls and empowers people to live as those who hear the Word of reconciliation in Jesus Christ and respond to it through the Spirit in witness and obedience.

On the one hand, then, the church is a nexus of particular human activities – a *visible* community, open to analysis in historical, psychological and sociological terms. On the other hand, as the definition also suggests, the church is more than this: there is a 'third dimension' to its existence, hidden to common perception but perceptible to Christian faith. This third dimension is that the church owes its existence to the work of the Spirit as the power of Jesus Christ, and is called to attest this invisible glory in visible ways.

To elucidate this third dimension of the Christian community, Barth describes the church as 'the earthly-historical form of existence of Jesus Christ Himself' (IV/1, 661). As Scripture attests, the church is the body of Christ: it is created and continually renewed by the power of the Spirit, and it belongs to Jesus Christ, its Head, as he belongs to it. The mystery of this dimension of the community's existence is grounded in the primary mystery of the eternal election of grace, by virtue of which its history is *included* in his history, such that 'His body … includes them all to their salvation and the salvation of the world' (IV/1, 664). To speak of the community and its members as the body of Christ is thus valid only with reference to the action of God, as the Spirit comes ever again to indwell them and thus makes the eternal election of the community a present reality.

In further developing this idea of the church as the body of Christ, Barth addresses the four predicates or 'notes' accorded to the church in the Nicene-Constantinopolitan Creed – one, holy, catholic and apostolic. Barth posits that each of these notes is a matter of confession and only visible in faith. Moreover, none of these notes is an ongoing possession of the church; instead they exist only as events in which Jesus Christ *acts* on the community by the power of his Spirit, and are therefore finally beyond its control.

Barth grounds the *oneness* of the community in the oneness of God, of Jesus Christ, and of the Spirit: 'In the same way His community as the gathering of men who know and confess Him can only be one' (IV/1, 668). Hence the current disunity of the church in the world is a scandal, something that is – like sin, as was seen in Chapter 4 – both ontologically impossible and yet real, and thus a cause for penitence. Barth finds the *holiness* of the community in its contradistinction to the world, but notes that this holiness only exists through the work of the Spirit which allows the church to reflect the holiness of Jesus Christ. Consequently, holiness is never a possession of the community or its members, but can only ever be an object of prayer – an asking after holiness. Barth roots the *catholicity* of the community in its universal character, in which 'the Church is the same in all races, languages, cultures and classes, in all forms of state and society' (IV/1, 703), in relation to all its members, and across its history. This catholicity does not exclude change or diversity; but it does mean that the church can never become anything other than the body of Christ. Finally, Barth sees the *apostolicity* of the community as expressing the faithful and obedient way in which the church, by the power of the Spirit, follows the present-day address of Jesus Christ as he speaks to the church through the apostolic witness. Hence Barth writes that 'the Church is apostolic … when it exists on the basis of Scripture and in conformity with it' (IV/1, 722).

Barth concludes with a description of the being of the Christian community in the 'time between the times', that is, between the ascension and the return of Jesus Christ. The strength of the church is that it exists on the basis of the Easter event and anticipates the return of Jesus Christ in the parousia. Yet this strength is also its weakness, for now the community walks by faith and not by sight. Nevertheless, the present is the time given by God to the community for its existence and its mission, and God does not will to be God without humanity. On this sure basis, the community is called to pursue its service of God with gladness in spite of its manifest weaknesses and worldly opponents.

In this first look at the church, we see evidenced Barth's highly *dynamic* understanding of the work of God as it gathers the Christian community. The church exists in the world as a concrete and identifiable entity, of course, but theologically it exists as an event in which the Spirit of Jesus Christ works in the community and its members by calling them to the activities of faith and obedience. In this way, there arises a subjective and historical correspondence in the life of the church to the objective reality of the reconciliation of humanity with God in Jesus Christ. This dimension of the life of the church – as with its oneness, holiness, catholicity and apostolicity – is not empirically demonstrable, but remains a matter revealed only to faith. And yet it is the strength of the church as it pursues its mission in this time between the times.

## IV/2: The upbuilding of the community

In turning to the upbuilding of the Christian community, its sanctification, Barth acknowledges that we have to do with the concrete being and visible activity of particular human agents. However, he emphasizes that we do not in any way leave behind at this point the action of God in Jesus Christ by the power of the Spirit – the third dimension of the existence of the community. Only this activity allows the community to offer a true witness to Jesus Christ in spite of its sinful tendencies and equivocal actions. In such moments, the true church becomes visible on earth, in the same way – Barth writes – that 'we can see and read the dark letters of an electric sign when the current is passed through it' (IV/2, 619). However, even this visibility is, again, only perceptible by faith.

For Barth, the upbuilding of the church in history has a clear purpose: 'to give a provisional representation of the sanctification of all humanity and human life as it has taken place in Him' (IV/2, 620). We have already noted that the sanctification of all humanity has *de iure* (by right) taken place already in Jesus Christ. It is the task of the church – the place where this sanctification is *de facto* (in fact) recognized – to offer a *provisional representation* of this sanctification to the world. This representation is necessary as an indication of the victory accomplished in Jesus Christ, and it is possible only on the basis of the activity of Jesus Christ in the power of the Spirit. Though God alone can build up the community, this does not absolve the community of its responsibility: the church is called not to passivity, but to free and obedient activity that corresponds to the divine work. The members of the community are thus commanded to participate in its upbuilding by way of a mutual love of neighbour which strives for the integration of the church as one body.

Barth proceeds to explore three distinct dimensions of the upbuilding of the community: growth, upholding and order.

First, Barth observes that there is a *growth* of the church in history as it increases in number and extent, even though he immediately remarks that 'It is not self-evident that this should be the case' (IV/2, 645). And he notes that the true growth which builds up the community is not so much its statistical growth horizontally as its intensive, vertical, spiritual growth. In this process, there is a movement, in Barth's words, 'from good to better faith and knowledge, ... from good to better communion of the saints in holy things' (IV/2, 648–9). Both types of increase take place as Jesus Christ lives as the power of the life of the community, and both take place in the power of the Spirit of Jesus Christ.

Second, Barth notes that as there is a growth of the community, so too there is an *upholding* of the community. This is a work both of the gracious God and of the grateful community. Such protection is necessary, for Barth, because the community is in danger: from the outside, it faces the threats of oppression and indifference; from the inside, it faces the threats of self-alienation and self-glorification. For Barth, these foes represent not merely the sinfulness of humanity but also the power of nothingness attacking the church. Yet Barth is confident that the community will not be destroyed: Jesus Christ is its Head, and, Barth writes, 'He does not fall, and so the Church cannot fall' (IV/2, 675).

Finally, Barth posits that the *order* of the community is the form essential for its upbuilding, including its growth and its upholding. This idea of order embraces for Barth the ordering not only of its worship, but also of its tasks and members, of its common cause and unity, of its discipline and oversight, of its relations to other communities and its unity with them, and of its relations to other bodies. The ordering in view, however, is always first and foremost that of Jesus Christ, the Head of the community, as attested in Scripture, and only then, and secondarily, the obedient, corresponding ordering of the community.

In this second look at the church, Barth particularly emphasizes the divine *activity* and human *activity* which lies at its centre. In careful dialogue with Scripture, Barth develops the idea that the event of the 'upbuilding' of the church – its increase, its upholding and its order – takes place in the ordered event of the communion of Jesus Christ with his body, the church, by the power of the Spirit. In other words, it takes place in the divine action of grace addressed to the community in Jesus Christ and the corresponding human action in gratitude that is empowered by the Spirit. This conception of the church is thus again thoroughly dynamic: the community exists and acts only in the sanctifying event of its encounter with Jesus Christ, who increases, upholds and orders its members and activities in the directing power of the Spirit.

## IV/3: The sending of the community

Just as, for Barth, there is no vocation without Christian witness, so too there is no vocation and no witness without the Christian community. Barth explains that in the act of witness the Christian is 'from the very outset ... united not only with some or many ... but with all those who are charged with this service' (IV/3, 682–3, revised). And as there is only one Word, so too this service of witness has but one theme – Jesus Christ.

Barth begins by exploring the *relationship* between the church and the world. Though the history of the world stands, as seen in Chapter 4, under the divine providence, it is also confronted, as seen in Chapter 5, by the disorder and corruption of humanity. However, Barth asserts, there is no static equilibrium between God's providence and human confusion, for as the world is reconciled to God in Jesus Christ, so this opposition has already been decisively overcome. As the church dares to hope in Jesus Christ, then, it dares to hope for the world, resolute and confident in its knowledge of the reconciliation achieved in him.

As the community of Jesus Christ, the church must be and become visible in the world, even as the basis and power of its life – its eternal election in Jesus Christ – is and remains invisible. In this way, for Barth, the church lives not only in total dependence upon the world, but also in absolute freedom over it; and correspondingly the church is not only desperately weak in face of the world but also immeasurably strong in relation to it. The basis of this paradoxical existence lies once again in its third dimension – its existence as the earthly historical form of the body of Christ. The church exists, Barth writes, as it is 'called into existence and maintained in existence by Jesus Christ as the people of His witnesses' (IV/3, 752). It exists, therefore, only in so far as he exists, and it exists as it witnesses to him. At the same time, the power of both its existence and its witness is the Spirit. It is the Spirit who, in Barth's words, 'is the power of God proper to the being of Jesus Christ in the exercise and operation of which He causes His community to become what it is' (IV/3, 759). In other words, the activity of the Spirit is the ground and mystery of the life of the church, guaranteeing its unity with Jesus Christ in its service of witness.

In delineating the *purpose* of the community, Barth writes that it is 'originally, essentially and *per definitionem* [by definition] summoned and impelled to exist for God and therefore for the world and men' (IV/3, 763). The church does not exist for its own sake, but for the world which God loves, and as a result, it is made responsible for the world. The *task* to which the community is called is to witness to Jesus Christ, the One who effects and reveals the love of God for humanity, and to humanity as elect and reconciled in him. This witness is to be addressed to all people in the sure hope that, as they hear and accept the Gospel, and as they become in fact who they already and truly are by right in Jesus Christ, the future which awaits them is one of joy and liberation. As this task is accomplished by the power of the Spirit, in an ongoing obedient listening to the Word of God, the community in its prophetic work in and for the world offers in a provisional way a likeness to the prophetic work of Jesus Christ.

Finally, Barth explicates the nature of the *service* of the community: the community fulfils its calling as its serves both God and humanity by means of its witness to Jesus Christ. For this to take place requires the community to pray for divine grace, and its witness remains at every point provisional. Nevertheless, its service stands under the unfailing promise of God, which establishes and sustains its work in face of all its limitations and pressures. The service of the church takes a variety of different forms, albeit they share an underlying unity in the Gospel. Barth enumerates and explores at some length here the twelve different forms in which he perceives the service of the community to take place. In the first six forms – praise of God, preaching of the Gospel, Christian education, evangelization, mission and theology – Barth discerns a priority of speech over action. In the second six forms – prayer, pastoral care, exemplary action, diaconal work, prophetic action and the establishment of community – Barth conversely discerns a priority of action over speech. These twelve forms represent for Barth forms of the witness of the community that are normative for its service in all times and places.

In this third and last look at the church, Barth indicates that the church is nothing without its activity of *witness*. There is no such thing, therefore, as a pure essence or static existence of the church without reference to its active vocation to the service of witness and its dynamic relationship with the world at large. Although the Christian community alone sees the world and humanity as they really are – estranged from but reconciled to God – nevertheless it understands that, without conforming to the world, the Christian community belongs to the world. This means that it stands in solidarity with the world precisely as it carries out its witness to Jesus Christ by the power of the Spirit. Its service of God and of humanity is thus a frail and human service, depending at every point upon the grace of God for its success; but precisely this *eccentric* existence, grounded beyond itself, is its hidden and enduring glory, the source of its life and its hope.

# *Comment*

In his ecclesiology, Barth offers a radical account of the Christian community as gathered, nourished, and sent by Jesus Christ in the power of the Spirit to witness to the reconciliation of God with humanity. The church exists in the event of grace in which this activity of God takes place – this is the third dimension of its character as a creature of Word and Spirit, as the earthly historical form of the body of Christ. For its part, the church corresponds to its holy foundation and calling as it seeks, in however provisional and limited a way, to proclaim to all people the good news that God is for humanity in Jesus Christ and that this Gospel is valid and effective for all those who hear. As such, the church is not only in the world, and of the world, but also for the world.

Among many points which could be elaborated at this juncture, there are four issues here which are worthy of particular comment.

First, Barth characterizes the church as the earthly historical form of the body of Christ. At the core of Barth's ecclesiology is the contention that when the doctrine of the church is investigated, there is no sense in which the person and work of Jesus Christ are left behind. As we observed in Chapter 3, the Christian community is elect in Jesus Christ before the foundation of the world: it cannot be considered without him, *nor he without it*. This is the third dimension of its existence, the dimension which is not empirically visible but is revealed to faith. It is this third dimension which fundamentally determines the existence and the history of the church. What takes place in the history of the church, then, is that the reconciliation of God with humanity which has been accomplished and manifested for all people in Jesus Christ is now – by grace – apprehended, appropriated and attested by the Christian community.

Second, Barth repeatedly affirms that the power of the life of this Christian community is the power of the Spirit of the risen Jesus Christ. At each stage in his ecclesiology – in the gathering, in the upbuilding and in the sending of the community – Barth has the activity of the Spirit clearly in view. This is a point at which Barth has been heavily criticized: it has been suggested that precisely here, where the Spirit should be the dominant figure, the person of Jesus Christ dominates Barth's reflections. Moreover, it has been argued that at this point the individual personhood of the Spirit risks being compromised in view of the ongoing material influence of Jesus Christ. Yet some of this criticism may be alleviated by the recognition that there is no competitive relation in view here: for Barth, to speak of the power of God proper to Jesus Christ in empowering the community to fulfil its calling simply *is* to speak of the Spirit. There is no independent work of the Spirit; the Spirit is the Spirit (of the Father and) of the Son, and thus both the eternal bond of peace between them and the Guarantor of the unity of Jesus Christ in his transcendence and his immanence.

Third, Barth repeatedly conceives of the existence of the church as event, strikingly emphasising the way in which divine activity and human response together determine the existence of the community. This is evidenced not only by the way in which the essence of the church is defined by its service of mission, but also by the way in which Barth here seeks to abandon absolutely any theological distinction between the being of the church and its act, its essence and its existence. This very dynamic conception of the life of the church as empowered by the Spirit resonates with the dynamic conception of the living God which was encountered in Chapter 3 and the dynamic conception of the history of Jesus Christ which was encountered in Chapter 5. Yet it has led to fears being expressed concerning the lack of attention Barth gives either to the church as an institution or to the role of the church as itself an instrument and mediator of the divine grace. While Barth clearly recognizes the immanent and visible dimension of the church, however, he is not prepared to identify the concrete church with the body of Christ without the qualification that the church must ever and again *take place* as an act of witness. Correspondingly, he is not prepared to identify the concrete church as a place through whose being and activities grace is *necessarily* mediated: as will be seen in Chapter 7, this has particular implications for how Barth conceives of the sacraments of the church.

Finally, Barth repeatedly seems to relativize the distinctions that other theologies can tend to draw between the church and the world.

This is encapsulated memorably in Barth's observations that 'the world would not necessarily be lost if there were no Church' but that 'the Church would be lost if it had no counterpart in the world' (IV/3, 826). What Barth is emphasizing here is that the church does not exist for itself, and indeed that it is not church at all if it does not engage in the task of witness. Hence not only the foundation of the church is extrinsic to itself, in Jesus Christ, but also the purpose of the church is extrinsic to itself, as it exists in a world awaiting news of the Gospel of Jesus Christ. This dynamic and purposive construal of the church has proven to be particularly important in the context of inspiring contemporary Christian communities to take seriously the full significance of the mission of the church. At the same time, however, it has made others nervous about the danger of eliding the distinction between the church and the world.

## III  The Christian life

Under this final heading, we turn to Barth's understanding of the three *individual* dimensions of the work and witness of the Spirit – the faith, the love and the hope of the individual Christian within the community. Barth asserts that in turning to the character of the Christian life, we are still within the scope of Christology, for 'although we are dealing with our existence, we are dealing with our existence in Jesus Christ as our true existence' (IV/1, 154). Each of these three concepts of faith, love and hope is accordingly *primarily* the work of Jesus Christ, *secondarily* his work in the community, and *lastly* his work in individuals. It is to these concepts in their final iteration, as together constituting *the* act of the Christian life of the individual, that Barth moves at this point in his doctrine of reconciliation.

### IV/1: Faith

In reaching the topic of Christian faith at the *end* of the first part-volume of the doctrine of reconciliation, Barth inverts the order of many dogmatic works in modernity which *begin* with the topic. The reason is Barth's view that Christian faith should know and confess itself as the *last thing* in Christianity, something which – theologically – can only follow the doctrine of Jesus Christ and the intermediate doctrines concerning sin, salvation, Spirit and church.

For Barth, Christian faith is a free and spontaneous act, an act which takes place only in relation to Jesus Christ, and this in three ways. First, faith consists in our orientation to him, such that we look to him, hold to him and depend on him. In faith, therefore, our existence is *eccentric* in the sense that the centre of our lives is no longer ourselves but Jesus Christ. Second, faith has its origin in him, in that it is only possible as a result of his victory over the human pride and unbelief that is contrary to faith. Indeed, in light of this victory, and given the awakening power of the Spirit, faith is no longer a matter of our arbitrary choice but a necessity of our genuine freedom. And third, the event of faith actualizes our constitution as a Christian subject in him, such that 'in this action [of faith] there begins and takes place a new and particular being of man' (IV/1, 749). Christians in their faith therefore not only recognize but also represent the salvific work of Jesus Christ that has relevance for all humanity.

On one level, then, the event of faith is a *cognitive* event, for it consists in the subject believing in the objective work of Jesus Christ for humanity that has already been completed. On another level, however, this event of faith is a *creative* act, for it is precisely here that there arises a new creation, a new subject of faith and obedience. It is precisely this new individual, as part of the community and as part of all humanity, who is eternally elect in Jesus Christ.

Turning to faith as a human act, Barth observes that 'in all the activity and individual acts of a man it is the most inward and central and decisive act of his heart' (IV/1, 757). It is an act which comprises three basic moments. The first – acknowledgement – indicates that in the encounter with Jesus Christ through the community, we submit to him obediently. Barth emphasizes that we submit neither to the community, nor to any creed or dogma, but only to the person of Jesus Christ. The second – recognition – signals that our acknowledgement is not abstract or formless, but relates to the Jesus Christ whom the community proclaims. Barth stresses that our faith is not merely theoretical but also *practical*, bearing implications both for our knowledge of ourselves and for our activity in response. In the attitude of faith, we recognize that in Jesus Christ our old self has been crucified and our new self has been given life. In this way, in the humility of faith and obedience, the Christian becomes 'a copy, a parallel, a likeness of His being and activity for him' (IV/1, 775). The third moment – confession – indicates that our acknowledgement and recognition of Jesus Christ moves us necessarily to confess our faith to others. Barth emphasizes here that this confession is not an optional extra for Christians, but is of the essence of the faith.

What Barth achieves in this presentation is a clear insistence on the complex nature of the event of faith. On the one hand, faith is the gift of the Spirit of Jesus Christ, and has Jesus Christ as its Object, orientation and origin. On the other hand, faith is also a fully human work, with radical consequences for the way that we think and act. Moreover, given the reconciliation with God attained for us in Jesus Christ, faith is not simply an option but a necessity if we wish correctly to use the freedom won for us in Jesus Christ. This indicates clearly once again – this time at the subjective level – the radicality of Barth's claim that reconciliation has been achieved for all people, not just for Christians, in Jesus Christ. At the subjective level, the true freedom of humanity is expressed in faith; any other expression is an impossible possibility.

## IV/2: Love

For Barth, Christianity consists wholly in the living, active reception of Jesus Christ in faith. But it does not consist exclusively in this. In the power of the Spirit, Barth writes, we confirm this act of receiving by 'the act of a pure and total giving, offering and surrender corresponding to this receiving' (IV/2, 730). Together, and indivisibly, the activities of faith and love constitute the one dynamic movement and act of Christian existence.

True Christian love – *agape* – is, for Barth, the movement in the power of the Spirit in which we turn away from ourselves and turn wholly towards the other for the sake of the other. *Agape* thus corresponds to our true human nature, as it is elected by God in Jesus Christ. In this movement of *agape*, we are freed by God, and rendered free for God, and free to be with other – in short, to be covenant partners of God. Barth contrasts this type of love with *eros*, which he defines here as the assertive, grasping, possessive self-love that is the opposite of *agape*. Given this definition, which is by no means uncontroversial or uncontested, *eros* contradicts our true nature, rejecting its corollaries of freedom and partnership, and thus demonstrates the absurdity and impossibility of sin. In the Christian life, *agape* and its antithesis *eros* are always found together. However, *eros* does not ultimately triumph over *agape*: Barth asserts that even the erotic person who lives in sinful self-contradiction remains loved and affirmed by God.

The basis of Christian love is the fact that God loves us first. As we saw in Chapter 3, the divine activity of love for us is grounded in the divine being as the One who elects to be for us in the humiliation and exaltation of Jesus Christ. Divine love is thus no mere disposition or attitude of the Christian God but characterizes God's very being. For Barth, then, God's love for humanity is an *electing* love that is absolutely free. But it is also more than this: it is also a *purifying* love that judges our sin and a *creative* love that transforms us for true communion with God.

The act of Christian love is, Barth writes, 'basically and comprehensively the form of life which characterises the existence of the community and its members' (IV/2, 784). This act, in which we respond to and correspond to the act of divine love, represents something new and unexpected within the world. On the one hand, Barth posits, it has a specific form: it takes place as a free act of human self-giving in the power of the Spirit, and reflects the love of God for the world. As this reflection, love is not simply a disposition or attitude; instead, it pertains to the whole life-act of the Christian, and brings with it real joy and blessedness and exaltation. On the other hand, Barth observes, it also has a specific content and meaning: on the basis of the reconciliation achieved in Jesus Christ, we are liberated (and commanded) to love God, and our freedom to love God is simultaneously our freedom to obey God. As this takes place, the divine covenant with humanity becomes genuinely two-sided.

On the basis of this covenant love, moreover, we are liberated (and commanded) to love our neighbour – even, Barth writes, 'in relationships in which its realisation is at the moment impossible' (IV/2, 809). In the self-giving act of Christian love in the Spirit, we attest to the other the love that God has for humanity. And as we love both God and neighbour, we offer a fragile but genuine witness to the One who achieves this love supremely and uniquely – Jesus Christ. Barth concludes his treatment of love with a sustained exposition of 1 Corinthians 13.

In this treatment of love, the fundamental point which Barth emphasizes is that the act of Christian love is a reflection of the eternal love of God and a necessary accompaniment to the act of faith. Love is of the very essence of God, and we are correspondingly liberated and commanded to love God and neighbour in a way which determines our whole being and action. Barth's dynamic construal of the relationship between *eros* and *agape* – developed in dialogue with Anders Nygren and Heinrich Scholz and drawing heavily on Scripture – emphasizes the way in which this possibility of Christian love corresponds to our true human nature. But it also indicates that this possibility is only actualized by the power of the Spirit, in the event in which our sinful tendency to self-love is overcome and we are liberated for obedience. It is in this obedience that we offer our most profound witness to the love of God.

## IV/3: Hope

In turning to the theme of Christian hope, Barth turns to the relationship between the Christian and their future, and, in particular, to their relationship with Jesus Christ as the One who is to come. For Barth, the existence of the Christian as one who both follows and obeys Jesus Christ becomes possible and actual as Jesus Christ causes us to stride towards the future in *hope* in him.

Barth recognizes immediately that, in this time between the times, the life of Christians has not attained its final goal. Though the resurrected Jesus Christ has spoken – and continues to speak – his Word of truth in the power of the Spirit, still this Word has not yet been spoken universally and definitively. Consequently, the life and witness of Christians can appear to be doubtful and vulnerable: it can appear, Barth writes, that the Christian is 'on the way into a future which seems to be for him an absolutely open and wholly unwritten page, or even an impenetrable sea of mist' (IV/3, 905). However, as Jesus Christ is the One who is the same yesterday, today and forever, the idea that our future is indeterminate or uncertain is comprehensively rejected by Barth. In its place stands Christian hope in the final return of Jesus Christ and the consummation of his revelation. This hope has its basis, not within the person of the Christian, but in Jesus Christ. Against this background, then, Barth writes that 'The Christian expectation of the future cannot be uncertain, nor unsettled, nor sceptical, but only assured and patient and cheerful expectation' (IV/3, 909).

At the same time, Barth observes, Christian hope also represents the free act of the Christian as they look at and move towards Jesus Christ in freedom. For that reason, we are called both to witness to the world in hope and to hope as we witness in the world. Even though we of ourselves are both justified and sinner, sanctified and unholy, we have in Jesus Christ the freedom to witness and to hope, transcending our present and indicating our future. In this way, our imperfect and fragile witness can participate in the prophetic work of Jesus Christ, and we can confidently hope in him as our Judge, for he was, is and will be the One in whom God is gracious to us. Indeed, Barth writes, we can confidently hope in Jesus Christ even in face of death, because our end, as coming from him, 'can only be an unequivocally welcome, because gracious, event' (IV/3, 927).

Barth proceeds to outline three dimensions of the Christian life determined by hope in Jesus Christ. First, Barth indicates that Christian hope is not a private hope, because the event of revelation for which the Christian hopes is not particular but universal. For this reason, the Christian is called to public witness to this hope, thereby offering a provisional representation of the work of Jesus Christ in the world. Second, Barth indicates that Christian hope is not a hope which abandons the world, because the penultimate events of this world – even and precisely considered alongside the ultimate return of Christ – have significance and meaning as determined by that goal and are thus deserving objects of Christian hope. Third, Barth reiterates that Christian hope is a hope which derives not from ourselves, but only from God, when God frees us by the power of the Spirit for the free human activity of hope. For Barth, it is in this Christian life in hope, awakened by the power of the Spirit, that we truly come to and may be ourselves.

Throughout this material on hope, Barth emphasizes the sure foundation of Christian hope in Jesus Christ. It is because Jesus Christ is the same yesterday – as the One crucified and resurrected for all humanity, today – as the One present and active in the power of the Spirit, and forever – as the One who will come again in glory, that Christians can have unwavering confidence in him and in his coming again in glory. On this basis, as attested in the Pauline letters in Scripture which are the focus of Barth's exegesis in these pages, Barth counsels that Christian hope should be assured, expectant and joyful. Despite the doubt and uncertainty caused by events in the world and the hesitation and anxiety caused by the prospect of judgement and death, nevertheless we are called to hope not only in Jesus Christ but also for the world in which we are called to be his witnesses.

# *Comment*

In this exploration of the concepts of faith, love and hope, Barth does not leave the work of Jesus Christ behind. Jesus Christ remains not only the primary Object of each of these characteristics, but also – in a very concrete way – their primary Subject. In other words, it is Jesus Christ in the power of the Spirit who determines our exercise of these characteristics and our Christian life as a whole. In this exploration of faith, love and hope, Barth also does not leave the community of Jesus Christ behind. It is the community which is the first subsidiary object of the election of Jesus Christ and it is the community which is the earthly historical form of his body. The individual, meantime, is only ever elect within the scope of the community. For this reason, at no point here is the Christian considered in abstraction or in isolation, but always as a member of this community, and dependent upon it.

At the same time, these three sections allow Barth to offer an account of the character of the life of the individual Christian. And they allow Barth to reflect upon the way in which the exercise of faith, love and hope represents a free activity of the Christian in which, by the power of the Spirit, they can correspond to the activity of God in Jesus Christ and become in actuality a genuine covenant partner of God – even in this time between the times. It is as they have faith in the One who came, love the One who is present and hope in the One who is to come that they realise their calling to be a witness of Jesus Christ. And with this step, a significant way-marker has been reached in the doctrine of reconciliation, indicating the end of a long path from Christology through the doctrine of sin, soteriology, pneumatology and ecclesiology to the Christian life. Only the ethics of reconciliation remain to be addressed.

# CHAPTER SEVEN

# Theological ethics

At the close of his dogmatic reflections in each of volumes II, III and IV of *Church Dogmatics*, Barth turns to matters of theological ethics. He thereby makes good in practice upon his insistence in volume I that because the theme of the Word of God is human existence *under* the Word of God, theology cannot be true to itself unless it is also prepared to be ethics. This chapter considers the ethical material presented in each of these volumes, beginning with his 'general' ethics – the section on the command of God in the doctrine of God (volume II/2). It then moves to his 'special' ethics – the sections on the command of God the Creator (volume III/4), and those on the command of God the Reconciler (volume IV/4) which were completed prior to Barth's death.

## I  General ethics

The material on 'general' ethics in volume II/2 lies within the doctrine of God. It seeks to understand the Word of God as the command of God, and to consider the command of God within the context of the *divine* being in action. In later volumes, in his 'special' ethics, Barth will attend to the command of God in its relation to the *human* being in action to whom it is addressed.

### Ethics as a task of the doctrine of God

The move by Barth to locate the material on general ethics deep within the doctrine of God and right after the doctrine of election is radical and innovative. After all, it draws the consideration of Christian ethics and the human being as ethical agent right into the centre of Barth's discourse concerning God. However, it is also absolutely intentional. For Barth, the Christian God is only known in Jesus Christ, the One in whom human beings are elected and realized as covenant partners of God, and so God cannot be considered apart from this covenant.

The covenant has two elements. First, there is the eternal election of grace, in which God determines to be gracious towards humanity in Jesus Christ – Barth considered this theme of *God for humanity* expansively in the first half of volume II/2, as was seen above in Chapter 3. But second, there is also the determination of humanity in election to be witnesses to God, and it is this theme of *humanity for God* that brings Barth here, at the close of his doctrine of God, to the discipline of theological ethics.

One significant way in which Barth indicates the twofold nature of the covenant is the language of Gospel and Law. The divine election of humanity is the good news of the Gospel; the divine determination of humanity is the command of the Law. Hence the one Word of God is, for Barth, both Gospel *and* Law: 'In its content, it is Gospel; in its form and fashion, it is Law' (II/2, 511). And it is never the one without the other. The election of God is thus election *for* a purpose – the conformity of our being and action to that of God. In response to the divine determination of the human being, then, there arises the question of the *self*-determination of the human being. The one who is elect exists in a position of responsibility, under the grace *and* the judgement of God.

In this position, only one person – Jesus Christ – fulfils the command of God. In Jesus Christ, we see the human image with which Adam was created to correspond, but from which Adam departed in sin. Yet Jesus Christ not only *reveals* what it is to be an obedient, and thus sanctified person; in his person he also *effects* the obedience and sanctification of humanity. And as we are elect in Jesus Christ, so he also *achieves* the obedience and sanctification in his person of all humanity. Barth therefore writes, 'The man Jesus ... does not *give* the answer, but by God's grace He *is* the answer to the ethical question put by God's grace' (II/2, 517).

In light of this view, Barth thinks that dogmatics cannot pursue any work on ethics that is abstracted from the history of God with humanity in Jesus Christ. Thus though Barth explores the possibilities of Christian ethics proceeding in an apologetic mode, or operating in parallel with yet distinction from philosophical ethics, or complementing the study of moral philosophy (as in Roman Catholic moral theology), each alternative is considered and robustly rejected in turn.

Instead, Barth posits, human action always takes place within the sphere of the divine command. And within this sphere, Barth asserts, 'the question of good and evil has been decided and settled once and for all in the decree of God, by the cross and the resurrection of Jesus Christ' (II/2, 536). It is Jesus Christ who both reveals *and* fulfils both the Gospel *and* the Law. And this means that the task of theological ethics is simply to witness to and confirm this decision in what it says about human action. In other terms, for Barth, the 'ethical problem' that is at stake in church dogmatics is to question 'whether and to what extent human action is a glorification of the grace of Jesus Christ' (II/2, 540). The goodness of human action – as obedient, responsible, Christian action – is thus never to be found in the human action itself. Instead, it is to be found in the goodness with which God acts towards humanity in Jesus Christ. Good human action which is commanded by and obedient to God thus points *away from* itself and *towards* the goodness of the Word of God which commands and sanctifies it.

There is only one command of God, Barth insists, but it encounters the human being in three distinct ways – as the creature of God, as the sinner pardoned by God and as the adopted heir of the kingdom of God. In later volumes, Barth offers distinct accounts of the command of God the Creator and of the command of God the Reconciler, and planned to do the same for God the Redeemer. In volume II/2, however, Barth continues with general ethics.

## *The command as the claim of God*

The claim which God has to the obedience of human beings is not grounded simply in absolute divine power, eternal divine goodness or unrequited human need. Instead, the fundamental basis of the divine claim is that God has given Godself to us and is therefore the God in whom we may believe. Barth writes, 'it is from the fact that He is this God that there derives the superiority and authority, basis and justice of His claim' (II/2, 557).

The *content* of the claim of God is that human action should correspond with and conform to the gracious action of God. In other words, Barth asserts that we and our action should present to the world an image of God: we and our action should *represent* God and God's action. There is no question of an identity of God and humanity in this correspondence, or of a lessening of the ontological difference between them. Instead, in our action we are to accept God's action in Jesus Christ as right – which means to recognize that we are God's and not our own – and to allow our action to be guided accordingly.

The claim of God encounters the human being in myriad different ways. As we saw in Chapter 3, the Word of God can be unveiled through the veil of any creaturely medium. What distinguishes the *form* of the command of God from other commands is that the command of God offers us *permission*, in that it grants us a very particular *freedom*. Whatever the particular and concrete *content* of this command, it will call us to an obedience in which lies our true freedom and to a freedom in which lies our true obedience. We see this unity of permission and obligation, which may seem counter-intuitive, revealed and fulfilled in Jesus Christ, in whose history we see both true freedom enacted *and* true obedience offered. The meaning of freedom for Barth, as was seen in Chapter 4, is thus radically different from the way in which we generally speak about freedom, which sinfully pretends that we enjoy absolute free will. And this means that the choice which confronts us here is not between possible obedience and possible disobedience, but between possible obedience and *impossible* disobedience. As we saw in Chapter 5, sin is for Barth an *impossible* possibility, even and precisely here, in face of the command of God. By contrast, the only true possibility of our freedom is to offer joyful obedience.

The command of God thus seeks both to claim us for Jesus Christ, and at the same time to make us free. It is a *personal* command, demanding our decision in relation to Jesus Christ, and it is a command which touches every aspect of our life. Therefore, there can be no room for neutrality before this command of God.

## *The command as the decision of God*

The command of God not only claims human obedience, but also decides in respect of our response to it. Our conformity or non-conformity to the divine command in time is measured both in time and in eternity by the will and act of God to be for us in Jesus Christ. For Barth, this sovereign decision of *God* therefore decides in respect of the decisions that *we* make in the course of our lives, and so we should make our decisions in a self-reflective way which examines the relationship between the command of God and our existence and takes seriously our ethical *responsibility* before God. It requires us continually to ask the question: 'What ought we to do?' (II/2, 645).

This is the question of *moral reflection* which confronts all human beings – the question of how our action and inaction has conformed, does conform, and will conform to the command of God. Yet in asking this question, it is not as if we have an answer ready. And this means for Barth that to approach the command of God responsibly means to be ready at each point for fresh divine instruction concerning what is good and obedient action, and thus to be willing to bracket all our existing knowledge or previous experience as merely hypothesis and opinion. This repeated movement of openness and bracketing in moral reflection never ceases throughout the Christian life.

The divine command, which as the divine decision confronts all our decisions, always has for Barth a particular content: it is always a *concrete* and *individual* command, communicating a *specific* meaning and purpose so as to *demand* obedience or disobedience. This is the view of the command of God which Barth finds in Scripture: the will of God is to be found in *particular* commands and prohibitions of God. Thus not even the Ten Commandments and the Sermon on the Mount provide universal rules; they are simply historical examples of particular commands to particular people at particular times. However, the foundation of all these individual commands of God is the one will of God to be merciful to *all* humanity in Jesus Christ and therefore the one desire of God that human beings witness to this covenant of grace. In all their variety, it is this one foundation which the various individual commands attest.

At the same time, Barth insists that the concrete divine commands that are found in Scripture are still relevant for us today. What God commands then, so too God commands now – *good* action, 'action which is integrally connected with the establishment and proclamation of His covenant, with His promised kingdom which has now drawn near' (II/2, 703). Moreover, Scripture attests not only the form but also the *content* of the command of God. This means that for all that we now inhabit a very different time and place, we are called to hear and respect the eternal and valid content of the command in Scripture.

Barth insists that the command of God, in all its diverse forms, is God's *good* decision. In its manifold goodness, both the command of God and the will of God are completely *indivisible*. And in its manifold goodness, as a corollary, the command of God *unites* human beings under the sovereign decision of God and *unifies* human beings to exist in inner harmony rather than internal conflict.

## The command as the judgement of God

In the claim and decision of the command of God, the judgement of God on human beings is both proclaimed and effected. Yet to observe this, Barth notes, is already to posit that God disposes over humanity, and does not will to be God without us. And this means, for Barth, that the judgement of God over humanity is always evidence of the love of God for humanity. It is in the history of *Jesus Christ* that God elects and actualizes and reveals the divine judgement of and the divine love for humanity. Obedience to the command in this perspective thus requires us simply to submit to this divine judgement, and to do so joyfully in recognition of the love of God that is directed to us within it.

In face of the divine command, Barth asserts that we neither satisfy its *claim* nor render obedient *decision*. The judgement upon us can therefore only be one of *condemnation*, and this judgement is executed as an event between God and humanity in the crucifixion of Jesus Christ. At the same time, the execution of this judgement brings with it the forgiveness of our sins – not on account of our own merits, but as we are elected, loved and blessed by God. Evidence of this gracious judgement comes in the resurrection of Jesus Christ, and demonstrates the *faithfulness* of God to those whom God has elected from all eternity.

The purpose of the judgement of God, for Barth, is that we might pass from judgement to a new life in covenant with God. On the one hand, our judgement lies behind us, in Jesus Christ; on the other hand, we continue to be judged by the command of God and thus are 'directed to live by the grace of God' (II/2, 765). The commanded response to the divine judgement is *faith*, and the final goal of the divine judgement is our sanctification before God as preparation for the eternal life that is to come. This sanctification does not become empirically visible to us, but is already fulfilled for us in Jesus Christ. As such, it belongs to our confession of faith, and to our response to God in prayer.

## *Comment*

The account of general ethics which Barth develops in *Church Dogmatics* is deeply embedded within his theological account of the relationship between God and humanity. More specifically, it follows both formally and materially from the doctrine of election which was discussed in Chapter 3. In light of God's gracious and eternal decision to be for humanity, the decision in respect of the good or evil of human action has already been made in Jesus Christ. And in the reconciliation effected in him there has already taken place the sanctification of all human beings, as explained in Chapter 6 above. The result is that the Christian needs neither to pose this question of good and evil for themselves, nor to seek to achieve their own sanctification.

Instead, we are called to hear the Word of God as it encounters us as Gospel, and to accept in faith the claim, decision and judgement on our human activity as these have taken place in Jesus Christ. And we are called to hear the Word of God as it encounters us as Law, and to respond in free obedience and obedient freedom to whatever it requires of us, thereby witnessing to God in our action. In each case, the Word of God will encounter us as a living, dynamic, personal reality that is directed to our particular situation and indicates to us our concrete obligations. Yet in all the multiplicity and specificity of its commanding, it remains the one, good command of God, arising within the one history of God with humanity for which God graciously elects Godself from all eternity.

Three features of this initial account of the command of God may be worthy of particular note at this point.

First, Barth's conception of the command of God leads him to an ethics of the divine command. Specific instruction is given directly to the individual in the concrete moment of ethical decision, and the only question for Barth is not whether God speaks but whether we hear. This conception emphasizes that God is the living Lord, and that God is radically *free* in God's revelation, themes that both featured prominently in Chapter 2. This conception also emphasizes that God exists in real and living *relationship* with the human agent who is the object of election in Jesus Christ. However, it may raise the fear that the command may be arbitrary or capricious – that there might be a certain *occasionalism* or disconnectedness at the heart of the divine command. Against this, one might consider the way in which Barth takes pains to assert the constancy and faithfulness of God as our covenant partner. Moreover, one might note that Barth repeatedly highlights the *unity* in multiplicity of the divine command, and its location within the *one* history of God with humanity centred in Jesus Christ. And finally, one might observe that Barth stresses the formal *and material* importance of the witness of Scripture in hearing the divine command.

Second, this ethics of the divine command leads Barth to a particular view of the place of moral reflection. Barth considers moral reflection to be important in so far as it attests the responsibility of the ethical agent before God, and contributes to a pattern of behaviour in which we learn progressively from each encounter with the command of God about how to approach it in future. Yet it is beyond the possibility of moral reflection, in Barth's view, to anticipate the command of God; indeed, in approaching the command, one's previous moral reflection must be utterly held in reserve. There may thus be a question as to whether this vision of ethical reflection empties the practice of moral reflection of *material* content or significance. For, as Barth indicates, perseverance in moral reflection means at heart that all our previous attempts to answer the ethical question are themselves perpetually called into question. Perhaps, for Barth, this simply is the central import of permissible moral reflection.

Third, this ethics of the divine command is rigorously attentive to the Word of God and denies the possibility of gaining knowledge of the command from any other source. Indeed, for Barth the more general conception of ethics corresponds exactly with sin, in so far as it fails to attend to the answer to the question of ethics that is given in Jesus Christ. There is an echo here of Barth's rejection of natural theology, as considered in Chapter 3. But precisely here, there may arise again a concern that Barth is unnecessarily closed to the insights and lessons of other disciplines which attend to human behaviour. In response, it might be noted that Barth nowhere denies the possibility of fruitful conversation with other disciplines at this point, and indeed that his own practice is to engage extensively with other views. At the same time, however, it is clear that the Word of God has absolute and unique priority in the domain of ethics.

Thus far, Barth's account of theological ethics as general ethics has been rather formal in its exposition; this changes markedly as Barth turns to special ethics.

# II  Special ethics:
# The doctrine of creation

Having focused in 'general' ethics on the command of God and the *divine* being and action, Barth moves in 'special' ethics to consider the *human* being and action encountered by the command of God. This encounter has three distinct aspects, corresponding to the spheres of creation, reconciliation and redemption. And though there is only one command, and not three, Barth considers the *distinction* of these spheres in special ethics to be helpful and necessary. At the end of the doctrine of creation, in volume III/4, Barth turns to the command as it relates to God the Creator and the human being as the creature of God.

## *Ethics as a task of the doctrine of creation*

Barth begins by considering how one might go about doing special ethics.

One possibility would be to think of the command of God as a list of prescribed norms and universal rules, whether derived from Scripture, tradition or natural law. These instructions could then be related to different situations in human life and applied to individual cases. Barth describes this conception of ethics by the term 'casuistry', and recognizes its historical importance and its theological attractiveness; however, he ultimately rejects it as a practice of ethics to be avoided. For Barth, such a conception implies that one can not only know but also master the command of God, suggests that the command of God is a fixed and universal rule, and obscures and obstructs the direct relationship which exists between the God who commands and the person commanded.

With the possibility of 'casuistry' ruled out, Barth proceeds to build his special ethics on rather different ground. On the one hand, he affirms as in his general ethics that the command of God is given afresh to each person in each new moment; on the other hand, he insists that the various instances of the divine command are not in any way disconnected but are all part of the one divine order that serves as the constant background to every ethical encounter.

The command of God thus has both has a punctiliar, *vertical* dimension which is the immediate encounter with God and a historical, *horizontal* dimension which is the history of the covenant of humanity with God. For Barth, even if we cannot predict *exactly* what the divine command will be at any point, still we can know the *context* within which it is given and the *agents* involved in its giving and receiving. And this means that we can know something of the *character* which the command will take. As special ethics investigates and illuminates this horizontal dimension, Barth writes, it can thus 'become a formed reference to the ethical event and therefore perform its service as instructional preparation' (III/4, 18). In seeking to indicate the contours and landscape of this formed reference, special ethics can only be derived from the Word of God – Barth again rejects the possibility of theological knowledge from any other source.

The task of special ethics is thus to describe and illuminate, on the basis of the revelation of the Word of God attested in Scripture, the *history* of encounter between God and humanity in which each concrete *event* of the command of God is but one moment. And although it can never predict or determine the command of God, it can offer in respect of the command a general description, an ethical lead, and a series of guiding directives. Ultimately, however, Barth considers that 'Ethics will still have to leave the final judgment to God' (III/4, 31).

This conception of special ethics means that Barth rejects a theology of 'orders of creation', as if the world of itself were able to offer instruction in respect of the relationship between God and humanity and the content of the divine command. Resisting this view, as he resists all natural theology, Barth argues that to speak of the command of God as that of the Creator is possible only with reference to Jesus Christ, in whom the true creature and true creaturely action is revealed and sanctified.

In organizing his treatment of the ethics of creation, Barth draws on the four dimensions of the human being as creature which he developed in volume III/2, explored in Chapter 4 above – the creature as responsible before God, as called to covenant partnership with God and living with other creatures, as dependent on God for life as body and soul, and as existing in limitation. The order of investigation thus moves again from God through life together to the individual. In the case of each dimension, Barth considers the extent to which the command of God has in view the sanctification of human action, and does so in each case by exploring the shape of the true *freedom* of the human as creature.

## *Freedom before God*

For Barth, the freedom of the human creature before God consists in being responsible before God. It is a responsibility which embraces the whole of human life and human action, and indicates that God the Creator is right in all God's works and that God alone is to be wholly trusted and freely obeyed. The command of God claims completely this responsibility of the human being.

This holistic responsibility before the divine command also encompasses one very particular responsibility which forms the middle and circumference of the whole. This claim finds expression in the fourth commandment – the command to observe the Sabbath. By considering the divine command to rest on the Sabbath right at the start of the ethics of creation, Barth seeks immediately to point *away* from what human beings can and do achieve and instead *towards* what God can and does achieve for humanity in the activity of Jesus Christ. In this way, Sabbath rest points towards the meaning of *all* human history, calling the human being to a faith in God which, for Barth, 'brings about the renunciation of ... all that he thinks and wills and effects and achieves' (III/4, 59). At the same time, the command to keep the Sabbath also calls human beings to corporate worship of God. Barth is not a strict Sabbatarian at this point. Instead, he desires simply to proclaim 'the call to renouncing faith in God in the concrete form of celebrating this day' (III/4, 66) – how this faith that renounces human possibility and achievement is enacted in any particular Christian life, Barth leaves undetermined.

Barth discusses here two further forms of creaturely responsibility before God – confession and prayer. On the former, Barth observes that God commands the human being to be and become a *witness* of God. On the latter, Barth posits that the human being is to seek everything that is needed from God in prayer. What these acts have in common with Sabbath rest is not only that they are undertaken in freedom and obedience, but also that they are self-renouncing activities. Thus in recognizing in faith the priority and ultimacy of God's action, in witnessing to the glory of God, and in petitioning God for all things, the creature who is responsible before God always points towards God and away from itself.

## *Freedom in fellowship*

As a creature, the human being stands in responsibility before God; but the human being is also destined to become the covenant partner of God. The corollary of this call to covenant partnership in the realm of creation is the call for human beings to live in encounter with other human beings. Barth writes, therefore, that God commands the human being 'not merely to allow his humanity as fellow-humanity to be his nature, but to affirm and exercise it in his own decision, in action and omission' (III/4, 116). We are not only to be free before God; we are also to be free in our relationship and communion with others, and in this way to become an image of the triune God who lives in relationship.

Barth explores here three different kinds of human relationship: between man and woman, between parents and children, and between near and distant neighbours. In each case, he describes the theological context of the relationship, and draws out the contours of the *formed reference* that can offer guidance and instruction – though not definitive answers – in respect of ethical questions.

The first human relationship explored is that of man and woman, which Barth considers to be the basic and unavoidable form of our creaturely life. The command of God that encounters us in this context is not limited to considerations of sexual ethics or of marriage, but claims our whole person. For Barth, the command of God confirms us as male *or* female, such that we cannot leave our gender behind or seek an identity beyond gender; but it also confirms us as male *and* female, in mutual co-ordination, such that the one cannot be without the other. This co-ordination, Barth writes, exists in a definite order: though man and woman are 'fully equal before God and therefore as human beings' (III/4, 169 revised), yet the man is to take 'the lead as the inspirer, leader and initiator in their common being and action' (III/4, 170). And so, for Barth, even if one can never know in advance exactly how the command will be specified in a given context, it will always require this *order* to be observed and maintained.

The central form of this encounter of male and female is marriage, though it is by no means a form to which all people or Christians are called. Marriage is the calling to full, exclusive and lasting life-partnership for which a couple is freed by God and which a couple receives as a task from God. In its characteristics as complete, unique and permanent, marriage offers an image of the gracious election of God, in which God from all eternity elects us as covenant partners. At the same time, a real standing in marriage is something which is determined by God and can only be known by human beings in faith; conversely, human beings do not dispose over the divine foundation of a marriage. For this reason, and despite much caution, Barth notes that we cannot exclude the possibility that a given marriage 'has no divine basis and is thus dissoluble' (III/4, 211).

The second human relationship explored is that of parents and children, which Barth considers to be the basic form of all familial relations. For Barth, the relationship between parent and child offers a pale, distant reflection of – and is grounded in – the relationship between God and the creature.

On the part of the child, the appropriate attitude towards the parent is one of subordination, as is suggested by the fifth commandment given to Moses. At the same time, however, Barth notes that parental authority must be measured against the authority of God on which it is based, and thus 'can no longer in practice remain unchallenged' (III/4, 248). The honouring of parents must therefore be a *free* decision: one should obey one's parents; but one should obey God first and above all. Again, the specific form of obedience will vary, according to the particular will of God commanded in the concrete situation. On the part of the parent, the responsibility of having children leads Barth in a preliminary excursus to consider the issue of birth control. Here again, there is no fixed or universal rule, and though Barth expresses reservations concerning the capricious or irresponsible use of birth control measures, he concludes that the will of God has in each relevant situation to be discovered afresh. Actually becoming a parent involves both honour and obligation: honour at involvement in the coming to life of a new human being, and obligation in responsibility for this new life as long as the parent lives. The parents are thus to witness to the child that their life is under the care of God, and to give the child the chance 'to encounter the God who is present, operative and revealed in Jesus Christ' (III/4, 283).

The third and final human relationship explored is that of near and distant neighbours. The command of God encounters us also in our relationships with people who are like us and with people who are unlike us, however opaque, fluid and transitory such a distinction may be. There are a number of variables in view here: there are different languages, different locations and different (yet still also common) history. And certainly these features shape the context of our personal encounter with the command of God. At the same time, there is no particular form of the command of God in this sphere, unlike in the previous two relationships explored, because, Barth observes, relations between different peoples are not fixed but reversible, fluid, even removable. And so Barth rejects the idea that human nature has a specific determination in this connection or that the state is an order of creation. The witness of Scripture has as its true theme neither the history of humanity nor that of the nations but the covenant of grace.

Throughout these sections on freedom for fellowship, Barth regularly engages with Scripture, exegeting a series of texts which pertain to human relationships, and with the theological tradition, considering a wide array of previous theological reflection on the themes explored. Yet Barth attends here in addition to a wide swathe of secular texts on human relationships, drawing creatively on diverse works of religion, psychology, physiology and literature.

## *Freedom for life*

As well as living in covenant with God and in relationship with other people, we are liberated and commanded to live our own lives as particular human beings. Barth writes that in encountering the creature, this particular aspect of the command 'pierces into the sphere of his humanity as such and therefore into the act of his existence' (III/4, 325). And while the command of God will enjoin *specific* acts and dispositions, it will be *characterized* at its heart by the demand that we will *to live* – that we affirm and will our existence and seek to preserve and continue it.

The first theme which Barth treats under the heading of freedom for life is that of *respect* for life. This respect is not based on the merits of life itself but on the divine command which *creates* respect for it. Barth recognizes here the need not only to appreciate the mysterious and the practical character of respect for life, but also to recognize the necessary *limitation* of respect for life in view of the will of God who is the Creator and Lord of life. This means that the respect for life which God commands cannot be made into a rigid principle or absolute rule without encroaching upon the freedom of the divine command. However, Barth immediately notes that this apparent *relativization* of respect for life cannot be applied without the greatest caution. Actually to suggest any limitation of this kind, Barth cautions, 'cannot have more than the character of an *ultima ratio* (last resort), an exceptional case' (III/4, 343). And even in such cases, the command itself is not relaxed or abrogated; rather, what is required is a deeper understanding of the will to live which here appears in broken form.

Barth briefly considers at this point respect for non-human life, acknowledging the need to think and act responsibly here too. Difficult questions arise here, and this is particularly true with regard to animal life, in respect of which Barth counsels respect, gratitude and considerate treatment. Barth concludes this excursus by noting that killing animals in obedience to the command of God is only possible 'as a deeply reverential act of repentance, gratitude and praise on the part of the forgiven sinner' (III/4, 355).

The idea of the will to live, which is basic to the respect for life, leads Barth to consider the *will to be healthy*, as well as the implicated phenomenon of human sickness in its character both as divine judgement and as creaturely limitation. And this leads Barth further to consider the *will for joy* or happiness in the will to live, particularly in its character as the simplest form of gratitude arising from the work of the Spirit and in its relation to the shadow of the cross. As the will to live is not simply a general truth, it is also the particular *will to be oneself*: to be the individual and particular human being whom God has called. And this leads Barth finally to consider the *will to power* – not in the sense of desiring to be a kind of superhuman, as is portrayed in the thought of Friedrich Nietzsche, but in the sense of obediently seeking to use the powers one has been given in gratitude, freedom and service of God.

The second theme which Barth develops in this section is the *protection* of life, in which he addresses the biblical commandment that we should not kill. In this connection, Barth again offers a qualification: 'The protection of life required of us is not unlimited nor absolute … [but] simply the protection which God wills to demand of man as the Creator of this life' (III/4, 397–8). Again, then, Barth refuses to countenance an absolute and universal rule at this point; however, Barth again refuses to accept that the command is ever relaxed or dismissed. Instead, Barth contends, echoing the line of the previous section, 'since human life is of relative greatness and limited value, its protection may also consist *ultima ratione* (in the last resort) in its surrender and sacrifice' (III/4, 398) – when God as the Lord of life so wills. It may be therefore that the divine command to protect life *exceptionally* requires that life be ended.

This concept of the 'exceptional case' dominates Barth's subsequent consideration of suicide, homicide (including abortion, euthanasia, self-defence and capital punishment) and war. Given that the command of God insists upon the protection of life, Barth explores in each case whether there can be cases in which the taking of life may nevertheless be commanded, and seeks where possible to outline what some of the relevant considerations may be.

In the case of *suicide*, Barth leaves open the possibility of the 'exceptional case' in which someone might be commanded to take their own life; but he remains clear that this would be rare and extraordinary, and refuses to articulate even in outline what sort of situation might qualify. As for *homicide*, Barth again proceeds from the assumption that terminating the life of another person can only take place exceptionally, in an act of obedience to the divine command; Barth does insist, however, that any instance of euthanasia to be nothing but murder. In respect of *abortion*, Barth considers that an exceptional case may arise in situations where the life or health of the mother has to be weighed against the life or health of the child. As for *self-defence*, the killing of an assailant can arise only on the extreme margin, though again Barth offers no detailed account of such a situation. On *capital punishment*, Barth analogously leaves room for the exceptional case where one has to make a choice between the life of those who are opposing the state and the existence of the state itself. Finally, in a similar vein, and despite pacifism having 'almost infinite arguments in its favour' (III/4, 455), Barth permits the extreme possibility, in exceptional circumstances, of taking another's life in the context of *war*.

Throughout this material, Barth again engages heavily with scriptural texts and ethical treatises, seeking to articulate clearly his rather delicate position. On the one hand, the dominant, even overwhelming, thrust of his argument commends the protection of human life across these ethical cases. On the other hand, however, he generally refuses to rule out the possibility that in extreme cases, under exceptional circumstances, this principle might be transgressed – not arbitrarily or capriciously, but in free, responsible and even joyful obedience to the will of God which may be encountered in such situations. The command of God is simply not bound by any general rules or universal laws.

The final theme which Barth addresses here is the theme of the *active life*, in recognition of the way in which the command of God summons us to free activity. In so far as this activity desires and achieves obedience to the divine command, Barth writes, it 'must obviously consist in a correspondence to divine action' (III/4, 474). And the best term for such correspondence is *service* – we do not live for ourselves, but for God, becoming disciples of Jesus Christ and serving the coming of the kingdom of God. This activity involves no human deification, but within our limits there is a creaturely co-operation in the work of God as we become witnesses of the will and work of God. That this takes place, in our true creaturely freedom, is for Barth a miracle of the grace of God, and depends simply on our creaturely ability to *work*.

## *Freedom in limitation*

In this final section of the ethics of creation, Barth turns to the human creature considered under the divinely determined *limitations* of creaturely existence: in this sphere too, we are summoned to obey the command of God in creaturely freedom. But Barth insists that we must recognize immediately that when we speak of creaturely limitation before God, it is not a matter of curse or affliction, but a case of delimitation and circumscription.

Indeed, more even than this, our limitation is God's definitive *affirmation* of our creaturely lives.

The principal limitation of human being is its finite life span. Yet it is precisely in the transience of this life that the Word of God encounters us. For Barth, the command of God in this context is simply that we may 'recognise, take seriously and occupy this place as our own, as the place allotted to us' (III/4, 579). This life is a unique opportunity presented to each human being. And so we are commanded, in full confidence in God, to accept our finitude with readiness and joy, and commend ourselves at every step into the hands of God.

The will of God which encounters each individual in their limitation always addresses them with a specific command. This brings Barth to the theme of *vocation* – a topic revisited in the context of the doctrine of reconciliation in volume IV/3, as noted above in Chapter 6. Here, in the ethics of creation, vocation refers to the specific creaturely circumstances and limitations in which we exist by the providence of God. The particular dimensions of vocation that Barth considers are our age, our historical context, our aptitudes and our sphere of everyday activity. These features of our life give the creaturely context within which the command of God encounters us, but cannot of themselves predict the command of God.

Finally, in this ethics of creation, Barth turns to the theme of honour. He recognizes that the terms 'command', 'obedience' and 'limitation' may seem to sit uneasily together with the idea of 'freedom'. However, he insists that where the human being in limitation hears and obeys the command of God, 'it is finally and decisively a matter of his elevation, establishment, encouragement and even exaltation' (III/4, 648). In this way, the command of God *honours* us before God as God calls us to exist in communion with God. But this covenant honour presupposes a prior honour which God also bestows upon us: the honour simply of being creatures of God.

## *Comment*

In this section of special ethics, Barth seeks to develop an account of the divine command with particular regard to its dimension as the command of the Creator encountering the creature of God. It should be noted immediately that the account which results in no way questions the Christocentric commitments which were made in the earlier general ethics. In this particular sphere of creation, as in general, the question of good and evil has been settled already in Jesus Christ, who has fulfilled both the Gospel and the Law, and therefore all that we are both commanded and freed to do as we encounter the Word of God is to witness to the glory and grace of God. At the same time, the ethics of creation retains its own theme and focus in so far as it pertains to the domain of creation in its character as the external basis of the covenant, to the creature in its character as the prospective covenant partner of God, and to God as the Lord of all things by virtue of being the Creator and Sustainer of all things.

What Barth is seeking to achieve with his special ethics of creation is to offer a formed reference to the creaturely encounter with the command of God. In other words, on the basis of the Word of God attested in Scripture, Barth aims as far as possible to describe and delineate the command of God the Creator by detailing the context within which it is issued and the character both of God as Creator and of us as creatures. It is clear to Barth that owing to the specific content with which the command of God is always filled, it is impossible to *predict* what the command of God in any given situation will be. However, by disciplined attention to the history of the covenant, Barth provides a series of contours, guidelines, indications and instructions which seek to aid the creature in hearing the command of God in this sphere of creation. And Barth does this in thematizing the creaturely *freedom* in which life is to be lived before God – both in relation to other people and in relation to ourselves.

The human creature is commanded and permitted to live in freedom in these relations, and as this takes place in obedience and responsibility, the result is that the creature genuinely co-operates in the will and work of God. There is no question here of the divinization of the human person or the human action, and no way in which the ontological divide between God and humanity is compromised. Yet in this event there arises within the sphere of creation an image of the Creator, as the work of the creature – in all its limitation – points to and thus corresponds to the work of the Creator. There can be no question of more than this witness; but precisely this is the glorification of God which God desires above all, and precisely this is, in turn and by reflection, the glorification of the creature.

Clearly, it would be possible to enter into debate with Barth at any given point in respect of the particular ethical positions described in his ethics of creation. However, in what follows, two areas of theological interest will be raised in which concerns have been expressed in respect of Barth's method.

First, it is explicit right at the start of Barth's ethics of creation that the practice of casuistry is to be rejected. The idea that there exists a fixed set of universal rules, scriptural or otherwise, and that we can then consider these and apply them to a given situation, is one which Barth strenuously rejects. And yet the fact that Barth proceeds to develop a series of criteria and stipulations in respect of various ethical situations might suggest that Barth is engaging in a *kind* of moral casuistry himself, albeit not one that is captured by the perhaps rather narrow definition of casuistry which Barth gives. At the same time, it is clear that Barth strives to avoid the introduction of casuistic moral principles into his theological ethics, so that even where he does offer criteria or stipulations, he still considers himself to be presenting only guidelines. Yet there may remain a level of tension here between his intention and his execution.

Second, it is clear in Barth's ethics that in respect of the command of God special ethics can only ever offer guidance to prepare us to hear that command – even as such guidance must be bracketed in the actual hearing of the command. Yet there may be concerns that his treatment of theological ethics is too abstract, either in the sense that it abstracts from the empirical situations in which the command is received or in the sense that it abstracts from the empirical difficulty of hearing the command of God. In respect of the first, it might be observed that Barth's conception of the command as entirely context-specific would render any *theological* attempt to address empirical situations rather redundant. In respect of the second, it might be noted that Barth's confidence at this point is supported by the clarity of the command as attested in Scripture; yet in truth this may not entirely address the underlying concern.

# III  Special ethics:
# The doctrine of reconciliation

Having addressed in volume III/4 the special ethics of creation, Barth turns in volume IV/4 to consider the special ethics of reconciliation. Here, he attends to the dimension of the command of God which relates to God as Reconciler and the human being as the sinner reconciled to God, and thus to Christian ethics as the human answer to the grace of God in Jesus Christ. Barth's plan was to write first on the doctrine of baptism as the foundation of the Christian life and last on the doctrine of the Lord's Supper as the thanksgiving for Jesus Christ, offering in between an ethical exposition of the Christian life under the guidance of the Lord's Prayer. In the event, the doctrine of baptism was published in his lifetime, and the material on the first two petitions of the Lord's Prayer was published posthumously as *The Christian Life*; work on the other petitions and on the doctrine of the Lord's Supper was never started.

## *Ethics as a task of the doctrine of reconciliation*

The introduction to Barth's ethics of reconciliation appears in *The Christian Life*. At this point, Barth considers himself to have reached the central theme of special ethics as a whole. He begins by rehearsing some of the initial material from the ethics of creation, concerning how one correctly pursues special ethics. But whereas the ethics of creation considered the human creature encountering God as its Creator, the ethics of reconciliation relates to the God who reconciles all humanity to Godself in Jesus Christ, the human being who is freed in Jesus Christ to be and become the covenant partner of God, and the covenant of grace in which they exist in specific and irreversible order. The task of special ethics here, as before, is not to decide concerning the command of God but to 'give instruction in the art of correct asking about God's will and open hearing of God's command' (TCL, 34). And for Barth, the one thing above all that characterizes the command of God in this sphere is that it frees and obligates the human being for the *invocation* of God. It is this action which principally corresponds to the fulfilment of the covenant in Jesus Christ.

The result of this focus is that the central section of Barth's exposition of the special ethics of reconciliation seeks to follow the course of the Lord's Prayer, which both teaches us what to pray and how to pray and instructs in the shape of the Christian life. As a prelude to this, Barth considers the foundation of the Christian life in the doctrine of baptism; and as a postlude to this, Barth had intended to consider the renewal of the Christian life in the Lord's Supper.

## *The doctrine of baptism*

The location of the doctrine of baptism at the start of Barth's ethics of reconciliation is significant in two respects. First, and in common with much of the theological tradition, Barth considers baptism to be the event of public entry into the Christian life, and thus a first step in witnessing to reconciliation. Second, and against much of the theological tradition, Barth considers the baptism of the church to belong to ethics as it is a *human* activity which does not convey grace to the one being baptized. At this point, Barth makes a careful distinction between baptism of the Spirit and baptism with water. For Barth, the event of baptism of the Spirit is the divine activity which founds the Christian life and to which the human activity of baptism with water in the church corresponds.

The first theme which Barth attends is the baptism of the Spirit. Barth begins by observing that there is such a thing as genuine human faithfulness to God, and thus, for all its evident problems, with the human activity of Christian faithfulness. On this basis, he poses the simple question: How does it take place that a human being becomes a covenant partner of God in freedom and in obedience? Immediately, Barth rules out certain other views as unsatisfactory: the Roman Catholic view which sees grace as infused into the individual, the liberal Protestant view which sees faithfulness simply as a fulfilment of nature, and the Reformation view which considers the human being to be unchanged by grace.

The true answer, for Barth, lies in the possibility of God to enable the human being 'to participate not just passively but actively in God's grace as one who may and will and can be set to work' (IV/4, 6). It is thus the power of God which draws and turns us to choose freely what God demands of us, and thus to become faithful in confession of and witness to God. The *basis* of this transformation is the history of Jesus Christ, in whose crucifixion and resurrection – as noted in Chapter 5 above – all people are reconciled to God and faithful human being is actualized. For this reason, it does not lie within our own capacity. At the same time, this transformation is not simply external to us, as if it only affected Jesus Christ: by contrast, for Barth, it is an event that is not only for us but also *in us*, such that Jesus Christ 'creates in the history of every man the beginning of his new history' (IV/4, 21). It is the work of the

Spirit which opens and frees the human being to seeing, hearing and comprehending this history of Jesus Christ as their own salvation history. And the goal of the divine act of reconciliation is reached when, as a result, the human being is freed and commanded to become faithful to God in response.

Barth refers to the event of divine change which founds the Christian life as 'baptism of the Spirit'. It is Jesus Christ in the power of the Spirit who alone effects this change, and this change therefore represents a form of the grace of the God who reconciles. The change demands our gratitude and obedience – as noted above, Barth never conceives of the Gospel apart from the Law – and incorporates us into the Christian community. Though radical and irrevocable, this change represents just the first step on the radical journey of faith and discipleship that lies ahead.

Having outlined the divine work in the foundation of the Christian life in terms of baptism of the Spirit, Barth turns to the faithful human response to this divine work. It is, for Barth, only as these distinct events of divine address and human response are seen together that there emerges a full picture of the foundation of the Christian life. The invited and commanded first form of this human response is the decision to undergo baptism with water in the church. This is the free and obedient human act which corresponds to baptism of the Spirit.

The *basis* of water baptism is the command of Jesus in Scripture to baptize as part of Christian mission, a command which Barth sees as itself grounded in Jesus' own baptism. When Jesus underwent baptism by John at the outset of his ministry, he submitted to the will of his Father, committed himself to solidarity with all humanity, and embarked upon his public service of God. For all the dissimilarity, something similar happens in our baptism: in freely following his act of obedience, we follow Jesus in his subjection to God, solidarity with all humanity and acceptance of service of both God and humanity.

The *goal* of water baptism is to look beyond itself, testifying as a human activity to the divine act of reconciliation between God and humanity in Jesus Christ. In this way, water baptism is not itself divine speech or action: Barth observes of Jesus Christ that 'He is He, and His work is His work, standing over against all Christian action, including Christian faith and Christian baptism' (IV/4, 88).

By contrast, as it is oriented in hope to its superior, transcendent and future goal, baptism is a profoundly human act – for Barth, it is 'the first form of the human answer to the divine change which was brought about in [Jesus Christ]' (IV/4, 90). As it thus witnesses to Jesus Christ, it is an act of confession on the part of both the individual baptized and the baptizing community.

The *meaning* of baptism is the final theme which Barth addresses at this point. He begins by denying any view of the meaning of baptism which seeks the sanctity of baptism in a 'supposedly immanent divine work' (IV/4, 101). Barth therefore opposes the idea that baptism is a sacrament, a bearer or means or instrument of grace, and thus opposes the traditional views of Roman Catholicism, Lutheranism and Calvinism. Nothing in the extensive exegesis of relevant passages of Scripture which he here presents leads Barth to consider baptism to be a sacrament. The one and only true sacrament, for Barth, is Jesus Christ.

The meaning of baptism thus resides not in its character as an immanent *divine* work, but in its character as a true and free *human* action which in obedience responds and corresponds to the divine action in Jesus Christ. It is precisely in this limitation that baptism finds its true purpose and glory. It is a sign of our *conversion* – of the transition 'from self-will to obedience to God, from anxiety before Him to hope in Him' (IV/4, 136). It is thus the first step in a new life, involving a free human decision in which their old nature is renounced and their new life is pledged. In this way, it corresponds dynamically to the justification and sanctification of humanity achieved in Jesus Christ, as considered in Chapter 6.

Given this emphasis on the freedom and obedience of the individual being baptised in the community, it is no surprise that Barth considers the practice of infant baptism to be deeply irregular. Although Barth carefully explores the various theological and exegetical grounds which have been given in support of this practice in different traditions, he finds them all ultimately to be wanting and misguided.

Finally, Barth returns to the theme of hope in relation to baptism. The new life marked by the human act of baptism can consist, Barth writes, 'only in a living hope which is continually confirmed and exercised' (IV/4, 197). In hope in Jesus Christ, each and every baptized person is assigned a place in the work of God's grace, witnessing in the world to the great acts of God. The life and witness that follows baptism is certainly in constant need of renewed conversion to God. However, as baptism takes place as a free and obedient act that is grounded in hopeful prayer, it is nonetheless rightly performed, whatever may lie ahead.

## *The Christian life*

The life of a Christian is obedient, for Barth, to the extent that its purpose, desire and work is centred on the invocation of God – in thanksgiving, praise and petition. Seeking concrete direction from the Lord's Prayer in expounding this idea, Barth begins with the observation that in its first words, Christians call upon God as *Father*. It is Jesus Christ who originally, properly and naturally calls upon God as Father, and who in his faithfulness and obedience reveals God to be the Father of all those to whom his work is now addressed. As we participate by election in the history of Jesus Christ, as considered in Chapter 3, so too we are also able to do as he does and thus call God Father.

The freedom of the children of God to call upon God as Father is a matter of sheer grace, grounded in the history of Jesus Christ who is both Son of Man and Son of God. This grace is given to Christians afresh with every new day and cannot be stored. For this reason, Barth writes, the Christian life is always in process of becoming, and must correspondingly always be 'the work of beginners' (TCL, 79). In invocation, we always come before God with empty hands, in our need and our helplessness, addressing God as *our* Father in recognition that God is the Father of all those who believe.

The act of invoking God as Father is the renewal from our side of relationship with God. That we can do this at all is the work of the Spirit of God who awakens, enables and impels us to exercise our freedom in this obedience. As they do this, Christians live from a centre that is beyond them, relying utterly upon God, and they live as *witnesses*, serving the world. And in response, God their Father will hear, and also – according to the will of God – answer, their prayer. So, Barth concludes, Christian action that takes place in the course of this free invocation of God will be action that is good and permitted and commanded.

The distinctive disposition and mode of action that is commanded alongside the invocation of God is a passion or zeal to honour God's name, as per the first petition of the Lord's Prayer, 'Hallowed be thy name'. This desire seeks to have God's name known and sanctified in every part of the world, the church and the life of the individual Christian. The knowledge and sanctification of God's name in the *world* has taken place in the history of Jesus Christ, but is opposed by the ignorance of God in the world's atheism, idolatry and equation of God with its own causes. The knowledge and sanctification of God's name in the *church* becomes real as it witnesses to the grace of God, but is also miserably opaque and greatly obscured through the tendency of the church to denial of and apostasy from Jesus Christ. Finally, the knowledge and sanctification of God's name in the *individual* takes place as they respond in faith and obedience to their divine election, yet they also persist in evil thoughts, words and deeds, and thus live in ignorance as well. In each of these spheres, there is knowledge and ignorance – not as equal and opposite alternatives, but as the existence together of commanded possibility and impossible possibility.

Given this ambiguity concerning the knowledge and sanctification of God, the petition of the Christian in freedom and obedience is that *God* take it upon Godself to hallow God's name, and thus to remove completely all ignorance and disregard. Christians know that God's name has already been perfectly hallowed in Jesus Christ; but they pray for the total and final sanctifying of God's name that will take place beyond the ambiguity of this time between the times. This can only be God's work, and Christians can only pray that it will take place.

At the same time, the zeal of Christians for the honouring of God's name will demand from Christians not only prayer but also action. In all its limitation and modesty, free and obedient human action 'will not just be unlike God's act but also like it, running parallel to it on our level' (TCL, 175). In such faithful activity, Christians will allow the Word of God to have precedence, which means that in their witness they will seek to resist and oppose the ignorance and disregard of God's name in their own lives, in the church and in the world.

A further element of the command that is given to the Christian – together with but inseparable from zeal for God's honour – is the struggle for human righteousness, in line with the second petition of the Lord's Prayer, 'Thy kingdom come'. The particular nature of this commanded and permitted struggle is what differentiates it from other struggles: it is not against people, but against the *lordless powers*. These powers encounter and threaten humanity, and are a form of *nothingness*, which was considered in Chapter 4. They belong therefore neither to the divine being nor to the creaturely realm, but to the same sphere of pseudo-reality and efficacy as human sin. Though originally created good, after the Fall these human powers rise up 'as lordless forces, against man himself' (TCL, 215) – and so against God.

Among the lordless powers, Barth names political absolutism ('Leviathan'), material possessions ('Mammon'), intellectual constructs (ideologies) and earthly forces such as technology, sport, pleasure and transportation. Of themselves, these aspects of human existence are all creaturely, even necessary; but in the domain of sin, they take on a life of their own, oppressing and enslaving human beings. Yet even as such, they remain, like sin and nothingness, under the lordship of God in which they find their limit. At this point, as throughout this part of the special ethics of reconciliation, Barth's text is rich in biblical exegesis, historical observation and references to contemporary events.

In calling upon God to vanquish the lordless powers, Christians pray that the kingdom of God will come within and over and against the apparent lordlessness of human life. The kingdom of God is, of course, already present in Jesus Christ, who definitively overcomes the unrighteousness and disorder of humanity. However, we still await the full and final appearance of the kingdom of God as the end and goal of human history. This is the work of God alone, coming from outwith human history, and therefore beyond human power. And yet Christians also become caught up with this prayer and petition such that 'their whole life and thought and word and deed are set in motion' (TCL, 262). They are thus summoned and freed to struggle for human righteousness, and thus to kingdom-like action as witnesses of God to and for other people.

## *Comment*

In this second section of special ethics, Barth seeks to develop an account of the divine command with particular regard to its dimension as the command of the Reconciler encountering the justified sinner and covenant partner of God. In one sense, the material from this ethics of reconciliation might be seen to be the internal basis of the previous ethics of creation, just as the covenant is itself, for Barth, the internal basis of creation. It is no surprise, then, that Barth thinks himself here to have reached the central theme of special ethics.

The basic presuppositions of theological ethics in this sphere of the Christian life are as before. Here again, the question of good and evil has been settled already in Jesus Christ so that what remains for the Christian to do is simply to witness to the glory and grace of God. And here again, it is impossible to *predict* what the command of God in any situation will be, thus only guidelines to aid in hearing the command can be given. Yet the overarching theme of the ethics of reconciliation is not freedom, as in the ethics of creation, but invocation.

What this means in practice is that as reconciled sinners Christians are commanded and permitted to live as covenant partners who *call upon God* in prayer as the fundamental and foundational act of their lives. As they do this in truly human obedience and responsibility, the result is – without any trace of divinization of either their work or their person – that their activity will respond to and correspond to the prior activity of God the Reconciler. And just as such, in its witness to Jesus Christ, it will participate in the work of the kingdom of God and, in all its human limitation, glorify God.

It should be noted that this does not represent any kind of permanent state of affairs, for Barth. By contrast, this participation and glorification takes place in the event of grace, one which is not at our disposal but for which we can only pray. The life of the Christian as justified sinner is thus not one of serene process in sanctification but of daily prayer and striving, on which path they can only ever be beginners who take relative, fragmentary and provisional steps towards fulfilling the command of God. And yet, for Barth, these steps of ours are real and definite steps: God does not will to be without them.

In the special ethics of reconciliation, the foundation of the Christian life is baptism, conceived by Barth as the inseparable unity of baptism of the Spirit and baptism with water. Barth considers himself here to be undertaking what he refers to as a demythologization, or demystification, of the traditional doctrine of baptism. His doctrine of baptism has been highly controversial ever since its publication. The theological distinction of these two aspects of baptism has been contested exegetically; the denial of baptism as a sacrament that communicates grace has been vigorously opposed; the rejection of infant baptism as an ecclesial practice has been widely denounced; and the continuity of this doctrine with the rest of *Church Dogmatics* has been questioned. At the same time, Barth's doctrine has also found strong support, notably among theologians and churches who enlist Barth in support of their own positions.

It is evidently the case that the scriptural material which lies at the heart of many of these questions has been deeply and widely disputed since the time of the Reformation, and the first three issues noted above cannot be resolved here. What is of more interest at this point is the final charge – that of material continuity. It certainly seems true that in the time between the early volumes of *Church Dogmatics* and this volume, Barth departed from a more traditional understanding of baptism. At the same time, however, in its basic structure, Barth's final doctrine of baptism evidences exactly the same pattern of divine action on one side and human response and correspondence on the other that we have seen to be a marked feature of his understanding of human action in general and theological ethics in particular from the very beginning. The idea of a radical departure in Barth's thought just prior to his doctrine of baptism thus seems rather unlikely.

This pattern of divine action and human response and correspondence in Christian baptism is clearly in evidence again in Barth's presentation of the ethical meaning of Christian life under the guidance and instruction of the Lord's Prayer. And Barth offers indication in his doctrine of baptism that the same pattern would also have been present in his doctrine of the Lord's Supper, though he did not survive to write it. The invocation of God which takes place across baptism, prayer and the Lord's Supper lies at the heart of the Christian life, responding with gratitude to God's gracious work on our behalf. Yet this invocation in free obedience leads not to any ethical quietism but irresistibly to human activity. In its witness to the grace of God, such human action seeks ever and again to hallow the divine name and oppose the lordless powers as we respond to the divine call to witness to the coming kingdom of God in all our lives.

# CHAPTER EIGHT

# Conclusion

From the early days of his parish labours in rural Switzerland, through his academic career in turbulent inter-war Germany, to his later years as a theological statesman in Basel, Karl Barth was a figure whose doctrinal views generated vigorous engagement and response. His influence was subsequently felt in the circles of both academy and church, and even, at times, beyond – in the wider circles of cultural, political and other public discourse. This book has sought to offer an introduction to the theology of this remarkably influential figure, and to do so by focusing on his major theological life-work – *Church Dogmatics*. In what follows, some concluding remarks will be offered in an effort to consider Barth's dogmatic legacy and ongoing significance.

## The dogmatic legacy of Barth

There are few works in the history of theology which demonstrate the commanding knowledge, intellectual vigour and considered reflection – not to mention sheer extensity – of *Church Dogmatics*. The legacy which this represents might be considered in two ways: first, in terms of the way Barth approached the task of dogmatics, and second, in terms of the dogmatic material which resulted.

First, in terms of Barth's approach to dogmatics, one way of characterizing his venture in *Church Dogmatics* would be to consider it as Barth's attempt to respond to the command of God to undertake dogmatic work. Such a conception would allow us to think of *Church Dogmatics* as a human venture undertaken not only in *obedient responsibility* but also in *joyful freedom* before God, and may allow us to grasp something of the particular character of Barth's approach.

From the start to the end of *Church Dogmatics*, Barth seeks to work in *obedience*, in the sense that at each point he seeks to be faithful to what he considers to be the norm and centre of all theological reflection – Jesus Christ as he is attested in Scripture. There is no other route to knowledge of God and no other way of proceeding in theology than to pray for the event of revelation in which God encounters us in this Word and empowers us to hear and respond in the work of the Spirit. Yet this is no easy or straightforward undertaking. Particularly at the more difficult and aporetic points in *Church Dogmatics* – in the doctrine of Israel, perhaps, or in the doctrine of nothingness – there is a corresponding and perceptible sense of Barth *wrestling* with the Word of God in Scripture, seeking in his response to be true to its witness and not to intrude upon it with his own desires or opinions.

Barth also seeks to work in *Church Dogmatics* in a way which is *responsible*, and this in respect of attending and being answerable not only to the Word of God, but also to other human beings. This is true particularly in respect of the attempts of others to confess the Word of God – Barth insists that one can only pursue work in dogmatics, and Christian confession more generally, when one *listens* to the attempts of others to do the same. And so the pages of *Church Dogmatics* are rich with all kinds of attentive (if fallible) readings of the dogmatic endeavours of all manner of theologians and churches through the ages. But not only this: for all Barth's insistent rootedness in the Word of God, scholars of many different disciplines are regularly cited and vigorously engaged.

For all its length, and for all its seriousness, it is clear that Barth undertakes the laborious work of *Church Dogmatics* with *joy*. There is an exuberance, an enthusiasm, a zest for the task on Barth's part that becomes apparent at different points in the text – at times in the most unexpected places, where a humorous aside or sharp exclamation gives sudden life to the writer behind the page. To attend to the work of dogmatics in joy is, for Barth, to recognize the merciful work of God which renders dogmatics both commanded and permitted, and to rejoice and be thankful for the grace of God to which dogmatics witnesses. Against this backdrop, even the unfinished nature of *Church Dogmatics* at his death was a matter for self-deprecating humour rather than any deep regret.

It is evident, finally, that Barth writes *Church Dogmatics* with a real sense of *freedom*. This is true not only in the sense that Barth feels able to map and follow his own course through the various topics of dogmatics and to structure his work in innovative (and fruitful) ways. It is also true in the sense that within each topic of dogmatics, and precisely in obedient responsibility before the Word of God in Scripture, Barth feels joyfully free to reject previous traditions and positions in theological work and to embark upon bold and new trajectories. Precisely in such cases, indeed, Barth attests the combination of freedom and compulsion which characterizes all standing before the command of God, as he considers himself not only permitted but also obligated to depart radically from historically well-trodden paths.

Instructive though Barth's approach to dogmatics may be, it is the theological content of *Church Dogmatics* which has generally garnered far more attention, and it is to this, second, that the briefest of consideration must here be given. Some of the broad, sometimes critical, contours of response to Barth's work have been mentioned in the course of the preceding chapters, and the places where Barth has offered particularly radical or controversial accounts of Christian doctrines have been signposted at appropriate points.

If one were to try and characterize the dominating *material* feature of *Church Dogmatics*, one might land on the Christological focus or Christocentricity which lies ontically and noetically at the heart of every major doctrine which Barth expounds. Single-minded attentiveness to the revealed Word of God in Jesus Christ is common in the theological tradition when it comes to doctrines of, say, Christology or soteriology; but it has not always been so rigorously pursued in the doctrines of, say, creation or providence. To some commentators, this is a great strength of Barth's work; to others, inevitably, it is a great weakness.

However one evaluates this Christological focus, it is clear that it has radical implications for the way in which certain doctrines in particular are developed by Barth. And it tends to be that it is at precisely those points – such as in the doctrine of Scripture, the account of knowledge of God, the doctrine of election, the account of soteriology and the theology of the sacraments – that the greatest theological controversies have arisen. And yet it is precisely on this Christological basis that Barth proceeds confidently and determinedly in theological enquiry in his time, reading the world by the Gospel and never the Gospel by the world.

## The ongoing significance of Barth

With five decades or so having passed since the death of Karl Barth, there is no sign of theological interest in his life and work diminishing. If anything, the rate of production of substantive monographs and research articles on his work has increased in recent years, and there is no sign of change on the horizon. Beyond the formal and material legacy of Barth's dogmatics itself, perhaps two factors may be suggested as to why this is the case: the first is ongoing issues of interpretation and the second is ongoing patterns of influence.

In respect of the first reason, it is instructive to note the varied ways in which Barth has been received and interpreted in the work of different theologians.

According to one account, Barth is considered a *neo-orthodox* theologian, which is to say someone who is involved in reappropriating and revisioning the work of older Protestant theologies, offering certain concessions to modernity on the way. Another significant way of understanding Barth's theology is as a thoroughly *modern* enterprise, one which not only responds to but is also circumscribed by the questions of the modern human being. A further manner of reading Barth is as one whose interests coincide with those of *postmodern* theology, a reading of Barth which tends to emphasize the early work of Barth and its dialectic emphasis on God as entirely other than humanity.

Two more recently prominent modes of reading the work of Barth might also be mentioned at this point. The first is to characterize his dogmatics as representing an 'evangelical catholicism', which is to say, a mode of pursuing theological enquiry which seeks to attest the Gospel of Jesus Christ but to attend in so doing to the theological tradition of the whole church, both before and since the time of the Reformation. The second is to interpret the theology of Barth as broadly consonant with and supportive of the instincts and themes of *liberation theology*, particularly by virtue of the way in which Barth prioritizes themes of freedom and justice, and recommends resistance against the powers that oppress.

It is precisely the depth and scope of Barth's work in *Church Dogmatics* and beyond which allows these questions to arise, and there is certainly no simple answer in respect of how to read Barth and of which of these interpretations to prefer. The danger of imposing an alien framework of presuppositions and questions upon Barth's theology is never far away. It is often correspondingly better to seek wherever possible to allow Barth's work to speak for itself, attentive to the directions in which it can be and has been appropriated and yet cautious about too hasty categorizations of his work under one heading or another.

In respect of the second reason, it is important to recognize both the intensity and the extensity of the influence which Barth has had on contemporary theology. It would be eminently possible, though perhaps not overly instructive, to provide a long list of names of those theologians over whom Barth has wielded significant influence, both during and after his lifetime. And it is certainly the case that reading the work of Barth has changed many people's minds in matters theological. Yet even where it has not changed minds, it has often had noticeable impact – furnishing new insights, challenging existing thoughts, spurring to new reflection.

What is particularly remarkable about this influence of Barth is the way in which it has crossed confessional boundaries. Barth was self-consciously within the Reformed tradition in terms of his church affiliation and his theological instincts, and yet his significance extends far beyond this one tradition. *Church Dogmatics* was, after all, not a narrowly confessional enterprise but a dogmatics written for the *whole* church, attending in its pages to theologians of all backgrounds. And for all its provenance in the academic training of pastors, *Church Dogmatics* was always deeply rooted in and oriented to the life of the actual church.

In light of the remarkable legacy and the ongoing significance of Barth, his work continues to demand attention in contemporary forays in theology. Yet Barth was more aware than anyone else of the incomplete, fragmentary and provisional nature of all dogmatic work, especially his own. For this reason, although theologians today should certainly think *about* Barth and *with* Barth, they are also called to think *after* Barth in their work, acknowledging that he does *not* have the final word. As they pursue this endeavour in this spirit, they will be true indeed to the spirit of Barth, for whom the last Word, like the first Word, is one to whom we can only seek to offer our modest, thankful and prayerful witness.

# FURTHER READING

To pursue the study of the work of Karl Barth further, the best place to start is undoubtedly with some of Barth's own writings. This book has intentionally focused on *Church Dogmatics*, and there would be many starting points within this vast work from which one could instructively begin reading. It might be profitable, for example, to begin reading from the opening pages of volume I/1, or volume II/1, or volume IV/1. Alternatively, it might be equally profitable to turn directly to a theme or doctrine of particular interest within one of the individual volumes or part-volumes, or to the exegesis which Barth offers of a particular passage of Scripture. If time is limited, much may be gained from exploring the excellent reader of R. Michael Allen, which helpfully introduces and reproduces some centrally significant readings selected from the wider text of *Church Dogmatics*.

Beyond *Church Dogmatics*, Barth at different points offered more concise presentations of his understanding of the Christian faith, such as in *Credo*, an exploration of the Apostles' Creed from 1935, *Dogmatics in Outline*, lectures on Christian theology from 1946, and *Evangelical Theology*, a lecture series from 1962. Also instructive within his corpus of publications are his commentaries on Scripture and collections of sermons. Among the former, the famous commentary on Romans from 1922 is particularly significant, as are the lectures on the opening chapters of John from 1926. Among the latter, one might attend to some of the early sermons of Barth from Safenwil collected in *Early Preaching of Karl Barth* or some of the later sermons of Barth in Basel Prison entitled *Deliverance to the Captives*. Bibliographical details of all these primary texts appear in the list that follows.

Allen, R. Michael. *Karl Barth's* Church Dogmatics: *An Introduction and Reader*. London: Continuum/T&T Clark, 2012.

Barth, Karl. *Church Dogmatics*. Edited by G. W. Bromiley and
T. F. Torrance. Translated by G. W. Bromiley and others. Student
edition in 31 volumes. London: Bloomsbury/T&T Clark, 2010.
Barth, Karl. *Credo*. Translated by J. Strathearn McNab. Eugene [OR]:
Wipf and Stock, 2005.
Barth, Karl. *Deliverance to the Captives*. Translated by Marguerite Wieser.
Eugene [OR]: Wipf and Stock, 2010.
Barth, Karl. *Dogmatics in Outline*. Translated by G. T. Thomson. London:
SCM Press, 2012.
Barth, Karl. *Evangelical Theology*. Translated by Grover Foley. Grand
Rapids [MI]: Eerdmans, 1979.
Barth, Karl. *The Early Preaching of Karl Barth: Fourteen Sermons with
Commentary by William H. Willimon*. Translated by William H.
Willimon. Louisville [KY]: WKJP, 2009.
Barth, Karl. *The Epistle to the Romans*. Translated by Edwin C. Hoskyns.
Oxford: OUP, 1968.
Barth, Karl. *Witness to the Word: A Commentary on John 1*. Translated
by Geoffrey W. Bromiley. Eugene [OR]: Wipf & Stock, 2003.

The secondary literature on the work of Karl Barth is simply vast,
stretching back to Barth's first commentary on Romans in 1919,
increasing over the course of his life, and continue to expand today
at a dizzying rate. Across research monographs, edited volumes,
journal articles and magazine contributions, Barth's work has
roused both passionate affirmation and robust dismissal, with
much by way of insightful analysis and critique along the way. It is
doubtful that a complete bibliography of this engagement is even
possible any more, let alone in a limited space such as this. What
is provided below, then, is a hugely concise and highly selective list
of broadly recent monographs in English on the theology of Karl
Barth, to encourage and illuminate further study. In what follows,
they are loosely grouped under headings which draw upon the
chapter titles that have been used in this book.

# The life and work of Karl Barth

Busch, Eberhard. *Karl Barth: His Life from Letters and Autobiographical
Texts*. London: SCM Press, 1976.
Gorringe, Timothy. *Karl Barth: Against Hegemony*. Oxford: OUP, 1999.
Jehle, Frank. *Ever Against the Stream*. Translated by Richard and Martha
Burnett. Grand Rapids [MI]: Eerdmans, 2002.

McCormack, Bruce. *Karl Barth's Critically Realistic Dialectical Theology: Its Genesis and Development, 1909–1936*. Oxford: Clarendon Press, 1997.

Webster, John B. *Barth's Earlier Theology*. London: T&T Clark, 2005.

# The doctrine of the Word of God

Currie, Thomas Christian. *The Only Sacrament Left to Us: The Threefold Word of God in the Theology and Ecclesiology of Karl Barth*. Eugene [OR]: Pickwick, 2015.

Ensminger, Sven. *Karl Barth's Theology as a Resource for a Christian Theology of Religions*. London: Bloomsbury/T&T Clark, 2016.

Greggs, Tom. *Theology against Religion: Constructive Dialogues with Bonhoeffer and Barth*. London: Bloomsbury/T&T Clark, 2011.

Jüngel, Eberhard, *God's Being is in Becoming: The Trinitarian Being of God in the Theology of Karl Barth*. Translated by John Webster. Edinburgh: T&T Clark, 2001.

Torrance, Alan J. *Persons in Communion: Essay on Trinitarian Description and Human Participation*. Edinburgh: T&T Clark, 1996.

Westerholm, Martin. *The Ordering of the Christian Mind: Karl Barth and Theological Rationality*. Oxford: OUP, 2015.

Wood, Donald. *Barth's Theology of Interpretation*. Aldershot: Ashgate, 2004.

Yuen, Alfred H. *Barth's Theological Ontology of Holy Scripture*. Eugene [OR]: Pickwick, 2014.

# The doctrine of God

Gibson, David. *Reading the Decree: Exegesis, Election and Christology in Calvin and Barth*. London: Bloomsbury/T&T Clark, 2011.

Gockel, Matthias. *Barth and Schleiermacher on the Doctrine of Election: A Systematic-Theological Comparison*. Oxford: OUP, 2007.

Greggs, Tom. *Barth, Origen, and Universal Salvation: Restoring Particularity*. Oxford: OUP, 2009.

Griswold, Daniel M. *Triune Eternality: God's Relationship to Time in the Theology of Karl Barth*. Minneapolis [MN]: Fortress Press, 2015.

Johnson, Keith L. *Karl Barth and the* Analogia Entis. London: Bloomsbury/T&T Clark, 2011.

La Montagne, D. Paul. *Barth and Rationality: Critical Realism in Theology*. Eugene [OR]: Cascade, 2012.

Lindsay, Mark R. *Barth, Israel, and Jesus: Karl Barth's Theology of Israel*. Aldershot: Ashgate, 2007.

Price, Robert B. *Letters of the Divine Word: The Perfections of God in Karl Barth's* Church Dogmatics. London: Bloomsbury/T&T Clark, 2012.

# The doctrine of creation

Gabriel, Andrew. *Barth's Doctrine of Creation: Creation, Nature, Jesus, and the Trinity*. Eugene [OR]: Cascade, 2014.

Green, Christopher. *Doxological Theology: Karl Barth on Divine Providence, Evil, and the Angels*. London: Bloomsbury/T&T Clark, 2011.

Kennedy, Darren. *Providence and Personalism: Karl Barth in Conversation with Austin Farrer, John Macmurray and Vincent Brümmer*. Oxford: Peter Lang, 2011.

Krötke, Wolf. *Sin and Nothingness in the Theology of Karl Barth*. Translated by Philip G. Ziegler and Christina-Maria Bammel. Studies in Reformed Theology and History, new series, 10; Princeton: Princeton Theological Seminary, 2005.

Price, Daniel J. *Karl Barth's Anthropology in Light of Modern Thought*. Grand Rapids [MI]: Eerdmans, 2002.

# The doctrine of reconciliation

Bender, Kimlyn. *Karl Barth's Christological Ecclesiology*. Aldershot: Ashgate, 2005.

Cocksworth, Ashley. *Karl Barth's Doctrine of Prayer*. London: Bloomsbury/T&T Clark, 2015.

Dafydd Jones, Paul. *The Humanity of Christ: Christology in Karl Barth's* Church Dogmatics. London: Bloomsbury/T&T Clark, 2011.

Drury, John L. *The Resurrected God: Karl Barth's Trinitarian Theology of Easter*. Minneapolis [MN]: Fortress Press, 2014.

Grebe, Matthias. *Election, Atonement, and the Holy Spirit: Through and Beyond Barth's Theological Interpretation of Scripture*. Eugene [OR]: Pickwick, 2014.

Johnson, Adam J. *God's Being in Reconciliation: The Theological Basis of the Unity and Diversity of the Atonement in the Theology of Karl Barth*. London: Bloomsbury/T&T Clark, 2013.

Kim, JinHyok. *The Spirit of God and the Christian Life: Reconstructing Karl Barth's Pneumatology*. Minneapolis [MN]: Fortress, 2014.

McMaken, W. Travis. *The Sign of the Gospel: Toward an Evangelical Doctrine of Infant Baptism after Karl Barth*. Minneapolis [MN]: Fortress, 2013.

Smith, Aaron T. *A Theology of the Third Article: Karl Barth and the Spirit of the Word*. Minneapolis [MN]: Fortress Press, 2014.

Sumner, Darren O. *Karl Barth and the Incarnation: Christology and the Humility of God*. London: Bloomsbury/T&T Clark, 2016.

# Theological ethics

Biggar, Nigel. *The Hastening that Waits: Karl Barth's Ethics*. Oxford: Clarendon Press, 1993.

Clough, David. *Ethics in Crisis: Interpreting Barth's Ethics*. Aldershot: Ashgate, 2005.

Haddorff, David. *Christian Ethics as Witness: Barth's Ethics for a World at Risk*. Eugene [OR]: Cascade, 2010.

McKenny, Gerald. *The Analogy of Grace: Karl Barth's Moral Theology*. Oxford: OUP, 2013.

Mangina, Joseph L. *Karl Barth on the Christian Life: the Practical Knowledge of God*. New York: Peter Lang, 2001.

Nimmo, Paul T. *Being in Action: The Theological Shape of Barth's Ethical Vision*. Continuum/T&T Clark, 2007.

Spencer, Archibald James. *Clearing a Space for Human Action: Ethical Ontology in the Theology of Karl Barth*. New York: Peter Lang, 2003.

Webster, John. *Barth's Ethics of Reconciliation*. Cambridge: CUP, 1995.

Webster, John. *Barth's Moral Theology: Human Action in Barth's Thought*. Edinburgh: T&T Clark, 1998.

Werpehowski, William. *Karl Barth and Christian Ethics: Living in Truth*. Burlington [VT]: Ashgate, 2014.

# INDEX